BECCLES SCHOOLDAYS

To Abbeyfield with thanks

BECCLES SCHOOLDAYS
1930 – 1948:
RECOLLECTIONS AND REFLECTIONS

by

David Woodward

DAVID WOODWARD

&

COLIN BAKER

MP

BECCLES SCHOOLDAYS

Published in 2012

by:

Mousehold Press
Victoria Cottage
Constitution Opening
Norwich NR3 4BD
www.mousehold-press.co.uk

ISBN 978 1 874739 63 0

All royalties accruing from the sale of this book will be donated to the friends of the Beccles War Memorial Hospital
and
the Waveney Stardust

printed by Mimeo, Huntingdon

A person who knows how to laugh at himself
will never cease to be amused.

Shirley Maclaine.

This book is dedicated to our Shirleys
with love and gratitude.

INTRODUCTION

Our friendship began seventy years ago in Beccles – the town where we were born and brought up – when we were school classmates and fellow members of the Air Training Corps, with its weekly parades and instruction and with its annual camps at RAF stations. We shared a teenage interest in playing snooker, billiards and table tennis, and spent many hours together and with other friends at the Men's Social Institute in Fair Close. We also shared an enthusiastic interest in cricket and football, though our actual participation in these games took different forms. In our teens we often had meals at each other's homes where our parents always warmly welcomed their son's guest. And we had mutual friends in a young married couple – former pupils of the Sir John Leman School who became school teachers – at whose home we spent many happy, memorable and entertaining hours. During Colin's postgraduate year in London, David stayed with him from time to time at his hall of residence in Knightsbridge, dining in hall, walking in the parks and visiting theatres. Though we stayed in touch during the following twenty years when Colin was in Africa, we inevitably saw less of each other during that period than previously. Our friendship has, however, been re-invigorated since his return to Britain, even though we live on opposite sides of the country. Now in our early eighties, we have had great fun in recalling our schooldays in Beccles and reviving memories of those far off days – memories which in some cases are recalled by one and forgotten by the other, and memories which in some other cases are interpreted differently and viewed from different perspectives.

We deliberately wrote the two main parts of this book separately, with as little knowledge as possible of what the other was writing. This was because we did not want the selectiveness of our separate and aging memories to be influenced, even though we knew there would be overlaps as each of us dealt separately with the same incidents. We felt that overlaps would highlight those things which we considered most important or, whether important or not, which remain most clearly in our individual minds. Approaching these overlap areas from different angles would, we felt, add colour and interest to the narratives. Curiously, in a few cases, far from there being an overlap, there are important gaps with which neither of us deals. The best example of this is the General Election of 1945, with its immense national, economic and social implications. Yet, despite the considerable general interest of one of us in political affairs, that election is mentioned in neither of our narratives. Perhaps, to us at the time, it was not as important as we would have expected it to be.

That we did approach many common matters from different angles may be the result of a number of differences in our individual backgrounds and experiences. Although there are many similarities in those backgrounds and experiences the differences ought to be explained or at least explored.

First, David lived in Fair Close in the older, northern and more urban part of the town, with industrial premises close by – the maltings, the iron foundry, the printing works, the railway station and a mineral water factory, and in the past a tannery – and with numerous and large shops, banks, hotels and churches nearby. One end of Fair Close was near the main part of this industrial area, and the other end was close to what geographers today call the CBA, the Central Business Area, the shops, banks, estate agents, building societies, etc. – an area through which traffic was constantly passing and pedestrians were coming and going all the time. This was especially true during the war when many soldiers were stationed in or passed through this part of the town. Beyond the built-up area of the town, people in this part of Beccles tended to look towards the Norfolk side of the Waveney River with its marshland and slightly higher land beyond; to a wide estuarine area, flooded in centuries past. They were more 'Norfolk orientated'.

Colin, on the other hand, lived in Pleasant Place, in the somewhat newer, southern, more rural, quieter, part of the town, with only Green's quietly whirring Castle Flour Mill nearby – and in the past a windmill – to disturb the peace, and with few shops, all of them very small, no banks, no hotels, no churches, no estate agents, and no building societies close by, and with no traffic passing through the area. At one end of Pleasant Place was a quiet road, little used by vehicles, and at the other there was open countryside. There were no folk passing through Pleasant Place to get to other places, because it was a cul-de-sac and there were no other places to go to. Apart from occasional individual visitors, the residents of this part of the town saw no military personnel or movements locally during the war, though they did meet men working relatively nearby on building the Ellough airfield. People in this area of Beccles tended to look towards the south, away from the river, away from the marshes and towards a mildly rolling landscape, towards an area where the receding glaciers had dumped their sands, gravels and clays in millennia past. They were more 'Suffolk orientated'.

It was their different home areas, and maybe different parental church backgrounds which influenced the places where they separately worshipped and sang for many years. David's father was a strong Church of England member, chorister and churchwarden. Although Colin's mother was a devout Anglican, his father had been brought up in the Baptist Church. Being very careful not to overstate the point, one might see David's father as the stronger churchman, and Colin's mother as the stronger churchwoman. David lived closer to the large Parish Church with its multi-gender choir of a full range of voices. Colin lived closer to the small Ingate Mission Church with its smaller choir, exclusively of boy sopranos. In the smaller church and smaller choir – with its shorter 'promotion ladder' – the relationships between the choir boys on the one hand and the parson, organist, churchwarden and helpers from the congregation, were more 'cosy', more like a family.

These differences in where we lived and went to church had their influences but should not be over emphasized. First, for example, we both supported Norwich City Football Club, in Norfolk, and not Ipswich Town Football Club, in Suffolk. Second, David, from the more urban, industrialized part of Beccles took up his long cherished desire to work in farming, while Colin, from the more rural and countryside part of the town, had no such desires – far from it – and his career had little to do with rural pursuits in Britain. For David – the farmer at heart – the attraction of Wordsworth's poem, 'Michael', was that Michael was a shepherd. For Colin – the geographer at heart – the attraction was the Cumbrian scenery. Third, living in different parts of the town did not affect our going to the same primary school, although other children living quite close to David's home went to the Ravensmere junior school and not Peddars Lane.

Next, David was one of two children in the family, both boys, and the age gap between them was four years. Colin was one of a family of two boys and two girls, and whilst the difference in ages between the eldest and the youngest was five years, his closest siblings were only either a year older or two years younger than him; the age gap between them was relatively small. Whereas David learned a good deal from his older brother about his experiences at the Sir John Leman School, Colin learned very little from his older sister about hers. In David's home, when he was growing up, his grandmother – and later his aunt – lived with them, en famille. There was always an older, third adult in the household. This was not the case in Colin's home. David has commented on the more boisterous atmosphere of mealtimes in Colin's family when compared to the more serious and formal atmosphere of mealtimes in his own home. Beyond this, we are not sure what influences these differences had, but we think there must have been some stemming from the presence in the home of a third adult and of girls as well as boys, from having more than one sibling, and from the age gaps. Perhaps others can see these influences more clearly than we can.

Since we were in the same class at the Sir John Leman School, it is easy to think that we were the same age and had always been in the same class, for example at the Peddars Lane Junior School. In fact, David was nine months younger than Colin and was in a form below him in primary school. This meant a year's difference at primary level, but Colin then went to the Area School for a year before going to the Leman School where he joined the same class as David. The effects of this difference in schooling – of Colin being at the Area School for a year – were four fold. First, he had the broadening effect of being in a school which drew its pupils from a very much larger area than had the primary school. Second, he was exposed to a wider range of teachers and their styles, and to more advanced equipment – for example in the science laboratories – than would have been the case if he had gone straight from Peddars Lane to the Leman School. Third, whereas Colin had the potentially disturbing experience of two changes of school – and the consequent disruption to friendships formed – from Peddars Lane to the Area School to the Leman School, David had only one – from Peddars Lane to the Leman School. Fourth, when we entered the first year of the Leman School, David was eleven years and four months old, and Colin was twelve years and one month old. A difference of nine months at that stage of growing up could be important. While we are not sure what precisely the effects of these differences were, it would be surprising if there were not significant effects. Again, these differences may be more apparent than real and should not be over emphasized.

There was probably little difference in our personal attitudes to school life in our early years at the Leman School. We larked around and found amusement in what was going on, equally the one with the other, save that David seems to have been caught out by the school authorities rather more quickly and frequently than was Colin – for whatever reasons. In our early years at the Leman School, too, our individual approaches to serious study were equally – how shall we put it? – unfocussed. In Colin's case, however, from the beginning of the run-up to the School Certificate examinations, he – it appears quite suddenly and unexplainedly – began to take his studies very much more seriously than he had done previously. At the same time David's diligence followed a more steady and consistent course.

But it was in the field of sports and athletics that there was a more marked difference between us. Both were very keen on football and cricket, David probably more so in his enthusiasm than Colin. The differences are described in our separate accounts in this book, but we think that in a school which prided itself on its games and athletic distinction, it was possibly inevitable that the successful players and athletes became on slightly closer terms with some male members of staff, some of whom may have found it difficult to give equal weight to enthusiasm and ability and to adjust their attention, tuition and encouragement sufficiently to balance these two aspects. It was also the case that in teams comprised of players from a range of classes and ages, friendships developed across class and age groups, friendships which might otherwise not have developed. At the rare reunions one might observe clusterings of old boys from the school teams rather than groups of old boys from the same classes.

A major difference was that David left school after the fifth form and Colin stayed on into the sixth form. The opportunities for boys and girls to learn more about the staff – and vice versa – were increased in the sixth form, as were the opportunities to develop whatever leadership potential a sixth former might have as a prefect or on the playing field. David's life during the two years after he left brought different experiences and different, but equally important, benefits.

The biggest difference of all, however, lies in the fact that David stayed in East Anglia while Colin went off to Africa for twenty years, and even when he returned to Britain he lived in Wales, paying only occasional and short visits to the Beccles area. Furthermore, David married a Beccles girl whereas Colin's wife was brought up in Argentina. How these difference impacted on our memories of our school days and our relationships with former pupils and with the staff, albeit as adults, is fundamental. Since leaving school David has been able almost continuously to refresh his memories through contacts and conversations with people with whom he was at school, and with others in the neighbourhood. Colin was more remote and his memories were not refreshed by local contacts. As the years passed, David's memories stayed alive while Colin's faded more quickly. Moreover, as an adult David got to know and learn more about a number of members of staff and their families. They became close friends and on personal name terms. Colin continued to know them only as his teachers and he knew little about their families. These differences show through in the narratives of our separate recollections – and consequently in our reflections on those recollections.

We are conscious that on many occasions we go off at a tangent and write about a matter which is but tenuously connected with the principal matter we are dealing with at the time. This, we fear, is the ways our minds have worked as we recall our early days – rather like telling stories in a pub – and reflect upon them, but we promise that we will always return, sooner or later, to our main themes.

We have tried to avoid falling into the error of using such expressions of complaint and regret as 'Things ain't what they used to be' and 'They don't make 'em like that nowadays', because things inevitably change and because the overwhelming balance of change, in our view, has been for the better. To take just one illustration, when we were born the life expectancy of men at birth in the United Kingdom was 59, today it is 78. For women it was and is about four years older. At the un-ripe age of eighty we are not sure how we should view these figures, but we are delighted to have got this far!

The memories of our school days, the pleasures of those years, and the influences of our early experiences – and of the people with whom we came in contact – are long lasting and in some cases they are indelible. Do we have any regrets? Only one – and it is a big one – the opportunities which we missed, either because we ignored them or, more usually, because we did not recognize them. The rest was good – very good!

BECCLES SCHOOLDAYS:
RECOLLECTIONS AND REFLECTIONS

Part One
by
David Woodward

CHILDHOOD MEMORIES

This is not a deeply researched account of my childhood. It comes simply from my memories as I write. It will, I hope, be of interest to folk who live in Beccles or the Waveney Valley now but also to a wider readership who may be interested in life in a small East Anglian town situated on the Norfolk and Suffolk border. I hope there is not too much 'me' in the book. My aim is to write about people and events that took place during the first 18 years of my life.

Of course, I cannot remember a lot about the first five years and pre-school days, but I do recall some things that my older brother, John (born August 1926) told me. We shared the same three-quarter size feather-bed for the first ten years of my life until he left to live in 'digs' in Lowestoft where he worked as a Youth in Training telephone engineer. John acted very much as my carer and had an almost paternalistic approach to his younger brother. I felt that he was always concerned that I did not let the good name of the family down. We were not a bit alike; in fact many people expressed amazement that two brothers so different came from the same stock. But this difference eventually drew us closer together. We did have very special subjects, like politics and literature that we agreed on. In the last few years of his life, as he bravely battled cancer, we became true brothers more than ever before. He seldom lost his sense of humour, and from his sick-bed we shared some of his childhood memories. He remembered that Mum told him when he was born that Dr. Wood-Hill attended but the mid-wife had arrived on her bike before him. On finding her raincoat across the foot of the bed he muttered about the dangers of microbes, picked it up and hurled it down the stairs.

We had a nanny-maid, Florence, who looked after us in the early years. It has always amazed me how my dad could afford to employ a maid. Most tradesmen, shopkeepers or professional people in the town could afford to have domestic help, but we lived in a humble terraced cottage in Fair Close. The area was very much working class, but the family had known more prosperous days. My late grandfather had been a well known grocer in the town and a Freemason. His daughter – my aunt – had a successful business career in London and she owned the house we lived in and may also have contributed towards expenses. My mum was also looking after 'Grandma', so it is possible the Freemasons also helped financially. We were soon aware that money was not plentiful but never did we go short of clothes or food. Dad was shrewd, thrifty and hardworking. He had other 'sidelines', as he called them, beyond his regular job as an auctioneer's clerk.

Florence would take us for walks along the avenue and on to the common. On Sunday afternoons when the weather was reasonable it was the rule to walk around St. Mary's Road. This was a steady half hour's stroll along Ballygate with splendid views across the marshes of the Waveney Valley, past the War Memorial and the hospital and thence home past the shops in Blyburgate with their blinds all drawn in observance of the Sabbath.

My brother was quieter than me and battled against a stammer, but I soon wanted to and did chat to everyone. My granddaughter Martha is the same or she certainly was at five years old.

I can just remember the celebrations that took place for the 1935 Jubilee. We all went to a special tea-party. This took place in a big marquee that had been erected especially for the occasion on the College Meadow football ground. We all sat at low trestle tables on small benches that had been taken from the local Infants Schools. There were egg and cress and ham sandwiches. But I do have one other vivid memory. Each child was allocated a jelly. It became quite hot in the marquee and the jelly had not set hard. It was almost like a raspberry coloured soup. To make matters worse the jelly had been placed in paper bun cups. Alas these were not solid enough to hold the jelly. There was much spillage, causing amusement to the boys, as they tried to funnel it into their mouths, and distress to the girls worried about staining their party frocks.

My dad told me a tale concerning an event that he was involved in at the time of the Jubilee. He worked for Durrants the local auctioneers and they had a big furniture sale that took place in a marquee somewhere near Bungay. Dad was given a lift home to Beccles in the lorry taking the marquee home to the owners at their base in Lowestoft. The firm was Clevelands and as well as supplying marquees, flags and bunting for festive celebrations they were also, and quite in contrast, undertakers. The term 'funeral directors' had not then arrived. As the lorry approached the Shipmeadow Workhouse the driver said to my dad, 'Jack, we have just got to call in at the "Wuck 'uss" as we have a suit of clothes for an old lady'. The lorry, bedecked with flags, bunting and various

14

packed tents, pulled round to the back of the building near the workhouse mortuary. The lorry driver and his mate got off, rolled some of the bunting back and hauled out a very plain coffin. This was the 'suit of clothes' for an old lady. After a few minutes they reappeared from the mortuary with the old lady in her coffin and this was pushed into the back of the lorry to be covered again with flags and bunting. The lorry pulled up near the church tower at Beccles so father could easily get to Durrant's office, and the poor old lady reposed in her flag bedecked coffin unseen by passers-by. Bless her heart. I expect she was finally laid to rest with full pauper's honours. My dad, a kindly man, never forgot that event and was into his eighties when he told me that story.

In these early years before starting school I can remember regular walks with Florence to feed the ducks on the wide dyke that flowed near the common. This dyke was bridged across the tree-lined avenue a quarter mile long that led to the common, and was always filled with water-lilies and king-cups. When a few years older, we used to dip jam-jars on string holders to try and catch tadpoles, and we also tried unsuccessfully to catch eels and sticklebacks. Just to the left of the elegant gates on to the common were two sets of swings. Mum would often be with us and give us a push. One swing was special for tiny-tots. It had rails around it – you were lifted in and pushed your legs through and thus could not fall when the swing was in motion.

A few years passed and Florence left to work for Dr. Grantham-Hill our doctor. No doubt it was a better paid job at the doctor's, more than my parents could afford, but the family wished her well. Then Winnie arrived. I never thought as a child of Winnie and Florence being in our employ. They were just two lovely girls – a bit older than my brother and me – who had come to care for us and help Mum to look after Grandma.

Eventually the common swings were extended into a real children's play area. There was a jump-on-jump-off small roundabout propelled by the children themselves as it rotated on a spindle. There was also a titta-ma-totter or see-saw and another boat-like object on huge springs which four children could sit in. The whole area was fenced around so that cattle grazing on the common did not foul the area. There were two bench seats for parents and carers to sit on while children played. Always in the summer the singing of larks soaring above the common were heard. Now over seventy years on, that sound-memory is still vivid.

DOWN OUR ROAD

Fair Close where I was born in 1930 was a close-knit community. Very few families moved house in the years I was growing up. I told you that I was a chatterer and I loved talking to everyone. There always seemed to be something going on in the road. The local Employment Exchange or as it was more suitably called the 'Unemployment Exchange' was on the other side of the road opposite our cottage. It was a busy office with comings and goings through the day and especially in the mornings. The Exchange was a green wooden hut in the garden of Mr. Jones the manager who lived in a part of the Old Hospital in Fair Close. In those days it had been divided into three dwellings. The centre portion of the building was the home of the Croucher family. I loved this part as it was thick with Virginia Creeper and in the autumn the leaves changed into vivid colours. When the war came the Croucher family had gone, moving into a modern bungalow on the Worlingham road, so this portion of the former hospital was commandeered by the military and used as living quarters for the various troops stationed in the town during the war years. The other end of the hospital was the home of two spinster school teachers, Miss Hunter and Miss Robinson, who were on the staff of the National School in Ravensmere. None of the occupants in the Old Hospital ever passed me without having a word. And then there was the added attraction of all the men who came to 'sign on' at the Exchange. Some of the regulars I got to know quite well.

There was a builders' supply yard in the road and it was interesting to see the activity there. In those early days the various tradesmen had long flat barrows rather than vans or lorries. These they pushed by hand with an apprentice boy putting his weight to the barrow as they trundled up and down the road.

Elliott and Garood's iron foundry was at the bottom of Fair Close and so there were lots of foundry workers going past our house on their way to work or returning home. A hooter sounded off at five minutes before 8 o'clock each morning to remind the slackers they needed to hurry. Most of the older men, clad in blue boiler suits, would saunter along in good time, but some of the younger lads would be almost running down the road and lane to the foundry when the hooter sounded. Even when very young we were allowed to play in the lane going between the factory buildings. It was exciting to stand in the open doorway watching the molten metal and the sparks fly. When the war came the factory was working twenty-four hours a day on munitions. There was a big bonus for us living near the foundry. Mr. and Mrs. Maurice Elliott lived at Hope Villa in Fair Close. Mr. Elliott invented a flying machine before the war. A small two-seater, it flew round their garden attached to a steel rope on a tall pole. Mrs. 'Bunny' Elliott gave wonderful Christmas parties for her family and all local children were invited.

A taxidermist also lived in the road and two postmen who did boot and shoe repairs as a spare time job. There were two other small builders in the row of cottages. They worked on their own but were always in demand for paper hanging, painting or small repairs. One of them, Mr. Smith, did all our house-painting and glazing or wall-papering. Even the most humble families used tradesmen for this work. Do-it-yourself had not arrived. The prelude to new wall papering always amused me. Mr. Smith would leave two or three books of sample patterns the week-end before work was due to commence. These were quite heavy objects and were laid on the dining room table for careful selection by Mum and Dad with Grandma adding her voice to the proceedings, notably if her room was to be decorated. Bedrooms were only done every ten years or so but the kitchen and living room had to be decorated more often. My mum favoured the brighter paper and paint while my dad looked for something he called 'more serviceable'. No doubt household economics played a part. Mr. Smith, I recall, had been in the Flying Corps in the First World War. During the Second World War he was a Special Constable. The other jobbing builder was Mr. Leighton. A great delight to us boys, he would cycle back and forth to his various jobs in an unhurried manner. As he approached the cross-roads he would call out to us 'Are there any sheep about?' There never were.

Three railway workers lived in the road. Mr. Pettingell was a signalman. He had a massive frame. A keen gardener, he kept his family and friends with produce off his fertile allotment. He also helped in the gardens of local widows or more genteel folk in the area. His two sons were playmates in the road. Another man, whose name I cannot recall, who lived at the bottom of the road also worked at the railway station. He always exchanged a few words with my mother. He knew her from the time she managed the refreshment rooms at the railway station before she and Father married. My parents first met in 1912 when there was a huge fire at Crisp's Maltings in Gosford Road that adjoins Fair Close. The fire blazed in the early hours of the morning. My father would have been 18 years old at the time, and with my granddad Mike he went for refreshment after the fire was extinguished. And so he met my Mum for the first time.

Mr. Oakley was another railwayman who lived in Fair Close, but he worked at the booking office issuing tickets to travellers. He and another fellow-worker shared the work and also booking in what was known as 'passenger goods'. All the heavy produce, such as sugar-beet, grain, coal and cattle, went by special goods trains. And their progress was often slow, as wagons would be shunted and added to the line as they travelled towards Lowestoft, Great Yarmouth or Ipswich and eventually London. But lighter and less bulky material, like 'luggage in advance', boxes of day-old chicks and even small calves, which were packed into sacks with their head peeping out, was able to be sent speedily by passenger rail and was carried in the guard's van. The local mail destined for Ipswich or London also went the same way. Incoming passenger goods were booked out by Mr. Oakley to the local postman or to individual collectors. Other items were also delivered in the town by a horse-drawn wagon.

A few folk who lived in the road also worked at the Caxton Printing Works in Newgate (now the site of a Tesco supermarket). The printers were the elite of the working class in the town, simply by the fact that their wages were highest. I remember especially Mr. Curtis who was secretary of the Men's Social Institute at the top of the road. The 'Tute', as we all called it, was ranked number three in the hierarchy of clubs and billiard halls in the town. Number one was of course the Conservative Club which was officially described as the Working Men's Conservative Club. Why a working man in those days would wish to be a conservative I have never been able to fathom out, but some did. I recall one grubby foundry worker proudly telling me that he was 'a bloody Tory and always would be'. The Caxton Club which adjoined the printing works was for the more affluent members of the printing fraternity. There were a lot of local people who worked at the Caxton Press but there were many who came from away to work in a flourishing industry. Much of the town's prosperity came from the result of the Caxton Press.

I was involved at the 'Tute' from the age of 13 years onward. There seemed to be no age restrictions on joining as luckily the 'bar' only sold soft drinks, crisps and nuts or packets of biscuits. These were all supplied from Lawrance's mineral water factory in Gaol Lane about a quarter mile away. The drinks were lemonade, grapefruit, Portello, Vimto and Cream Soda. During the war years the supply of these was restricted, the caretaker always trying to allocate the drinks fairly to members.

The 'Tute' had three billiard tables. No. 1 was exclusively for billiards which was more popular then but gradually giving way to snooker. Snooker was played on tables 2 and 3. You paid 6d for half an hour (2½ p) to hire a table. The person in charge of the bar allocated the bookings. He had three cut out cardboard clock faces. The hands he was able to propel to show the time each half hour was up. During the week and especially in the early evening there might be plenty of free access. Then the half hour allocation was less rigidly applied. But on Friday and Saturday nights on dark evenings the tables would be fully booked. It was the custom for lots of folk to have a game of snooker and read the Eastern Evening News or 'Pink-un' before going to the second house at the Regal Cinema in Ballygate or to the 'Old Cinema', now Prezzo's Italian Restaurant. We all spoke about the 'Old Cinema' but the official title was 'Beccles Little Luxury Theatre'. My dad sang behind the silent screen there in the 1920s with Mrs. Esling (who with her husband John kept a newsagents in Blyburgate) playing the piano.

On Friday and Saturday nights it was possible to have a bath at the 'Tute' for sixpence. There were two bathrooms. Each had a small changing area with a wooden bench and a peg to hang clothes on. There was no carpeting but a wooden duck-board to stand on rather than a cold cement floor. The caretaker, a retired foundry worker from Elliott and Garood, who lived in a cottage nearby, would light the boiler for the bath-water early on Friday afternoon. He and his wife would then have a free bath as one of the perks of the job. The secretary's wife, who also helped with the cleaning and bookwork, was allowed the same benefit. But they would have left the premises long before the members arrived.

There were a few towns-people who became members of the 'Tute' at six shillings a year (30 p) solely to be able to use the bathing facilities. In the cold weather it was always best to get the first bathroom as it was next to the Crane boiler. If the wind was wrong the coke fumes might be strong but the extra warmth made up for this. You were expected to supply your own towels and although no rigid time limit was set anyone who took longer than twenty minutes over their ablutions was frowned upon. Sometimes the person in charge of the 'bar' that night would go and lump on the bathroom door if it was thought a culprit was too long bathing.

A local dentist who lived in Station Road lodgings was a regular for his weekly bath. He strolled along each Friday at 6.00 p.m. so he was sure of an early bath. He was tall with a bald head and, strangely in those days, never wore a cap. But always he dressed in a navy blue suit. As the colder weather arrived he had a heavy woollen blue overcoat and a blue muffler. He was a man of few words, smiled at everyone, but did not engage in much conversation. After his ablutions were over he'd quietly pay his dues and leave. On the few occasions when he had to wait for a spare bath he would sit quietly on one of the benches around the billiard room and read the paper. Curiously, these benches can still be seen. Although the 'Tute' closed years ago they still have a bowling green at the rear of the Beccles Library, accessed via Fair Close. And these benches which have a high seat, reached by a step which acts as a long footrest, are still in use. Originally they gave spectators an excellent view of the snooker or billiard tables – now they provide the same service to people watching bowls. In their former use they were varnished, now they have a strong coat of all-weather gloss paint.

Another regular for the baths but not a person who got involved in any of the other 'Tute' activities was 'Slippery'. He never spoke to anyone but came in every Saturday night early in the evening for his bath. Slippery was the most dilatory of all the bathers. Someone timed him one night and he took over fifty minutes. An impatient customer waiting his turn banged on the door but, as always, Slippery appeared some time later, apparently oblivious of any problems he had given. Silently he paid his money without uttering a word. Then, giving the person taking his dues a cursory nod, disappeared into the night.

When I went to the Institute we had no bathroom at home, so I made use of the facilities. But I was the only one in the family who did. In those days a weekly bath was the custom in most households. Some of my more affluent friends like Derek Lawrance or Christopher Elliott, whose parents owned the mineral water factory and iron foundry respectively, had a bathroom in the house. But most families relied on a galvanized bath that was kept in a shed outside and came into the house on bath-night and was filled with water heated in the copper. This was either in a corner of the kitchen or in some dwellings in a wash-house outside. The tin bath was a splendid haven in the shed for spiders. These were brushed out before the bath was carried into the kitchen. Our particular bath was different from the norm. It was round and only about eight inches in depth. I discovered many years later that is was in fact a Victorian cream skimming vessel rescued from an old dairy, but it was adequate for its changed use in our household.

Our kitchen was the scene of all ablutions. Father shaved there every morning, using a 'cut-throat' razor which he sharpened on a leather strap which hung from a small hand-pump beside the kitchen sink. There was a bundle of old newspaper squares about eight inches wide hung next to the strap and on these squares Dad wiped the shaving soap and beard from his razor. His business of shaving was a daily ritual. And my grandma, who was still living with us and in her eighties, told me that my granddad, who died before I was born, followed the same procedure. The small hand-pump over the sink gave access to soft water which had collected in a small 'well' just outside the back door. It was not a true well but a reservoir for rainwater collected from the roof. This soft water was pumped into a jug and then boiled in an old black kettle designated solely for this purpose. Besides shaving, this water was used for hair-washing or special clothes washing such as silk stockings and other delicate lingerie. Father's pre-shaving lathering was vigorous and methodical. He would lather his face using a stick of shaving soap and a brush. Or at times he was given a present at Christmas of a more select scented soap in a bowl. He told me that when I grew up and shaved I must never buy a cheap brush because of a risk of anthrax germs entering nicks in the skin. He would go over his face with the razor twice, lathering again before the second shave. By the time my brother and I arrived on the scene at 7.45 a.m. he had almost finished and then he would help Mum supervise breakfast. It was one of the 'rules' that we did not enter the kitchen before then. Restless lads around him were not ideal for Dad when his cut-throat was in use.

All meals in the household were formal but breakfast was the only one where we did not have to sit and eat together. Egg and bacon followed by toast and marmalade was the usual fare. But there were days when kippers or bloaters and even smoked haddock were eaten. Once or twice in the year sweet-breads would be fried. And in the autumn field mushrooms might be available. They often came from Mr. Alec Gill's farm in Ringsfield. Cereals were sometimes eaten – more so in the war-years. Farmers' Glory wheat flakes and porridge in the cold winter months was thought to be a good filler before school. My brother and I always drank two beakers of tea before leaving for school or play in the holidays. The first beaker was brought to us in the bedroom by Winnie who had arrived to help in the house after Florence left.

This is a good time to tell you about Winnie Alexander who had such an influence on my young life. She came to work as a full-time domestic help. Everyone loved her and she grew to love us. Winnie was such a contented and placid girl and got on with everyone. She was a deeply sincere religious person who eventually left our family to work full time for the Church Army in Scotland where she met her future husband. Sadly, over the years we lost touch with her although her sister Laura eventually came to live in Fair Close when she married. We always said 'hello' if we passed in the street. Winnie's dad was a fisherman out of Lowestoft and the family lived in one of the council houses built in the 1930's on the Ellough Road and Castle Hill estate. Winnie walked daily from there to Fair Close each morning, arriving at the house at 6.30 a.m. She must have been only about 14 years of age when she started. But she was luckier than some girls going into domestic service in that my mum treated her in some ways as one of the family. Nevertheless I shudder at the thought that Winnie must have got up at least two hours before we did. Letting herself in by her own key, she made a cup of tea for Mum, Dad and Grandma, which she carried to them on a tray. She then lit the fire if required and busied herself in the kitchen, preparing breakfast and laying the table. She herself had breakfast and all other meals with us. If there were special guests Winnie sat at our table but was up and down all the time, fetching and carrying. Sometimes she preferred quietly to eat alone in the kitchen. Until we reached more mature years Winnie walked part of the way to school with us. For all this devoted work for the family she was paid the princely sum of five shillings (25p) per week, plus her keep. I hope that she was happy with us, but I think she must have been, because she visited the family household many years after she left. On her half day off on Saturday she would sometimes take my brother and me to Norwich, Lowestoft or Great Yarmouth for an afternoon trip. I believe my parents then paid the costs. Nearly all the families who could afford it paid for someone to help them in the house. Usually they were young girls from working families who left school at fourteen and had no chance for further education. I have often wondered since who helped those girls' parents. For housework and running the home was a full-time job. All the washing was done by hand. The vacuum cleaner was just starting to be used, but one did not come into our home in Fair Close until the 1940s when Aunt Marge arrived to escape London's Blitz. My mum was beginning to suffer poor health and was overjoyed to have this mechanical time-saving cleaning aid.

Another eccentric but interesting character who lived at the top of Fair Close was Clifford Grinter. There was no one else in the town like Clifford.

And never have I met anyone else quite like him. He always addressed me as 'young fellow'. Clifford had a terrible phobia about suffering from the cold or damp weather. He was never outside without a very light raincoat even on boiling hot days when most folk were in shirt sleeves. Today half the population would be in shorts, including postmen, on the days Clifford was attired in his light raincoat. As the days got cooler in the autumn Clifford progressed to a heavier raincoat. In the depth of winter when ice and snow was on the ground he had a thick grey woollen overcoat that came below his knees. He always wore a trilby and this was attached to his coat by a 'hat-guard' even in a light breeze. This was a very light chain or strap that clipped on the rim and then was fixed through the over-coat buttonhole. No one else have I ever seen wear one. To withstand the elements Clifford also wore buskins or leggings which protected his legs up to the knees. These he wore for most of the year except on the light raincoat days of high summer. He worked for a time in the office of a local builder. As a prank, anyone who entered used to leave the door open so Clifford became the victim of a draught. This was one of his great fears. Perched high with various ledgers around him at a Victorian desk, he kept a very long rule beside him. This he used to poke the offending door shut. He often had to repeat the process as most visitors left the door ajar when they left, but he never seemed to admonish anyone or complain. Like all the cottages at that time the lavatories were outside and down the yard or garden. It was said that Clifford kept a special old hat and coat on a hook by the back door. These he put on when he made a trip to the lavatory. Poor Clifford, he must have been concerned about draughts when his trousers had perforce to be lowered. Many, many years later I met a native of the town who told me he started his early married life in 'rooms' they hired from Clifford which he let to augment his income after his mother's death and he had a room to spare. On a Sunday morning when the newly-weds were enjoying a lie in and a Sabbath kiss and cuddle Clifford would tap on their bedroom door at 11 o'clock calling out 'its time you young people were up'. But, although strange, he was an accepted part of the locality. Few spoke ill of him, he was always in work albeit at his own steady pace. One wonders how he would have coped in the modern world today, or how it would have coped with him. Fair Close held a host of characters.

Mr Smith, an elderly retired man, had a small plot of land adjoining his house. It was not a large area but it did house a big greenhouse and a plum tree. As a lad I would be sent on an 'errand' in season to buy tomatoes or plums. His greenhouse enchanted me. It was lower than ground level and you stepped down into it to be among the tomato plants growing in the soil on either side. Things like grow-bags were unheard of. It was heated by a coke boiler in a small entrance lobby to the house. Here he had a table for the scales with which he weighed the tomatoes for sale and a chair on which he sat for a lot of the day. Two single hot water pipes ran along the length of each side of the greenhouse walls which were bricked for the first couple of feet or so. The heat was never on when I went in the early summer to get tomatoes, but had been used earlier to bring the fruit on. A pound of tomatoes cost 6d and they were often a feature on our tea-time menu in the summer months.

Now is a good time perhaps to mention a bit about the tea-time. We ate at 5.30 p.m. or soon after when Father returned from the office. The preparation for tea would have begun some time earlier. Two plates of bread and butter were cut in the kitchen – one plate of brown cut from a small loaf and the other white from a larger loaf. Sliced bread was not available and I'm certain would not have been used in our household if it was. My mum always baked various cakes and biscuits every Friday and these were kept in tins and consumed through the week. But the main bulk for tea was the bread and butter. The bread came from a variety of small local bakers in the town. I will try to recall them all. Dusty Farman had a small bake-house and shop in St. Anne's Road. He was famous for rasped loaves and saffron buns. A rasped loaf had been purposely overcooked so that the crust was slightly charred. This was then scraped off by Dusty with his own home-made rasp made from old crown beer-bottle tops tacked on to a flat board. He would strike the crust several times with the side of the board to loosen and break it. And then he would rub the charred pieces off, using the beer-bottle tops as a very effective rasp. The charred crumbs were eventually swept up and placed on a bird table in the yard. The St. Anne's Road birds were well fed. Mr. Farman died in 1953. The business had been started by his father when he, the father, was only 17, and when he died, aged only 46, his son took it over but had to close it during the First World War when he served in the Suffolk Regiment. He reopened it when he was demobbed. Farman's was the last brick oven left in the town.

Another baker was Billy Dawson whose shop was in Blyburgate and the family lived above. There was and still is a small arched alley-way leading into Hungate, passing the then Seppings slaughter house. As children we always called this Dawson's alley. Billy Dawson also sold dough buns at a farthing each. Quite a good return on my pocket money. Filby's was another local baker and their shop was at the entrance to Ballygate from the New Market Square. Percy Filby was a friend of my father and they were both members of the Conservative Club. He had a collection of Lowestoft Porcelain and Dad took an interest in this. Most of the local tradesmen belonged to 'the Club' and my dad was the secretary for many years and certainly all through my childhood. Filby's were famous for their hot-cross buns which were baked on Good Fridays only, when there would be small queues at all the local bakers for folk collecting their traditional breakfast, the early callers being there soon after 7.00 a.m. Filby's also produced a variety of mock cream cakes some of them covered in shocking pink icing. Clarkes were local bakers and had shops in Northgate and at the end of Blyburgate opposite the Black Boy public house. Many of these bakers delivered bread in the town. We were thus served, one day a week, from Tooks whose shop was in New Market. The bread arrived at the door, packed high in a huge basket and selection was made thus. 'Dipper' Pluck was the delivery man and he pushed a huge barrow with two shafts. When fully laden it must have been hard work as it was propelled by his power alone. Dipper got his nickname because he was a great swimmer, and he gave displays at the annual regatta in August. He would dive from a high platform erected on Darby's wharf into a flaming hoop in the river. He was one of the stalwarts of the water-polo team between the wars. In the year 1959 he and I were fellow patients at Beccles War Memorial Hospital. It was the middle of a long hot summer and the then new swimming pool had just opened in Puddingmoor. Dipper was pleased about this recent addition to the town's swimming amenities. We watched a continuous procession of folk young and old making their way along Priory Road to the pool. The numbers were even greater at this time, for the local print workers from the Caxton Press were on strike. The interest shown in the town on swimming and water sports prompted Dipper's memories of his former aquatic glories. Although by then elderly and in failing health, he was always jolly company. I seem to recall that he had also delivered for Money's the bakers. Their shop was at the entrance to Hungate from Exchange Square. This eventually in my time became Drury's and finally Ford's bakery. I think it was the only bake-house in the town that had a few café chairs and tables at one end where it was possible to get tea and cakes. A small haven for tired shoppers. When it became Ford's bakery in the 1950's the owner, Reginald Ford, was a stalwart of the local hockey team of which I was a member. At the end of each home game both teams would repair to Ford's bakery for a sandwich and cake tea. This was generously supplied by Mr. Ford at a cost of one shilling (5p) paid by each home team member. His wife had prepared this refreshment during the afternoon.

But back to Fair Close again. A small cottage at the top of the road was the home of Miss Bradnum. The front room had been converted into a small shop, selling sweets and other bits and pieces. She was quite an elderly lady and I suppose the few pence she took each day from local boys and girls helped to eke out the pension. I went there to get aniseed balls, slab toffee and sugar mice. Miss Bradnum also sold some wood kindling and paraffin for oil lamps and heaters. The only source of heat in the early days was from solid fuel or paraffin oil. There were two other sweet shops near enough for me to visit as a child on my own. Miss Ellwood's in Newgate which was always referred to as the back street. A Mrs. Eagle kept a similar sweet shop and small stores in a cottage in Gosford Road. I think her late husband had been one of the earlier workers at Elliott and Garood's iron foundry. Other local tradesmen and shopkeepers delivered regularly in the road in addition to the bakers.

Let me tell you about the green-grocers. Our regular deliverer was a Mr. Spratt who I think was based somewhere in the Swines Green-St. Anne's Road area. I cannot remember if he grew many of his own vegetables to sell but the supply was certainly local. He certainly kept chickens – as Colin tells us later. Vegetables of course came strictly in season, but he did supply, when wartime restrictions were not in force, citrus fruits like oranges, lemons, bananas and, especially at Christmas time, tangerines and boxed dates. Fruit such as plums, apples, pears, bullaces and blackberries came from local growers. He had a very docile pony drawing his cart who plodded steadily up the road unattended, stopping every few yards to allow his owner to supply each group of cottages in the road. Mr. Spratt came twice a week I think on Tuesday and Saturday.

Mr. Bloomfield another green-grocer was also a regular but on different days. We did not buy from him but he always had a cheery word for children playing in the road. His pony was a cryptorchid i.e. he had not been castrated because the testicles had not descended into the scrotum. This made him a bit aggressive and you could not venture too near and coax his nose, like you could Mr. Spratt's gentle pony, or he would try and bite you. Mr. Bloomfield led him up the road and then 'anchored' him at each stop by fastening the rein to a heavy 7lb weight carried on his cart for this purpose. Mr. Bloomfield supplied very large Jaffa oranges which were individually wrapped in tissue paper. These wrappers were smoothed out carefully by his customers and used in their lavatories as toilet paper.

A Mr. Banns from Burgh St. Peter also came with eggs, flowers and vegetables during the war years. He came to Beccles sale-yard on a Friday to sell rabbits, chickens and vegetables but provided some for my mum at a reasonable price. My mum and aunt looked forward to his visits. Often they would have a mock argument between themselves about who was going to answer the door when he arrived. Mr. Banns was a tall man with an hussar-like moustache.

Milkmen were regular daily callers, coming with fresh milk. The milk in those days had to be used, especially in the warm weather, within twenty-four hours. Mum would scald the milk to keep it longer in the high summer. I can remember three milkmen who came to Fair Close: Mr. Alec Gill, Mr. Buckenham and Mr. Boast. They each used pony drawn milk floats (carts). Mr. Gill's was very elegant, his ponies were dashing. He had to employ a 'boy' to hold the pony on Saturday mornings when his stops were longer as he collected the week's money at the door. I did this job for two years during the war in 1943 and 1944. Some of the milk was bottled in half, one and two pint glass bottles. Skimmed and semi-skimmed milk was unheard of, but many of his customers took their milk straight into a jug proffered at the door-step. Mr. Gill carried this milk in a small hand-churn to the door and then measured the milk, using a half pint measure that hooked on to the lid of his churn. He did this with quite a flourish and always gave a small amount more 'for good measure'.

Another regular caller was Mr. Simmonds who visited from time to time to renew the wireless accumulator. These were heavy-duty and Mr. Simmonds carried a few on his trade bike. He brought them to the back door, and the wireless was conveniently placed on a table against the living room window. To access it Mr. Simmonds only had to lift the sash and he was able to change the accumulator without even entering the house. The back lane in Fair Close was wide enough to allow the corporation dust cart drawn by Prince, a Suffolk Punch. The dustmen lifted the bins on to their shoulders easily and then tipped the contents into the dust-cart. In hot weather they carried packets of disinfectant powder which they sprinkled in the emptied galvanized bins. Mr. Fairweather also came up the lane with a horse-drawn cart. He supplied logs for the fire and smaller cut wood which folk chopped themselves for kindling. It must be pointed out how important this wood was in the 1930s and wartime years. In our household the copper and Dutch oven in the kitchen, plus two more fires in the living and front room all required good kindling to light them. As soon as I was old enough one of my favourite tasks was to sit on a stool in the shed and chop the kindling on a special wooden block. Our next-door neighbour, Mr. Ernest Shiplee, was a keen tomato grower and whenever the ponies or horses were about he kept a look-out for supplies of manure. This he stored some months before using it.

I can remember two window cleaners. The most notable was Nicky Goffin who would go along a terrace of houses cleaning the front windows and then repeat the process at the rear. Most of his customers left money on the step for him to collect. His charge for a small cottage was 6d. Nicky had a 'secret ingredient' he added to the water and was recognized in the town and beyond as a window cleaner supreme. He had been quite a sportsman in his younger days, playing football for Beccles Town. He was, when I knew him, a most artful spinner of a table tennis ball. He would wait and hit the ball below the surface of the table so you could not see which way the spin would take the ball. Often it would go away at right angles in a different direction from that which his opponent was expecting. I played against him at times after the war when the 'Tute' team was reformed and he often beat me although some 25 years older. Nicky was one of the town's characters – he loved his pint and a joke, but worked hard and did no one harm. But it was what he called the 'chat' (spin) he put on a table-tennis ball that made him famous and memorable in my eyes.

Another notable up and down the road was 'Uncle Jimmy Cutler'. He worked until his retirement at the Caxton Printing Works. A plump jolly man, he had a Churchillian look about him. He had a 'collar and tie' job at the printing works, and mostly he sported a blue spotted bow-tie. He was seen in the road going to and from work or, later in life, on the way to the shops for his wife, basket in hand and his Skye terrier dog on a lead. This little dog was adored by Jimmy and the children in the road. But it did not fit his grandiose image. He was the conductor of the Beccles Light Symphony orchestra who appeared at lots of events in the town and surrounding area. They performed in the Public Hall at the first play I ever saw, 'Charlie's Aunt', in 1937. Lindsey Tilney the gunsmith took the leading role.

Poor Uncle Jimmy! I witnessed his demise as I stood beside him on the touch-line at the College Meadow watching a football match. Suddenly he keeled over and rolled on his back like an upturned turtle. His breath seemed to come in spurts and his whole body vibrated and rattled. I stood back aghast as the football trainer and other first aiders came to give assistance. With difficulty he was carried into the dressing room. Later that evening, as we were having our bed-time cocoa, Aunt Marge suddenly exclaimed 'Poor old Jimmy Cutler dropped dead at the football this afternoon'. Slowly it sunk into my mind that I had witnessed his death. I cried myself to sleep. But by morning my thoughts were on other things.

Our next-door neighbours in Fair Close were Mr. and Mrs. Shiplee and their daughters. Mrs. Shiplee was a very special lady. If this Part of the book achieves nothing else the fact that Mrs. Nell Shiplee features in it makes it all worth while. She took so much pride in caring for husband, family and their home. But her lively personality and zest for life spread not only around her family but to everyone in the area who passed by or called at their home. She was so energetic, enthusiastic and hard working in everything she did, happily doing the most mundane house-work. And in her younger days she did not consider using modern cleaning aids. Every morning, around six thirty, all household mats and rugs were collected and banged with a beater on the brick wall in the lane near their back gate. There were a lot of brass instruments in the household and these were always kept shining. Lino on the floor was polished. Once a year in the spring a big carpet in the front room was folded up and placed on a little go-cart and trundled to the nearby common to receive a beating. Mr. Shiplee was enrolled on this mission. And I suspect a stop was made for refreshment at the Star Public House en-route.

Mrs. Shiplee was such a cheery little soul, greeting everyone she came in contact with joyously. Whether trades or delivery men, workers at the nearby iron foundry of Elliott and Garood, or folks calling to collect shoes her husband had repaired, and even us boys playing in the lane, everyone got a smile. Life could not have been easy for her bringing up three girls in wartime Suffolk, and her husband did not enjoy the best of health. Gassed in the Great War, his hacking cough was often heard. But whatever cares she had she kept to herself. The girls played the piano in the front room which was against our joint wall. We were serenaded on special occasions, most notably at Christmas when everyone had a fire in the front room.

Mrs. Shiplee's diet was sensible and basic. Maybe this accounted for her long term vitality and good health. They all ate an abundance of good fresh potatoes and vegetables and she was a great believer in onions. Every midday she drank a half-pint bottle of stout with bread, cheese and onion. She and Mr. Shiplee's main source of entertainment was the wireless and Daily Mirror on weekday evenings and a visit to the Star Hotel on Saturday night for a drink, a bit of a laugh and a sing-song. Maybe their stable family life owed much to the fact that Mr. Shiplee, although in poor health after the war, was always in regular work as a postman. The oldest daughter on leaving school worked for Dr. McLaren, the local doctor and surgeon. And at one time Mrs. Shiplee did their laundry and ironing. Even into her old age and widowhood she continued to be active in helping my dad and aunt. She would come bustling up the back garden path in the early evening to exchange her Daily Mirror for our Eastern Daily Press. Devoted to her grandchildren, when they were young she would put a weekly fixed amount in a tin for each child. Then as birthdays came round she had funds for their presents. Lord Beveridge and the new welfare state enabled this gem of a lady to reach old age with the dignity she so richly deserved.

Mr. and Mrs. Lee lived next door on the other side of us, together with Miss Lee who lived en famille. It was much more the custom in those days for a single person to make their home with a married sibling. It seemed to work without friction and often to their mutual benefit. My brother when young was very friendly with the Lees. Mrs. Lee was a retired school teacher and helped us both as we prepared to take the entrance exam for the Sir John Leman School. As brother John grew up he became the handyman in the family. He left school before the end of the war and trained as an apprentice telephone engineer, known as a 'Youth in Training'. But he was skilled at electrical work and helped us and neighbours in this respect. He put power on to Mr. Shiplee's cobbler's shed so that his shoe repair work continued after dark – a mixed blessing as the sound of the hammer reverberated into our kitchen. But we only laughed. Then John laid an underground cable down our garden to the privy. There was a two-way switch in the kitchen so winter visits could be made without a torch or candle. A blessed relief! But still a cold one when it blew a wind frost, although the privy door faced west and was sheltered from the prevailing winter east wind. In the summer evenings the setting sun shone comfortably through a ventilating gap at the top of the door.

It is hard to believe now, but soon after John had started work as a telephone engineer I was allowed to accompany him in the evenings and weekends if he had an emergency call-out. There were no concerns about health and safety or insurance risks. His local inspector, based at Lowestoft, must have known about this but turned a blind eye. My dad, who always wanted to do the right thing, never queried our outings together. The telephone engineer's vehicle was a small green Austin Seven van and it was fun to trundle around the leafy lanes of the Waveney Valley. We often visited a small telephone exchange at the village of Brampton. The building is still there on the A145 before you reach the Brampton Dog, a former public house, now a guest house run by Mr. Benson, a former member of Kenny Ball's Jazz Band. Alas, I let John down one day. It was dark in the blackout and no moonshine to help. He asked me to watch the rear of his van as he turned in the road. My warning shout was late and we went thump into the hedge. But no damage was done. One day at Hopton-on-Sea I was allowed to climb the telephone pole when my brother requested a different spanner or similar tool. John was strapped at the top of an extra tall pole swaying in a strong breeze. I had a few steps to climb on the small ladder carried on the top of his van. From this you transferred to permanent metal steps which went up the pole. The strength of the wind and movement of the pole startled me. I was glad of the adventure and proud to have helped but not sorry to be back again on terra firma. Other interesting trips we made to the Royal Naval Base H.M.S. Europa at the Sparrows Nest in Lowestoft. I was not allowed on to the base so waited in the van near the entrance. John's work was helping to maintain the teleprinters used at the camp. These were at the time the most modern information technology. It was exciting sitting in the comfort of the van on a wild winter's night with rain and sleet lashing on the windows, and listening to the roar of the nearby North Sea. A naval rating in white gaiters and belt on guard duty came and talked to me. His must have been a bleak, cold and lonely duty. John always took with him a thermos flask of chocolate drink. This was made from a powder mixture of chocolate, dried milk and sugar. It was called 'Namco', and it was issued to young telephone engineers and others on similar duties during the war. He kindly always shared his ration with me.

John also had another official wartime activity when he reached the age of 16 years. In August 1942 or soon after, he volunteered to be an A.R.P. (Air Raid Precautions) messenger. Issued with a blue uniform and a black steel helmet with a white 'M' painted on the front, his mission was to take messages on his bicycle. Every town and village in the country was ready to take on Hitler if he did arrive. Beccles had a series of police and A.R.P. stations, fire watchers, Home Guard units, the hospital, munitions factory, printing works and railway needing to be in contact with each other. Sometimes the telephone or electricity supply might fail. Then brother John provided that contact on his bicycle. My dad was proud of him. We all were.

After the Lee family left next door, Miss Jeffries arrived from Ipswich. She was a palmist and fortune teller with a big black cat. During the war for a time two soldiers were billeted in her house. I was fascinated by their accent, so different from our Waveney sound. I was in the back-yard one sunny weekend afternoon and the Air Raid Warning had just sounded. Suddenly the sound of a low flying air-craft was heard overhead. One of the troopers ran into the garden to warn me to get indoors. But he soon calmed everyone as he shouted: 'Eeh – It's only a Lysander – going like the duvvel'.

In the next house down the road lived Don and Kate Martin. Don was a very steady and reliable chief engineer at Elliott and Garood's. He was high enough in the factory hierarchy to wear an overall coat and collar and tie as he had risen above the usual garb of boiler suit. During the war he worked very long hours, and he was on standby twenty four hours a day for any problems at the iron foundry. Don was also one of my dad's fellow members at the Conservative Club. But his other great interest when possible was working behind the scenes with the Beccles Amateur Dramatic Society as assistant stage manager. Together with Mr. Wilson the furniture shop owner, they built the scenery and did the lighting for the B.A.D.S. as the society was affectionately known. Before the war they produced a farce each year in the Public Hall, including Charlie's Aunt, Leave It to Psmith and The Middle Watch. And later during the war I can remember one production they did to boost local morale called 'According To Plan' by no lesser writer than L. du-Garde Peach. The play featured the Home Guard or Local Defence Volunteers, with fire-watchers and Air Raid Wardens all playing a part. I have often wondered if this was a fore-runner of Dad's Army, the well known T.V. programme. Certainly the Public Hall was packed each night for a week. And I want you to imagine the problems that folks had to overcome in the blackout at the end of the show. But I think it took place in June when daylight was long. For weeks after, quotes from the play became catch-phrases in the town. One still retains in our household. A young female telephonist at an out-post for the Home Guard had to report every ten minutes or so to the Brigade Headquarters. Sitting on the edge of the stage and using the old fashioned link phone wound with a handle, she blurted out in a broad Waveney dialect. 'O.P. report, there's narthen to report'. The part was played by Dot Darby, one of the jolliest ladies in the town.

Kate Martin was a real joker and a pal of Aunt Marge. When ladies took on jobs to replace men in the armed forces she worked in the office of Poll's the local timber merchants and she became an Air Raid Warden at the same post where my dad was the Senior Warden. Kate was keen on sports and played tennis, belonging to a rather exclusive club at Homefield Paddock in Ballygate. In the winter time most of the members played badminton on a court in the Corn Hall in Exchange Square. This was originally one of the old Fisher Theatres. Kate acquired a pedigree Welsh Corgi dog at a time when most pets were mongrels. The dog was spoiled by her and all dog lovers in the road, but it was nevertheless a nice little pet. Kate was always one for a joke or a saucy tale. A few neighbours might gather for a chat in the back-lane or across a garden wall. If Kate was present a sudden peel of laughter was frequently heard. Kate and Aunt Marge would swap risqué paper back books. She let me borrow her copy of 'No Orchids For Miss Blandish' by James Hadlee Chase. I found it rather brutal and sordid. Aunt Marge and Kate agreed. What they wanted was a bit of saucy fun. Sadly Kate did not live to a great age and eventually Don had to soldier on without her.

They shared their accommodation, a three storey terraced house, with Ernest Goldsmith, Kate's bachelor brother. They kept to their separate rooms but ate a main meal, cooked by Kate, together and got along very well in this way. Ernest was quite different in character and held a senior position at the Caxton Printing Works. He walked to work well dressed in a tailor made suit. He worked office, not factory, hours and was a solitary man but not unfriendly. After his retirement he had more time for his two great hobbies. A keen lepidopterist, he had a well kept collection of moths and butterflies. He let me and my brother see them. But his other interest was the railway and railway travel. He always returned home to sleep, often on the last train from Liverpool Street. He would take his meals in the dining car on the train and he planned his itinerary so he visited towns like Ely, Cambridge or Bury St. Edmonds. Often stopping at small stations and halts, he would walk in the countryside looking for the wildlife, especially butterflies. He lived with Don after his sister died. Growing older and frail, his walks and journeys became shorter and eventually ceased. I can remember seeing him resting on a low wall at the top of Fair Close as he returned from the shops. Don called my father one day to say 'I think Ernest is really ill this time – will you come?' Dad went back into the house with Don and confirmed that Ernest had died.

Probably because of his propensity for walking, Ernest was a collector of shoes. There was a stack in the bedroom and about five pairs were unopened in their boxes. Being the same size I took, they were passed on to me as a gift and kept me shod for years. One pair was in the moccasin style and extremely comfortable.

Another Mr. Shiplee lived further down the road. He was also a postman and again worked at spare-time boot and shoe repairs. Many postmen and railway men were keen gardeners. Because of an early start or shift work they found it hard to take part in an active evening social life. But they had free-time in the afternoon to garden, often on allotments where the vegetables produced were a great aid to their families, especially in wartime.

HOW THE ROAD AND TOWN CHANGED IN WARTIME

It's good to reflect how our lives changed when war came. Some months before hostilities commenced, Dad became an Air Raid Warden and was soon promoted to Senior Warden in charge of the local station, a special building at Hipperson's builders' yard in Station Road. There were several of these in the town and were called A.R.P. posts. Sadly, the building, used post-war for years as a store and office, was pulled down in 2005 when a new furniture shop opened on the site. We felt the loss as stories around it have lived on in family history. But things change and not all for the worst – many alterations in Beccles are a great benefit to the town. How our old folk of the time would have loved the Waveney Centre! And what a tremendous asset the Museum in Ballygate is. But talking of the wardens' post, I was asked to read a John Clare poem at the Requiem Mass for Reg Jones, a former neighbour in Fair Close. Keith Hipperson was waiting to speak to me afterwards in Grange Road. He told me he had memories of my dad giving him sweets when as a toddler he visited the wardens' post. I think his dad, Percy Hipperson, was a warden, but the family certainly lived next door to the post.

One can not write of Fair Close without mentioning its proximity to the railway station and railway life. Before her marriage Mum had worked with her sisters for the railway company, the L.N.E.R. (London North Eastern Railway). Eventually she became a popular manageress of the refreshment rooms at Beccles railway station. As a little boy I loved to be taken by her to watch the trains. Always at that time a hub of activity and employment, things changed when the war began. A considerable amount of troop movement was by rail. There was also transport of other wartime equipment and munitions. But the first major wartime use entailed the transport of evacuees. A few days before war was declared many arrived from the Romford-Dagenham area by boat, I think pleasure paddle-steamers, into Lowestoft. Poor little souls, some of them were shipped by rail the short journey to Beccles. I have somewhat hazy memories of them coming in a large group slowly up the road, late in the afternoon. They stopped at various houses and were allocated into accommodation for fostering. What a way to treat children, many of them of only primary school age. No doubt it was all meant for the best but to billet children into foster homes with scant enquiries into the suitability of the homes was dreadful. No doubt there were many acts of kindness, care and love – but not in every case, I fear. We did not have an evacuee because my six year old cousin Michael, whose home was in Croydon, came to live with us. His family were on their annual holidays with us when war was declared. In his case and in many cases the evacuees did not stay in Beccles for long. Lowestoft and the east coast area was, in the early days of the war, subject to more air raids than London, so many of them went home after some months – alas just in time for the commencement of the London Blitz and the Battle of Britain.

But it was the soldiers billeted in Fair Close that made the biggest impact on the road and the town. They took over the whole of the central part of the Old Hospital. They had a big air-raid shelter built outside. It was across half the pavement and into part of the road so it left space for transport to go up and down one side and pedestrians on the other. The old adult school and teachers centre at the top of the road eventually was turned into a cook house and mess for all the troops in town and area. And the military took over the top floor of the Men's Social Institute. This was used as sleeping quarters and offices. Some of the houses also had troops billeted with them. What excitement for a young boy to have all this going on in the road.

It must have been after Dunkirk when a Czechoslovak regiment was stationed in the town and surrounding areas. They used to parade before meals in Fair Close and march round to the cook-house for dinner. They carried an enamel mug and their own knife, fork and spoon in their right hand as they marched. After eating, they would drift away in a more leisurely manner back to their living quarters. One of them used to chat to me in broken English and used to give me smoked sausages to eat. The skins were very tough but I loved the spiciness. I regretted in later years not attempting to learn any of their language. Some of the Czech soldiers were also in Lowestoft. A lass I worked with in the Civil Service in the 1960s told me she had a crush on one of them. They were wonderful dancers and very gallant, she told me. Made a girl feel special.

Later in the war and not long before 'D Day' a Belgian Armoured Car Battalion came to town. They moved into the quarters formerly occupied by the Czechs. With their fast moving armoured cars they caused great excitement. They would often go out on manoeuvres in the country surrounding the town and would fight mock battles on Beccles Common. With American and RAF bases at Ellough, Flixton, Seething and elsewhere in Norfolk and Suffolk, the whole area had so much more added interest. Strangely, this all seemed to be detached from the dreadful war going on in Europe. No doubt our mums and dads, many with husbands or sons involved in the conflict, viewed it differently. I did, growing older, as the war progressed and I heard of boys who had left school and had gone into the war and had been killed, wounded or taken prisoner. Some families had to cope with news of a member 'missing'. After months of anxiety came grief or joy.

Another group of servicemen, who were scattered in the villages on farms around the town, manned the anti-aircraft guns and search-light batteries. Their bright lights in the sky, weaving and criss-crossing the heavens, were a feature some nights, notably in the winter months when the darkened sky arrived before bed time.

We were visited here in Frostenden by an ex-soldier some years ago who was on a searchlight a few hundred yards from our present home. He said that in the cold winter of 1941 they were sleeping in tents. But the village folk invited them to use the warmth of their beds in the day-time. They were allowed to snuggle into the soft feather mattresses vacated by the farm men and their wives. He told us that they also managed to catch a few pheasants and rabbits during their night-time vigil.

I have one vivid memory of the Belgian Troops. It was on Good Friday in 1943. I was still a boy chorister in St. Michael's choir. And we were to give a performance of John Stainer's Crucifixion in the evening. My father was the bass-baritone soloist. After a hard day at the sale-yard livestock collecting centre he had a bad spell of nervous flatulence over tea. He left early for the church so as to meet Mr. Mitchell, the tenor soloist who had travelled on the train from Ipswich. I was told not to be late. Alas, the Belgians were all lined up in their armoured cars along Newgate. There was much activity and inspection going on as ammunition was loaded on to the vehicles. My thoughts were carried away watching all this, and my progress to the church was delayed. But luckily for all concerned I just made it, sprinting across the church-yard and up the vestry steps in time to don my robes and 'Fling Wide The Gates'. The fact that it was Good Friday and my dad had worked all day at the sale-yard and the Belgians were on manoeuvres illustrates once again how the war changed our lives in so many ways. Until 1940 Good Friday was kept in sombre devotion, the hot cross buns alone providing a little relief at breakfast. The normal routine was 'Sunday best' clothes or 'Wolf Cub' uniform. A short children's service was held in the church at 10.00 a.m. Afterwards we would go in an orderly manner across the Gillingham Dam with Miss Robinson, the cub-mistress 'Baghera', and gather primroses in Dog's Lane at Gillingham. These were given to old ladies in the parish on our return. You never gave men flowers.

But the sale-yard business was held on Good Friday during the war like any other Friday. The fat cattle, pigs, plus a few sheep were collected at the sale-yard. After being weighed and graded they were sent to the local slaughter houses in Caxton Road Beccles plus another at Benacre. The meat was then distributed to local butchers, and housewives got the family rations. Some of the pigs destined for the bacon curing went to Elmswell near Bury St. Edmonds. The farmers were then paid by the 'Ministry' according to the weight and grade of their stock. And this had to continue regardless of former religious scruples concerning Good Friday behaviour. But I recall we still had boiled cod with egg sauce for tea that day.

Something else has struck me as I write. Peering out of one of the Belgian Vehicles was their Padre, his dog collar clearly visible. He had no problems about Good Friday military exercises. Everyone truly believed we were fighting a just war that needed to be won at all costs.

Since those days my wife Shirley and I have had a close affinity with the Belgians. Living in Lowestoft in the 1960s we got to know a Belgian family. Over the years we made several family trips to Brussels, Flanders, Namur,

Dinant and the Ardenne. Our friends took us to the beaches at Dunkirk, the site of the Battle of the Bulge in the Ardenne, and to the First Great War museums and war graves at Menin and Namur. Going further back in history we visited Waterloo.

We were always made so welcome by the Belgian families. And even more so when we told them of their armoured car soldiers we got to know in the War. All wars are hideous and ought to be unnecessary but strangely they can bring out the best in human qualities. Sadly they also brutalize others.

The war also changed sporting activities. Cricket and football were played on Sundays. Beccles formed its strongest possible side made up from the pick of local clubs, calling it Beccles United. They played against strong local Army, Navy and RAF teams on College Meadow. The Beccles team varied over the years as many themselves were 'called up'. But I can recount a few names. Arthur and Jack Moore; the Woolfson brothers, Bernard and Roy; Kelly (Harold) Baker, Colin's cousin; two senior Leman School boys, Arthur Pye and Peter Chatters; and Dick Sparkes from Bungay. The local museum at Beccles has, I believe, some records of this team.

Mr. Glover, the sports master at the Leman School, used to organize cricket matches at the school against servicemen teams. He would augment the boys' team by playing himself, and Mr. Reginald Firth, another teacher, plus any local 'old boys' on leave in the town. These games were all 'friendlies' but played in a competitive spirit. The senior girls and Mrs. Pegram, the caretaker's wife, would provide a special tea for the troops. The matches were well attended and many spectators lined the boundary.

Sailing races took place on Sunday afternoons during the war. I have mentioned that I was a choir-boy. One of the men in the choir was a Mr. Knights who lived with his wife in a tiny bungalow in Station Road near the junction with Newgate. He owned a Waveney One Design half-decker sailing boat called 'Picotee' (a carnation with dark petals). I was his crew and manned the jib sail. All through the summer on Sunday afternoon any boat able to produce a sail and crew took part. Most of the boats were skippered by 'ancient mariners' too old to be in the services. And many like Mr. Knights had a 'boy' as crew. A motley flotilla of yachts came to the starting line and the race was made even by a skilfully adjusted time handicap. The prize for the winner was a jack-pot of florins collected from each entrant. I don't know if I was, but I believed myself to have become, an expert on the jib sail. We never won a race but did come second once. And Mr. Knights was very complimentary about my efforts that day in a high wind. The sailing races were enhanced by the fact that Mr. Knights was a representative for McVitie's biscuits and carried a tin on the boat.

Alas, the wartime summers seemed to fly. When the nights pulled in it was back to choirboy duties on Sunday afternoons in the Rectory Room where evensong took place at 2.30 p.m. to beat the blackout, as the church could not be lit. But even in this came a wartime hidden bonus. The entrance lobby of the Rectory Room covered a wide area. This was left open at all times for people to leave salvage newspapers. We choirboys used to arrive early and scan through the old copies of the Daily Mirror to see how 'Jane' had managed to divest herself of her outer garments. Her skirt might be caught in the filing cabinet or similar and off it would come, displaying her shapely cartoon body and frilly underwear. All good for young choirboy morale. And it certainly brought a saucy connotation to 'All Things Bright And Beautiful'.

It is hard as I write this to put the various events that took place during the war in accurate chronological order. Was I ever fearful of the likely consequence of the war on our lives? In the most part, no. But there was one event that did terrify me. Early one morning around 6 00 a.m. an enemy Italian plane circled the town and, presumably seeking to bomb Elliott and Garood's iron foundry, discharged a stick of bombs. The first exploded on the allotments between Fair Close and Grove Road and was only about fifty yards from our back gate. The sound and blast were terrifying. I can remember jumping out of bed and hurtling down the stairs to see what had happened. Strangely, none of our cottage windows was broken, possibly because they were all ill-fitting sash ones which rattled back and forth in the blast. But they were spattered all over with thick sticky mud blown out of the crater the bomb made. That piece of allotment was more than double dug that morning. Families, as a precaution against window blast, were encouraged to paste see-through gauze netting in crosses on each window pane. This prevented or minimized the danger of flying glass. For the life of me I cannot recall if we had done that. But, knowing my father's wish to follow all civil defence guides, I think we must have done so. Sadly, some of the other bombs did cause causalities. The last one landed on houses in Kilbrack. Mr. and Mrs. Tricker who were retired stewards from the Conservative Club were killed. Their sons were great sportsmen. One became a professional boxer and another played football for Woolwich Arsenal. Elizabeth Gothard, who was in my wife's class at the Peddars Lane school, was also injured as were both her parents. Mrs. Gothard never got over the incident and was in poor health for the rest of her days. There were other raids in the area, and bombs were dropped in the surrounding countryside. And incendiary bombs also fell in the town – but I do not believe other high explosive bombs. But there were several incidents of machine gun attacks.

It will seem strange today that the Army Drill Hall near our junior school was the scene of much local military activity. I believe the Belgian Armoured Cars were sometimes parked on the Black Boy meadow but we continued at school without any qualms. It was a war; everyone was in together.

We did have air-raid shelters at all schools. They were underground and quite damp and dark. I can remember going down them in the early days of the war if the air-raid warning sounded. The siren was on the police station in London Road and eventually another was put on the Fire Station in Ravensmere.

We had to take a tin of 'iron-rations' to school to use in the shelter in case we were marooned for some time. We filed in pairs holding hands. I was pleased because I had to hold Patricia Beezley's hand. It was the first time I'd held a girl's hand, and found it very pleasant. After that I held as many as let me. I hope that holding Pat's hand helped her as we filed into the shelter and sat side by side on a low wooden bench. We pooled our iron rations, each tasting some of the other mums' biscuits. I can recall vividly going into the shelter on that occasion but I do not think that we often used them. There were shelters at the Sir John Leman School situated in the school ground near the corner of Ringsfield and Ashmans Road. We never used them as in the winter they became flooded.

As the war progressed various activities took place in the town to raise funds for the war effort. There was a "War Weapons Week" and a "Wings for Victory Week". I wonder how the Royal Navy managed! House to house collections took place and there were various fund-raising events going on, local raffles, whist drives, and special football matches. These often took place in the summer months in 1940 or 1941 during the war's darkest days. At the end of a fund-raising week we would all gather in the Exchange Square. A long banner was unfurled by Mr. Baxendale across the front of the Corn Hall, stating how much money had been raised. It was always more than expected and a loud cheer went up from the assembled company.

Mr. Baxendale was one of the town's elite. He had an interest in Pickfords Removals and the Circus. His wife, a lively lady, was a former trapeze artist. She worked in the munitions factory. Her war effort was very practical. Through their circus connections they got to know the Norfolk artist Edward Seago. He was Field Marshal Auckinleck's camouflage advisor during the war. Edward Seago had also toured with the circus earlier in his life. Eventually Field Marshal Auckinleck lived in the former Baxendale home in Northgate.

National Savings stamp books were also encouraged. I had one, but not many stamps went into mine I'm afraid, only those given me as birthday or Christmas presents. There were also National or War Savings Certificates, pronounced by locals as 'cerstificates'. They cost 15 shillings each (75p) and at the end of five years they were worth £1.00. Not a bad investment. A Miss Turney was the local organiser for War Savings. She was a genteel lady who lived in Barsham and would go to local schools, factories and other groups, extolling the virtue of National Savings.

Another event that took place during the summer was 'Holidays At Home Week'. Trips away from home were out of the question. So to give relief and boost morale for everyone, young and old, this special week was organized in the town during the first week in August. Something in some form or other took place daily in the town. Local school teachers and voluntary helpers willingly gave their time to organize the programme. The principal venue was the natural arena of the 'Dell' accessed from the Ringsfield and Bungay roads. A big covered stage was erected on scaffolding and deal boards provided by local builders. No doubt Mr. and Mrs. Baxendale with their Big-Top experience gave advice. It looked a splendid affair. There were bench seats and chairs taken from local schools. Those not seated were able to stand on the raised part of the surrounding area. Local groups such as the Choral Society, church choirs and the Beccles Amateur Dramatic Society joined forces to put on evening concerts. In the daytime the local school children entertained.

Mr. A E Groom, the conductor of the local church choir, was the principal organizer. What stalwart work that gentleman did through the war. The local manager of the Stead and Simpson shop in the New Market, he was an inspiration to us all. He could not have been a young man at the time but he threw himself into such activities. A Mr. John Hammond from Lowestoft was choir master at the commencement of hostilities. He was called into the Army and eventually became a Far East prisoner of war. So Mr. Groom stepped into the job unpaid as he wanted the job to be available to John on his return from the war. And it was. But Mr. Groom was not content with letting the church choir tick over. He organized as many extra concerts or oratorios as possible. There will be more on 'Daddy' Groom later.

There were other holiday and weekend attractions in wartime. Cycle rides were easy and safe on the roads surrounding the town. I had learnt to ride and cycle in the middle of the war at about 12 years of age. A neighbour and friend, Cliff Curtis, about two years older, was my principal instructor. Early instruction took place in the back lane or along the avenue to the common. Eventually it was decided I was expert enough to ride with Cliff out to Weston, a nearby village. All went well until we turned for home and down a steady incline. At the side of the road a large wooden wheelbarrow was parked. 'Watch that', said Cliff, riding 'shot-gun' beside me, and moved on to the crown of the road. The wheelbarrow mesmerized me like a rabbit by a stoat. And I rode slap bang between the barrow shafts. Cliff said in amusement, 'If I'd asked you to do that you could not have made a better job of it.' Luckily no damage resulted either to myself or the bike.

We never rode our cycles after the blackout restrictions came in at dusk. It was during these hours that most road accidents occurred. A few years ago I was surprised to read an article which said that the figure for road accidents in the wartime blackout was higher then than the present day. Many folks found this fact hard to believe.

There was, however, one group of lorries on the road for part of the war whose speed as they drove through parts of the town and countryside raised alarm and concern. These were the tipper trucks carrying the sand and gravel for the aerodromes being built in Norfolk and Suffolk. They did cause at least two local accidents that I was aware of. One tragic one (in this case not due to speeding) took place at the low railway bridge where the Waveney Valley line crossed the road in Ravensmere. This bridge and line are now long since gone. The driver of an empty lorry had given a lift to a serviceman. He was standing in the rear, leaning over the top of the driver's cabin. The poor man was decapitated. I myself was involved in an adventure with one of these lorries. I was on the milk float with Mr. Alec Gill and holding the reins of his pony Kitty. We had turned into Grove Road from Blyburgate and were making our way to his dairy. One of the tipper lorries met us, travelling at a stupid speed in the other direction. We met near a row of terraced cottages just in Grove Road. There was no time for either to stop. Alec Gill swore as he quickly took the reins from me and pulled as far as he dare across the pavement. Luckily no pedestrians were about, and he was able to prevent the terrified Kitty from bolting. The lorry scraped the road-side wheel of his elegant float, causing minor damage. But it also scraped all alongside the side of one cottage. The main marks were made on the brickwork across an arched way that gave access to the rear of the cottages. Deep grooves were cut into the bricks. These remained for many years. I would proudly take my school-mates and show them where 'I had been in an accident'. Luckily there was no great damage done to anyone or anything, but it might have been much worse. I believe the reason why the lorries hurtled at such break-neck speed was two fold. The air-fields were needed as soon as possible for the war effort, and the drivers were paid a bonus for each load they delivered.

Other lorry transport on the road was the fleet of cattle trucks belonging to Mr. J W Leggett in Blyburgate. They were a bright blue with an inscription on the front 'Here comes J W Leggett', and at the rear, yes you have guessed it 'There goes J W Leggett'. Mr. A W Denney ran a haulage business. He had a small fleet of lorries based on premises formerly used as a blacksmiths and engineers at the corner of Blyburgate and Peddars Lane. Likewise, Robinsons ran a similar fleet in London Road beyond the railway crossing going south from the town. When the post-war Labour government nationalized the transport system Mr. Denney became the manager. He lived in a purpose built house on that site. During the war the general hauliers might transport coal, grain, sugar beet and other farm products. They also, I believe, carried goods for William Clowes, the printers. A lot of their books were sent by rail. They were taken to the railway station from the printing works on a mechanized low flat trolley with packaged books and other printed material stacked high. The gentleman who was the last person to do this was Mr. Wright and he is still affectionately known by everyone as 'Trolley'. As I write I am wondering how he got on in inclement weather. I cannot recall that there was any protection on the conveyance against wind and rain. Maybe Clowes only sent books out on sunny days.

But you must realize how many more cattle and goods were sent by railway before, during and in the early post-war years. If you visit Beccles or any small railway station in Norfolk or Suffolk today, it certainly bears no comparison to these stations in the 1930s to 1950s. At that time the railway was busy all day long. Several times a day a lengthy goods train would leave the town and proceed to either Lowestoft or Great Yarmouth on the coast or to Ipswich and London. Beccles was the junction for trains coming from Yarmouth and Lowestoft on their way to London. There was always an interesting and busy delay when trains, either goods or passenger, linked up, destined for all stations 'up the line' to Ipswich and Liverpool Street. Thus coal, cattle, fish, corn, munitions, troops and their armaments were transported efficiently by rail.

I must not forget to mention the Waveney Valley line. This started from Beccles and meandered across the marshlands, calling at Geldeston, Ditchingham, Homersfield, Forncett and Tivetshall where it joined up with the Ipswich to Norwich line. These lovely village communities were thus provided with a link to the market towns of Beccles and Bungay and the City of Norwich. During the war this line carried equipment and munitions to a large arms dump isolated on the marshes.

One of my happy childhood memories was of the view from Beccles church-yard and watching the Waveney Valley steam train slowly vanishing into the autumn mist and the cattle gazing at this regular disturbance. What a shame the line is no longer there. What a tourist attraction it would have been for Beccles and Broadland visitors.

In my childhood the railway at Beccles had a large staff. Now an unmanned halt in dilapidation, in its glory days it boasted the following: a station-master who lived conveniently in Station Road, with gold braid like scrambled egg on his hat, his assistant came next with slightly less braid, and there were three uniformed ticket collectors. All were keen gardeners and for most of the year sported a rose or carnation buttonhole. They worked shifts so the platform was served by one of them throughout the day including weekends. When they were not required collecting tickets between train arrivals they busied themselves in attending to flower beds around the station, and keeping the waiting rooms and toilets polished and spotless. And then about four porters were always busying themselves about. They helped passengers on and off the train with their luggage. They also aided the postman to deal with outgoing and incoming mail from or destined for London and all stations in between. Another duty of the porters was linking the carriages or trucks as they proceeded to Liverpool Street, or dividing those from the metropolis en-route to Lowestoft and Yarmouth. A booking clerk issued tickets to passengers. You had to buy a penny platform ticket to see someone on to a train or meet family or friends arriving. A machine in the forecourt dispensed these.

In the station entrance hallway, which was a spacious square room with upholstered bench seats along the walls, a roaring fire burnt bright all day and evening in the winter. It became a favourite meeting place for some of the elderly or disabled folk who lived nearby. It was a warm spot for them, seated on the plush benches, and the activities at the railway station added interest for them.

The book stall on the platform run by Smiths was busy all day. Customers were excused the platform tickets. Apart from newspapers and magazines it was possible to join their library. I think this cost 3d. a week. For this you were allowed to borrow two books. My dad was a regular patron.

Long before I arrived on this earth there were also refreshment rooms. My mother had been the manageress. She told me that in the early 1920s they might serve up to 24 dinners for businessmen arriving on the train from Liverpool Street. I assume that the advent of the restaurant cars on the trains led to their closure. But the one on Lowestoft Station kept going until after the war. Because of her association with railway catering Mum always got special treatment. When I was quite a small child she would take me there to have lemonade and a doughnut filled with jam. In fact, all railway workers got special treatment. Mum said the porters, ticket collectors and clerks got a cup of tea and a bun for a halfpenny. The tea was served in larger cups than the usual customers, but always heavy white china – no paper or plastic and nothing from a machine!

HOLIDAYS BEFORE THE WAR

We always had a holiday away from home every year before the war. It is possible to give a fair estimate of the dates by estimating my age at the time. The first I can faintly recall must have been in the summer of 1933. We all went with some of my father's cousins to Southwold and stayed at a holiday bungalow down Ferry Road. One episode was to leave its mark on me for the rest of my life. I sat too briskly on a small juvenile chamber pot. It shattered and a sharp fragment of china was embedded in the base of my spine. I was treated at the local hospital, but a scar was to remain. On my Naval Pay Book in 1948 it was noted I had 'hazel eyes and a small scar at the base of the spine'. A memory I have of this trip was that I loved to watch the sailing of model yachts. It was the forerunner of the interest I had in my early youth in Waveney sailing boats. I never had the skill or prowess my older brother had as a helmsman, but I was a useful 'crew' for him sometimes. At the time of that holiday he was around 8 years old and I watched his boat with interest. We also had nets to catch butterflies or tiddlers in the marsh dykes, but with little success.

However, most pre-war years the usual family holiday was a week in Lowestoft. We stayed around 1935 to 1938 with a Mrs. King at 9 Marine Parade. I enjoyed the anticipation and preparation for the holiday as much as the event. We went the week following Beccles Regatta. This took place the week after August Bank Holiday which in those days was the first Monday in August. No sensible or loyal Becclesian left the town when the regatta and amusement fair took place at Beccles Quay. For some days before we left for Lowestoft my mum, ably assisted and advised by Grandma, who lived with us and was then in her seventies, would be arranging the clothes and gear we needed to take. The bulk of this was carefully packed into a huge trunk. This was about four feet six inches long and two and a half feet in depth and width. When full, it could only be lifted by two strong men and placed in the boot of the taxi taking us to Lowestoft. Dick Rix was the local taxi driver who drove one of the two Nightingale 'charabancs' owned by the Moyse family based in Blyburgate near the old sale-yard. The Moyse family were Salvation Army stalwarts. Eventually the 'Army' moved their Citadel from Northgate into Blyburgate on the site of the former charabanc depot.

We must have had at least three such holidays at Lowestoft, staying with Mrs. King. Bed and breakfast was provided and, if we wished, my mum and dad would buy food for 'high tea' which Mrs. King or a maid cooked for us. Fish or, to my greater delight, sausages, figured in this plan. One day in the week cold ham and pork pie with a salad would be taken. Salad was always simple tomato, lettuce, cucumber and spring onion, Heinz salad cream being the only garnish. But a saucepan of boiled new potatoes added bulk to the meal. Aunt Marge, if present, to my amazement, always sprinkled sugar over her salad. Grandma, disgusted, stated 'it's some trick she's learnt in London'.

The main feature of the holiday was time spent on the beach. But there were additional highlights. These took the form of Punch and Judy shows and a ride along the promenade on donkeys. Boat trips were popular. Large row-boats, mostly kept by retired fishermen, were situated at intervals along the tideline. Into these were packed a number of children who sat on seats athwart and around the side of the boat. With assistance from his 'mate', the skipper pushed the vessel into the sea and we were rowed a hundred or so yards out along the shoreline between the breakers. I wonder what present day 'health and safety' would think. But the trips only took place on calm days, and life guards were on duty. The cost for the trip was 3d. per child. Yet another boat trip took place once in the week. All the family would slowly promenade on the seafront to the Kensington Gardens at Kirkley. Here electric powered boats carrying two passengers voyaged around a small lake. The waterways traversed around small islands in the lake. Attendants, wearing thigh-boot waders and a peaked cap, stood in the water to help you aboard. I was always a little distressed because my older brother and I were fellow passengers. And he, being more mature, held the steering wheel. Years later in the 1960s we lived near this boating lake. My son was then at primary school and I used to take him for a boat trip at weekends. I had done a favour for one of the then thigh-booted attendants. And my son had as long a trip as I wished. He was only called ashore at my request. The boats were all numbered, and as the scheduled time was up the attendant called them in with a haler 'Come in number 7' or whatever. This special privilege was only allowed my son out of the peak holiday periods. In August there were queues of youngsters waiting to board the boats. What a shame this popular and delightful treat is no longer available.

On days to be spent on the beach, Grandma, Mum and Dad always staked their claim to a section of the beach as near to our guest house as possible. Deckchairs were hired from the local Town Council. The collector, again in a blue peaked cap, came around selling tickets for each chair at 3d. a session for morning and afternoon. Children did not have deckchairs but sat on a blanket on the beach. We were allowed to sit on the chairs if a grown-up went for a short stroll or visited a nearby cafe for tea or coffee. This was always served in a white cup and saucer. No plastic or paper cups. And there were no selections of coffee such as espresso and cappuccino. The coffee was usually dispensed from a large urn and the milk had already been added.

Some of the less salubrious cafés – a series of small huts along the promenade – did provide a cheaper beverage in the form of Bev or Camp coffee, a liquid instant coffee with added chicory, supplied to the cafés in enormous catering jars. Camp coffee is still available and my wife still uses it in icing and flavouring for cakes and buns. To a discriminating palate its flavour has little resemblance to ground coffee.

There was a special treat during the week. Usually this was on the Thursday evening. We all went, Grandma included, to the 'pictures' at the Odeon cinema. Before watching the film we had tea in Waller's Restaurant opposite the cinema. My choice was baked beans on toast served with thick lashings of butter followed by creamed meringue. Two films I remember were 'Elephant Boy', starring Sabu, and 'The Charge of the Light Brigade', featuring Errol Flynn. I lost myself in the films. Soon I was in India on an elephant with Sabu, or riding a horse, flashing my sabre, beside Errol Flynn. But it was all unreal. The true significance of the story did not register. There were only goodies and baddies. And the goodies triumphed. The only film that ever upset me as a child was the newsreel coverage of the Japanese bombing of China in the 1930s and the Italian invasion of Abyssinia.

The Odeon had a special smell about it. A mixture of a hygienic heady scented spray they used, tobacco and the new deep cushioned sofas that were around the upper entrance lobby to the circle. We sat in the best seats on holiday. Grandma paid. I loved it when we left the cinema. It was getting dark and the lights were shining all along the sea-front that we walked along before going into 9 Marine Parade.

Poor Father never spent the Friday of our holiday with us. It being sale day, he returned to Beccles on an early train to fulfil his duty as clerk for the auctioneers. Our landlady kindly packed him some sandwiches and a flask of coffee. He never once thought to question the fact that this was expected of him. Possibly, he would have missed not being on duty at the sale-yard. His work was a great part of his life. But he was back in the evening for our Friday night fish supper. Not fried,alas, and no chips. It was boiled cod with mashed potatoes and parsley sauce.

Some memories of other events stand out from those pre-war holidays in Lowestoft. Mr. Lobby Lud of the News Chronicle visited the town one August. He was making a tour of popular sea-side resorts. The aim was to promote interest in, and sales of, the newspaper by visiting Great Yarmouth, Clacton, Felixtowe and Southend. Southwold, Aldeburgh and Frinton-on-Sea were too high-class for such a visit. The News Chronicle supported the Liberal Party but was popular among all the working class because it gave very good sports and racing coverage. Charlie Buchan was its highly acclaimed sports editor. Now, my father was a Daily Telegraph man as was my grandmother. And they did also purchase an Eastern Daily Press at holiday time. But never would they stoop so low as to buy the News Chronicle. Not so Mum when she heard and also read on the hoardings that Lobby Lud was in town. He was scheduled to walk along the seafront and shopping area and mingle among the crowds after 10.00 a.m. Anyone thinking they recognized him could challenge him as long as they carried a copy of that day's News Chronicle. Mum purchased a copy from a stall on the promenade and we went in search of Lobby Lud with hope of claiming the prize. We strolled up and down the promenade for about an hour. And just when we were thinking it was getting towards lunch Mum espied a man slowly walking on his own. It was one of those chilly, cloudy days with an easterly breeze. Few people were bathing and those brave enough to venture on the beach were clad in thick pullovers. So it was no surprise to see a man in a light raincoat and his trilby pulled down on his forehead against the breeze. 'That's him!' Mum said, 'I'm sure!' And boldly she stood in his path exclaiming 'You are Lobby Lud. And I claim the News Chronicle prize.' The man paused for a second; and said not a word. Then, with a hint of a smile on his face, he stepped gently to one side and progressed on his way. We sat despondent on one of the seats on the promenade. My mother, still certain it was him, scanned her News Chronicle again. 'Oh dear', she eventually said. 'It must have been him but I missed a word out in my challenge. I ought to have called him <u>Mr.</u> Lobby Lud.' We hurried back to seek him again but he was gone, probably over the old swing bridge and into the High Street. The prize was £50, a small fortune in those days. It would have more than paid for our holiday. Never down hearted, Mum consoled us both with an ice-cream cornet.

On another of those pre-war holidays we had a very special treat and adventure. I realize now that it was most probably due to my mum being left a small legacy from a relative in Australia. Not a fortune, but that year we were able to replace the furniture in the front room. My parents had a new bed and Dad seemed less agitated when bills came through the letter box. During that August holiday we were able to afford a paddle steamer cruise from Lowestoft to Clacton-on-Sea. The steamer had commenced its journey from Great Yarmouth but berthed en route at the end of Claremont Pier to embark the passengers from Lowestoft. It was a bright sunny August morning when we boarded the ship around ten thirty in the morning. The cruise down the coast was enjoyable but uneventful. Arriving at Clacton in the early afternoon we must have met up with some of my mother's sisters. They lived at that end of the county and most likely had taken a day's charabanc trip to the coast. Due to their good offices, my brother and I consumed a few ice-cream cornets. And together we all had tea later in the day with scones and jam. Then around six o'clock the steamer set out on the homeward voyage to Lowestoft and Great Yarmouth. We had only left Clacton about an hour when the wind suddenly changed from a gentle off-shore breeze to considerable, nearly gale force, gusts. We were advised by the crew to stay below deck and not to venture on the weather deck and observation areas. From below it was exciting to see the huge waves and white horses as the North Sea became turbulent. The tempest did rage o'er the deep. 'Ere long, quite a few passengers started to feel sick and many looked almost green in colour. But we found our sea legs that day. Mum told me to keep eating a little at a time – we had some packed food and chocolate. And then, contrary to normal parental procedures, my brother and I were allowed to play the 'fruit' machines. I cannot remember if we won much money but certainly, as the steamer neared Claremont Pier, we may have been a little in pocket. Perhaps the rolling sea upset the equilibrium of pay-out. But what was important, none of us were sick and we were all in good spirits. There was more adventure to follow; over the skipper's loud hailer it was announced that because of the rough seas the steamer could not dock at the Claremont Pier. We were to get the bonus of a trip down the coast into the harbour at Great Yarmouth and a free ride by coach back to Lowestoft. My brother and I were almost looking forward to getting back to school so we could tell our chums about our maritime adventure.

The mother of one of my more affluent chums always took us both on a day trip to Lowestoft in the summer holidays. These outings were notable in that we spent the day at the children's corner near the South Pier. This I enjoyed because we always had pork pie and ham rolls and these did not figure in our usual family diet.

Miss Jeffries, the palmist and fortune teller who lived next door to us in Fair Close, also took me for a day on the beach. Known as Madam Pauline she dressed in long flowing robes on arrival at her tented site on the sea-front. But she took a lengthy lunch hour and we went to a fish and chip restaurant in London Road South. Yet another gastronomic delight as fried fish and chips never graced our table at home. But purchase of a 'pennuth' of chips secretly did occur when possible.

We did have holidays once or twice in London, staying with Aunt Marge in her flat. It was here I first spoke on a telephone and used a bathroom and a lavatory indoors. Also we once visited an uncle on my mother's side. His wife, Auntie Gert, came from Devonshire and I loved her speaking so differently from the Waveney accent. They lived near Epping Forest and we had great fun walking and playing midst the trees. I loved to ride in black taxi-cabs which we did on rare occasions. But sitting on the top deck of the bus or the excitement of a journey on the underground was such a contrast from sedate East Anglian life. Aunt Marge could whisk us around the West End or the City, hopping from one bus to the next. The pace of life was different from the Suffolk countryside but people had time to speak and smile even on the underground. The conductors on the buses were entertaining with their banter. My brother told me later that on a bus journey to Regents Park, Father requested tickets for the stop nearest to the Zoological Gardens. The 'clippie' stood bemused for a minute, then a wide smile broke on his face and he exclaimed 'Oh Guv, you want the zoo'. On this holiday we went to a West End show and saw Fred Emney and Richard Hearn – Mr. Pastry. We also saw an Ice Skating Spectacular. A visit to the Science Museum, my brother and I loved. The only blot on this holiday was four tedious hours at the Victoria and Albert Museum. But I was adjured by Mum to accept this because 'your dad does love these things'.

IN QUIRES AND PLACES WHERE THEY SING

Why was choir spelt like that in our old prayer books? My dictionary gives quire as 24 or 25 sheets of paper. But as a young choirboy, during the sermon I'd often scan the prayer book. It has always kept in my mind 'in quires and places where they sing – here followeth the anthem'. I was a reluctant chorister, but I'm glad my parents ensured I became one. The Anglican Church in Beccles was so much a part of my early life. And to please my mother I went along with most of it gladly. Perhaps it is a good idea to deal with Mum's involvement first. Unlike my dad, in no way could she be described as pious.

There was nothing sanctimonious in her attitude. Most of her involvement was through the Mothers' Union. She would tell me tales about their meetings and discussions when we went on one of our frequent strolls together. Some of the tales were hilarious. Mum had an ability to see lots of the people in the town as cartoon figures. She'd describe a facet of someone in a few words. 'Saw Mrs. G. in the town this morning. Her backside was outside Gipsons's the Grocers and her head was in the Exchange Square.' Or 'Miss F can break wind from the Rectory room to the Catholic Church. And that's at walking pace'.

But there was never a hint of malice in it all. I can hark back to the time she told me about a delicate young curate who was visiting the Hospital Fete before the war. Bless his heart, in a token of casualness she was amused to see that he'd got on a straw hat and an open neck shirt but beneath and quite visible was a thick woollen, buttoned-up vest. Beccles at this time – it may still be – was riddled with an amusing and stupid class system but Mum ignored all this. And this was one of the great things she did for me – to believe there must be richer, cleverer folk than you, but no one is your superior. Be polite and kind to everyone. If they do not treat you likewise, ignore them as much as possible. My son, years later gave me equally good advice, 'Never argue with a fool'. Like me, Mum was short in stature; 'hold your head up', she said, 'and you'll gain a couple of inches'

Mr. Storeton West from Lowestoft was choirmaster when I joined in 1937. He was a cheery gentleman known as 'Storty', who travelled on the train from Lowestoft to take choir practice on Mondays (boys only) and Fridays (full choir). He kept discipline easily and practices were entertaining. We were paid each quarter on our attendance record. He was able to look around the choir and at a glance knew at once who was missing. I loved the Psalms and singing them. One incident remains. We were singing Psalm 75 and had got to verse six, 'Set up not your horn on high, and speak not with a stiff neck' – giggling by the boys – and going to verse seven, 'For promotion cometh neither from the east, nor from the west: nor yet from the south'. Realizing a bit of tomfoolery was going on, he banged the piano lid down with a clatter and shouted to us startled choristers, 'Where does promotion come from then?' Silence from the boys. 'Must come from the North. Can't make that out. All we get from there in winter at Lowestoft is cold wind and snow'. Storty was popular with the boys. When we knew the quarterly pay day was due we met him off the train at Beccles Station and marched up the road escorting him to the church. No one minded that the practice that Monday was longer, because we could not begin until we had received our wages.

John Hammond, a much younger man, followed when Storty retired. He also lived in Lowestoft but there the similarity ends. He was debonair, quietly spoken and refined. An outstanding musician, he was not only an accomplished organist but excelled even more as a pianist. He quietly kept us in order, aided by a droll sense of humour. Had it not been for the war I am sure he would have had a career as a concert pianist. But eventually he had to enlist and we all wondered how such a tender man would cope even just wearing heavy army boots. How wrong we were. John Hammond not only withstood army life but he coped with the harshness of being a Japanese Prisoner of War. Unable to play the piano in captivity he made himself a cardboard keyboard to practice on. He played the piano again for the first time after the war when he gave a concert on the troopship bringing fellow prisoners home. After his return, he often used to spend a Sunday in our household, taking his meals with us. Various members of the church took it in turn offering him hospitality. By then I was working on the farm. He expressed amazement at the quantity of food I ate when I returned in the evening. It must have been in sharp contrast to the deprivations he had suffered as a prisoner. Such a thought never crossed my mind at the time. In the 1960s, when we were living in Kirkley, John was the organist at Pakefield Church and part-time music teacher at St. Felix School in Southwold. My wife and I joined his choir. He was surprised and amused that I had volunteered to sing for him again. Shirley was a valued soprano, having perfect pitch and the ability to sight read. I sang bass, and he told me I might not always sing the correct notes but was generally in tune.

Rear Admiral Paymaster C S Johnson used to stand in, or rather sit in, for other organists during the war. Poor man, he was a butt to our boyish pranks. He wasted a good half an hour at the boys' Monday practice trying to mark the attendance register. He would peer at the list placed on the top of the piano and, not raising his head, call out our names. We used to cover up for those absent, shouting 'Yup' when the Admiral called an absentee's name. When he had finished, the poor old boy – he was probably 20 years younger than I am now – looked in despair when he found he'd got 25 boys present on the register but only 15 sitting in the two practice pews. He would sigh and decide to go through the hymns and psalms for the following Sunday. We always had some amusement if he played the organ for a Sunday service. He played rather slowly. So when we arrived in the choir stalls, having processed down the aisle singing the first hymn, he was by then about two lines behind. He'd be 'scatter all my unbelief' and the choir 'shining to the perfect day.' We corrected him by singing a very loud Amen at the end of the hymn. Also at least once during the service his foot would slip on the pedal during the lesson or sermon and the organ would break wind, much to us boys' amusement and the tenors' and basses' chagrin.

The Evangelicals

There was a group of regular attendees at St. Michael's who did not fit into the normal mould. It would be wrong to say they were in conflict or divisive, but they were identified by being more active and robust in their worship. They would frequently be at the Sunday morning matins at 11 o'clock each week, and would be at the 8 o'clock communion service once a month. But later in the day they followed their Christian commitment along a different route. No one doubted their sincerity. All were evangelically minded and knew the bible better than most.

I cannot remember any of them being choir members, but at whatever act of worship they attended, their singing was always lively and animated. Their presence was agreed by the rector and the Anglican community to be a great asset. They tended to form in groups both male and female and were involved with various fringe organisations of the church. Some were Sunday school teachers and others took bible classes for older children. These took place at either the Ravensmere or Ingate Mission churches on a Sunday afternoon, and in their own homes. On Sunday evenings they were involved at an evensong which took place at 6.30 p.m. at both the mission rooms at Ravensmere – now converted to a private dwelling – and at Ingate – presently used to store building supplies. There was a full house at these events and Ingate had a flourishing choir which rivalled the one at St. Michael's. Mission-room work at Ravensmere was especially suited to their calling. They at times had a chance to take part of the service and read a lesson or lead the congregation in prayer. Sometimes this prayer might be extempore and tended to go on a bit. Choruses might also be sung. Evensong always closed with 'Round me falls the night, Saviour be my light – etc.'

As a group they tended to be left wing in outlook. Socialism was, in their eyes, a natural expression of the Christian way of life. The father of one once told me that they were not Conservatives 'as we have nothing to conserve'. At least one of them was involved in the trade union movement. Some years ago a gentleman who knew her well told me the following anecdote. It illustrates fully their commitment and zeal. This lady was quiet, small and, at first appearance, timid. She worked at the local printing works and had risen to be in charge of a department; I believe it was the bindery. They were a close-knit community and looked to the welfare of each other. Sadly, one of the young ladies in this department was ill for some time and eventually died. The management decreed that two representatives from the department would be allowed to attend the funeral in working hours. Not satisfied with this, our timid lady requested that all members attend and pay due respect to their colleague. She pointed out that as the church was only about three minutes walk they would only be away from the shop floor for about an hour. I believe an offer was made to make up lost time in their lunch hour during the week. But the management was obdurate; no way would they agree. So on the given afternoon the whole department downed tools and, led by their union leader, quietly processed to the church to say farewell to their comrade. 'The meek shall inherit the earth.' No further action was taken.

Daddy Groom

Mr. A E Groom, who had been the manager of Stead and Simpson in the town, sang tenor in John Hammond's choir. A talented musician himself, he had a fine lyric tenor voice. We boys listened in wonder when we first heard his melodic rendering at practice as he sang 'Happy Art Thou oh Israel'. But John Hammond left for the army and 'Daddy Groom', as we affectionately knew him, took over the choir. His main aim was to keep the position open for John on his return. Mr. Groom did me one special favour; he had a grandson, Brian Patrick, who was evacuated to him during the war. As fellow choristers we became friends and that valued friendship continues to this day. And will do, I know, until one of us 'falls off the wagon'. Brian only recently told me his grandfather had been badly wounded in the Great War and had also been affected by a poisonous mustard gas attack. This makes his efforts with the church and choir during the war nothing short of heroic. He put his own mark on the proceedings. Realizing the value of music in the town as a boost to morale in war time, he recruited new choir members, many of them young ladies and girls in their late teens. The presence of these attractive damsels in the choir stalls enhanced us choir-boys' interest. Daddy Groom had no problem adding to his list of boy trebles. Believe it or not, at the time females in the choir had to be heard but not seen. They entered by a small priest door and quietly took up their seats in the rear stalls, virtually out of sight of the congregation.

Mr. Groom had a service with anthems for special occasions like the Patronal Festival, Easter, Harvest Festivals and Remembrance Sunday when a large congregation gathered. The church was full at the Christmas Carol Service. As many boys as possible sang a solo in the carols. Their proud mums, dads and family all turned up and swelled the numbers. One year my dad and I were the King and Page in Good King Wenceslas.

Daddy Groom had an effective way in maintaining discipline. When a lad's behaviour went beyond the pale he was described by him as a blitherin, blatherin, hydrocushinized, fat-headed, kipper-kitted, monstrosity. This, of course, produced much amusement among the boys, culprit included. I am grateful to his grandson Brian for helping me with the order and spelling.

He also had little breaks in choir practice to lighten proceedings. He'd play the piano for us, and Richard Adinsell's Warsaw Concerto, featured in the 1941 film 'Dangerous Moonlight' was often requested. He had a trick whereby you folded one hand across the other, bent both thumbs and moved one hand so it looked just as if you were pulling the end of your thumb off. Later he taught me the trick and I used it to amuse my grandchildren and other youngsters. Colin tells me that he amuses his grandchildren in the same way. One of the great pleasures in writing this Part of the book is that Daddy Groom's outstanding contribution to life in wartime Beccles is recorded.

Mr. Groom extended his hospitality in various ways. A Young Fleet Air Arm pilot, Eric Waterson, was stationed at the Ellough Airfield towards the end of the war. A squadron of Barracudas was engaged on anti-submarine patrols. Eric was a gifted organist and was allowed to practice at St. Michael's Church. His wife and small baby came to stay in Beccles for a week and my mother gave them meals. Life is full of co-incidence. Many years later, on holiday at St. David's in Wales, we visited the cathedral. When stationed at an airfield in Wales after the war, Eric Waterson had become assistant organist at the cathedral. We spoke to a gentleman who had been playing the organ and he told us that Eric Waterson had taught him to play. As a boy I idolized this young pilot. It was with a heavy heart that I went to the airfield and watched the Barracudas fly off when they left Ellough.

The Reverend Harold Lea Birch was rector when I joined the choir. He came to the town in 1934. An amicable if sometimes distant man, he and my brother became friendly. For relaxation during the week he used to knock a golf ball about on the common. John went to retrieve any balls lost in the gorse, and in return the Rev. Birch gave him one of his old clubs. The rector caused amusement to us boys. He did not have a melodic voice. And his Adam's apple was unusually prominent. When he chanted the 'responses' it appeared to go up and down like a yo-yo on a string. His sermons, shamefully long, were always itemized – firstly, secondly, thirdly, and finally, and to our dismay one last thrust – in conclusion.

The organist always sat in the comfort of the choir-stalls during the sermon and would hurry back to the organ loft when the rector got to 'finally' in the sermon. The organ would then be warmed up when 'in conclusion' arrived. One warm, sultry, evening he nodded off into a doze. Luckily, the rector spied this as he turned east for the concluding prayer. He then belted out in the loudest voice he could muster 'hymn number so and so'. It would have been a wonderful end to this tale if it had been number 474, Awaked From Sleep We Fall Before Thee, God Of Love.

Mr. Birch was an ARP first aider. I can still picture his Adam's apple going up and down as he bent over me as I lay on the floor in a farm building in Shadingfield. A big Civil Defence exercise was taking place. Boys from local 'cubs' had been enlisted as willing mock casualties. 'You look to be in quite a bad way', said the rector, reading the label on my tunic which said I had a fractured spine and other injuries!

The Reverend Barnes was a popular young curate. He took an interest in the boys and organized various sporting and social activities. He had charm and lots of the young ladies in the choir and congregation fell for him. The Reverend Hulbert was another curate. His wife sang in the choir and had lovely curly blonde hair. When the Rev. Birch retired, the Reverend Wilkinson-Rideal came. He was sedate, serious and devout. A genuine man, he was devoted to the church, congregation and the town in general. He invited my father to become Rector's Warden. So father proudly changed from an Air Raid to Rector's Warden. When he came home from his inauguration ceremony, my brother and I had got his old White Air Raid steel helmet out and printed 'Church' in black letters on it. We also festooned the table with empty beer bottles. Luckily for us, Father came home alone and took it in good part. He was elated by his new position in the church hierarchy.

But soon I was made to attend dreaded confirmation classes with the Rev. Rideal. I was certainly not a willing pupil. But Father's word had to be obeyed. Mum said, 'Don't upset him.' So I went and hated a lot of it. The bit I found unreasonable was not being able to query the various doctrinal things that came up. But the Reverend Rideal was a kind, gentle, man, and eventually the classes were not such an endurance as at the outset, and we chatted more informally.

The men in the choir fascinated me. Most of them had their own individual foibles. Little Jimmy Howes we called Sharpe's Creamy Nut, because he resembled the dapper little man who appeared in the toffee adverts. He took the choir very seriously and was a constant attendee. He sang bass with a rather nasal sound but took bit-part solos in anthems and oratorios. Always one of the malefactors in Stainer's Crucifixion, he was also a regular Wise Man in the carol service. It always perplexed me that sometimes they called them Kings and at others Wise Men.

In his way Little Jimmy was kindly disposed to us boys. At times three or four of us would be invited to his home in Gosford Road where he lived with his elderly mother. He had a radiogram, a very up-to-date model for those times. He had the complete recording of Handel's Messiah on 78 inch vinyl records. He was able to load them six at a time on to an automatic turn-table which clattered loudly as each record dropped. Occasionally there would be a hitch in proceedings. Exclaiming 'darn the thing', Jimmy made adjustments and 'My redeemer' was able to live again. We went joyfully to these evenings for coffee and biscuits following the Hallelujah chorus. Eventually Jimmy, who had an office job at Elliott and Garood's, became the verger at St. Michael's, a post he filled with dignity and enthusiasm.

Rowland Reynolds – Roly – was another long-serving bass and regular Wise Man. His voice had a very open sound, as though he sang with something the size of a walnut in his mouth. For all that, it had a notably pleasing sound. In charge of the local Co-op grocery store at a warehouse in Gosford Road, he was a familiar figure in Fair Close as he wheeled a trade-bike to and from his workplace. He was involved in various musical events in the town, serving on different committees. He arranged and organized visiting soloists and musicians and helped with the staging and preparations. He would be dodging about behind the scenes. The conductor would be on the rostrum ready to commence proceedings and a curtain or screen at the rear would move and Roly, unsuccessfully trying to be inconspicuous, would appear, take up his place, pushing past a few fellow singers on his way.

Roly organized coach trips to attend concerts by other local choirs and did sterling work to foster musical and other arts in the town and district. His wife, 'Win', also sang in the church choir and other musical societies. She had the palest face imaginable.

Sammy White, a respected watch-maker and jeweller, was the senior tenor when I joined the choir. He had a lovely half-hunter gold pocket watch. This he wore in a waistcoat pocket on a gold chain. It chimed the hours when he opened it, and he delighted in showing it to the boys after choir practice. A popular townsman, when he died the church was packed for his funeral. There was a full choir. We sang an anthem and Sam's favourite hymns.

Harry Carr, who worked at the Printing Works, was another long serving bass. He sang the odd solo at carol services and was a stand-in Wise Man if needed. The boys liked him: he often had boiled sweets in his pocket, especially near Christmas. He had a pronounced stutter but never once was the butt of our mirth.

There was a man whose name I forget, who sang alto. He arrived around the start of the war. All boys turned and 'gauped' in amazement when we first heard his falsetto voice. Colonel Baker – no relation to Colin – was the archetypal retired colonel. Every Sunday he quietly took up his seat in one of the rear choir stalls, near the organ. He had his own large Hymn and Prayer Books with the musical scores. Never did he robe or process with the choir. I think he had sung in choirs earlier in life and wanted to be around the singing without having to attend practice. This was accepted without question – well, he was a colonel! He lived in a house called the 'Cage'. Perhaps he thought he sang like a bird. He took a constitutional walk every afternoon along the Ringsfield Road past the Leman School playing fields.

Mr. Hubert Byles was another tenor, and was out of step with the other men, although they appeared to get on satisfactorily. He was a member of the communist party, although he did not proselytize his political beliefs. But others mentioned it, for he was out of the accepted thoughts of most Anglicans. The Church of England was often described in those days as the Tory Party at Prayer. For all that, Hubert Byles attended church regularly and was a loyal choir member. He helped to run a choirboy cricket team; we played on Beccles Common and he was often umpire. I can hear him now as the batsman took guard. 'Do you wish me to give it from where he bowls or from behind the stumps?' Or hear him calling to the scorer to ensure accuracy in records. 'He was runned out'. As I write this I can picture his ruddy face and the ever present sound of skylarks soaring above us on the common. When there was no organized game he'd coach and bowl to us. An accurate spinner, he took only two paces before delivering a deceptively flighted ball. An engine driver on the Waveney Valley line owned then by the LNER (London North Eastern Railway), he took choirboys one at a time to ride on the footplate during the summer holidays. What an experience! On my appointed day I joined him and his fireman at a small siding about 200 yards from the station. We went out to a turntable and set off to Tivetshall across the Waveney Marshes. His shift that day lasted longer than expected. To get me home by teatime I was given a half single Geldeston to Beccles ticket costing one penny. And although I boarded the passenger train at Tivetshall this ticket got me past the carnation buttonholed collector at Beccles Station. No doubt everyone on the railway knew what was going on, but for the sake of decorum such formalities had to be obeyed. My fellow chorister and friend, Brian Patrick, told me of his trip. Mr Byles gave him the opportunity to stop a passenger train at Geldeston Station. Alas, he missed and the train ended up 300 yards past the platform. So Hubert, undeterred, took over the controls, put the engine into reverse and they shunted back to the platform. Not a difficult manoeuvre on this line which was without doubt a push-me, pull-me, slow speed one.

Another bass in the choir was Mr. Goodin. My dad reckoned his voice had the richest tone and he sang perfectly in tune. When available, he sang solos in anthems. The manager of Lloyds bank in the town, he was one of a few bank managers who played a prominent part in church life. Baron S. George at Barclays was a churchwarden and close friend of my father. Who better to keep tabs on the parish finances or speedily count the collection than a bank manager?

The two churchwardens when I first joined the choir around 1937 were Mr. Bunn, who was a managing clerk at a local solicitors, and Mr. Fowler, who ran a coal-merchants business in the area. He lived in Fair Close and was the father of Eric Fowler who, as Jonathon Mardle, for years wrote a feature column in the Eastern Daily Press every Wednesday. One article that sticks in my mind was when he bemoaned the fact that no one played sport or took part in activities just for the fun of it. We had lost the art of doing something not very well. Everyone had to be a winner and this was not possible. As he got near to retirement he extolled the virtues of a bowls club he had joined where you just turned up to have a game. Happily, like those of his contemporary, Adrian Bell, who wrote in the same paper every Saturday, his articles have recently been repeated. At Sunday evensong, as the curate might be at either the Ingate or Ravensmere Misssion Church, the wardens read a lesson each, in those days from the King James authorized version of the Bible. I always listened to and loved the poetry of the words. I am so glad we then had not drifted into this modern stuff which I heard so aptly described as 'filing cabinet English'.

As choirboys we gathered a whole list of misquotes or changes in the sense of the text. I think it all started when a reader turned over two pages and the result was gibberish. You may like to read some!

> 'And Saul took to him a wife
> Twenty cubits wide and thirty cubits in length'.

> 'And behold Abraham was sick
> And the lot fell upon Isaac'.

> 'And the Lord said to Moses, Come Forth!
> And he came fifth and lost his beer money'.

After the recessional hymn, when the choir was at the rear of the church, the rector always gave us a final prayer chant. A stand-in rural priest taking evensong changed the format and intoned 'Let Us Depart In Peace'. There was a deathly hush from the choir. And then Fred Lawrance – who else? – quietly, so only we boys could hear, sang 'And not in pieces'. We hurtled hurriedly up the spiral staircase to the vestry. This vestry over the South Porch was cold and damp in the winter. The only heat was from a small electric fire. Before we robed we took it in turns to air our cassocks. You could see the steam rising from the material. Fussy as he was about us not wearing damp clothes, Dad was content for us to endure these rigours in the name of religion.

Church attendance was regular, and certain folk were in the congregation every week morning and evening. But one must not run away with the idea that everyone in those days went to church. I suppose only about four families in our road were regular attendees. Another six or seven would go on special days – Christmas, Easter, and of course Harvest Festival. The latter event always filled the Parish Church. I knew of one young jolly village clergyman who jokingly wished non-regular folk a Happy Christmas as he shook their hands in the porch at the Harvest Service, saying 'I don't suppose I'll see you again before'.

But everyone, with few exceptions, got married, christened and had their funeral at a church or chapel – hatched, matched and dispatched as the saying puts it. No one had the right to a certain pew in the church apart from the wardens and the rector's family. These had a brass plaque denoting their purpose. But most regulars had their usual seat and their unofficial right to it was accepted.

One lady soon took my eye, as a boy. She sat in a front pew visible from the choir stalls. Immaculately groomed, she had the habit of genuflecting almost to the floor when the Virgin Mary was mentioned in the creed. She lived a mile or so outside the town, and during the week in favourable weather she walked into Beccles to shop, basket in hand and with her two pure-breed Fox Terrier dogs. The dogs were as well groomed as she was and were a kind of fashion accessory. But what was even more incomprehensible to us country lads, she called them darling in an over enthused manner. She normally had a brusque manner of speech but she softened when she talked to her spoilt dogs. But they probably gave a lonely and aging lady something to shower her affection on.

The Three Bees café was a meeting place for such genteel ladies of the town and district. Wives of doctors, bank managers and other professional men in the town would congregate there. I only ever went in the place if Aunt Marge took me. The owner had a pug dog who prowled around in the kitchen but had to be removed when the Fox Terriers were in the tearoom. I have two particular memories of the Three Bees café. Customers sat on wicker Lloyd Loom type chairs at tables with glass tops. But the entrance to the kitchen was by Western cowboy saloon type doors which easily opened when the waitress pushed the laden tray against them. Also the pug could easily negotiate biscuit-scrounging access to the customers. Now and again in the course of the year this led to a fracas with the Fox Terriers and a withering look from their owner.

A great bonus of being a choirboy was the activities we indulged in on our way home. The length of a choir practice varied, so one had about an hour's free time before arrival home was questioned. On pay night, and for a few weeks after if funds allowed, we visited the fish and chip shop. On our way it was fun to spin around in the revolving doors of the King's Head Hotel. When it was blackout dark we'd make forays along Ballygate to the grand Georgian houses, including the Rectory. We activated their 'pull-out-of-wall' door bells whose ring resounded loudly in the building. We'd then scamper down the steps into Puddingmoor. One day a colleague was too energetic in his effort, and the bell pull came away in his hand. He stood transfixed! 'What shall I do?' he cried – 'Drop it and run', I advised. Fortunately, he did, for later he rose to an elevated position in the Anglican ministry and was awarded the MBE.

On a more serious note, do not imagine, dear reader, that we were permanently flippant. One night after a Friday evening practice near Christmas we were walking across the Market Square and the voices of men quietly singing 'Silent Night' could be heard. It was still, moonlit and frosty. Curious, we walked toward the music, soon realizing the voices were singing in German. They were prisoners of war and their lorry was parked near the Falcon inn. The canvas cover at the rear was rolled back and we could just discern them sitting on benches, their legs beyond the knees covered by thick straw, wisely lain on the floor of the lorry against the cold. Whenever 'Silent Night' is sung, my thoughts go back to that time.

I would not have missed those choirboy days for anything. They did not make me a devout person, but they gave a spiritual dimension to life and are a great source of comfort as we grow old. 'Oh clap your hands together all ye people, and sing unto the Lord with a voice of melody.'

SCHOOL DAYS

Peddars Lane

Lots of my friends have memories of their first day at school. I do not. But I have recall of events at the infant's school in Peddars Lane where I commenced my education in 1935.

Miss West supervised what was called the 'babies' class which we all joined on arrival. She was soft spoken and gentle, and as I write is still living in the town. Recently I saw her doing her shopping at the new Tesco supermarket only a few hundred yards from her home. We all thought her to be very grown up but she must have only finished her training in 1935, when she taught me.

The main worry for young infants was a fear of having to use the lavatories. These were dark, dank and smelly places, with tarred walls and were outside in the playground. I had to wear short flannel trousers with thick woollen itchy underpants in winter. These were secured by braces that slipped through a loop so they held both garments in place. Mum or brother John helped me dress before we left for school. And with a bit of luck I could get through the morning or afternoon session at school without recourse to trouser lowering. But there were days, notably when scrumped apples were only half ripened, that a crisis might arise. It was on these occasions that a dear Miss Newson who lived in Alexandra Road near the playground came to my aid. A retired former nanny or governess to a member of the Spanish Royal family, she befriended a few of us infants. Now and again I made use of her expertise in fastening difficult trouser buttons. Sometimes I would head for the security and comfort of her home when the final school bell rang. She proudly showed us photographs and postcards collected during her time in Spain. Quite in contrast to her gentle nature, and to my horror, some were scenes of the bullfight. Miss Newson would give me tea and Marie biscuits to eat. Often Mum joined us and escorted me home.

Other teachers at the school as we rose through the ranks were Miss Hewin, Miss Jeffries, Miss Watson and Mrs Johnson. The headmistress was a Miss Bertha or 'Bessie' Snell, one of three spinster sisters who lived together in Ballygate. Devout chapel-goers, they were respected in the borough. One sister was the manageress of Shields, a high class stationers and supplier of school pens and pencils, and you could buy foreign stamps of top quality there. But Shields was too high class to trade in newspapers, magazines or tobacco. The third sister kept house and ran the home and also was the local agent for the Westminster Fire and Household Insurance Agency. When she eventually retired from this part-time job my dad became the local agent in her place. The plaque outside Miss Snell's house was moved to our home and placed near the front door. Every quarter, a lot of townsfolk called at the house to pay their premiums. Often on the more humble dwellings it was only about six shillings (30p) for the three months. But Dad certainly had some more affluent clients who posted their premiums in by cheque. To keep his expenses down, I used to be sent on 'errands' to deliver the receipts by hand. I found if I knocked on the door and handed the envelope to the householder a tip of a few pence was often forthcoming. Dad discovered this and I was told to quietly put the envelope through the letter box. After this, as most of the grand houses had a long front drive, I sang and whistled so my arrival did not go unnoticed and the tips continued. Father could hardly tell his choirboy son not to sing.

But back to headmistress, Bessie Snell. She was a popular head of the infant and junior school. With no disrespect intended, I named my favourite sow in my toy farmyard Bessie in her honour. Miss Hewin was notable because during her lessons I developed a love of writing 'compositions'. This was the name for essays or stories. She once told me that if my spelling and grammar could equal the ideas I might achieve some success and even get to the grammar school. This was something I had no desire for. They were all 'sissies' who went to the 'Centre School'. All I wanted was the chance to work on a farm and look after animals. However, I did for a few months, after seeing a film about David Livingstone, wish to become a missionary and go to Africa. I must have rather startled my father one night when I told him this as he was tucking me in for the night. His reply was 'we'll have to see – do you say your prayers every night?' Oh dear, seldom, I thought, and not as he did, kneeling by the bed after he had read his daily passage from the bible.

Mrs. Johnson was a teacher we all feared. A strict disciplinarian she was the only teacher at the school whose behaviour bordered on brutality. My wife, who was at the school about five years later, told me that her mother once went to the school complaining about her treatment from Mrs. Johnson, a very rare happening and response from parents at that time. My unforgettable episode with Mrs. Johnson took place thus. She took prayers sometimes with her class. We all had to stand at our desks with closed eyes and our hands clasped in front in suppliant manner, then together recite the Lord's prayer. Just as we got into the piece about not being led into temptation I suddenly sensed a presence behind me. Instinctively I turned slightly towards it, my eyes squinting open a little to see who it was. Sadly, unbeknown to the class, Mrs. Johnson had quietly left her position in the front. Walking up and down the rows of pupils, she was anxious to see everyone was praying with due reverence. Alas, I was not. Unlike the Almighty, Mrs. Johnson did not 'forgive our trespasses'. The result was that I received two resounding blows across the ears. As I bit back the tears, I was sent from the class to the headmistress. Happily, her reaction was kinder. I did not get the anticipated ruler across the hand as some did. I was told to try and be a good boy in future. No doubt she had seen my eyes, red with tears, and felt sorry for me.

Before the school milk allocation came in during the war we were all given a small mug of very watery Horlicks to drink in the winter months at playtime. I believe this was provided by one or a group of wealthy local benefactors. Many of the children from the poorer families in the town came to school perforce cold, badly clothed and undernourished. I can remember one girl who came barefoot sometimes and, poor lass, she did not smell very sweet either.

Each classroom had a coal fire to keep us warm in winter. This was attended to by the caretaker who made regular visits keeping it topped up with coal. There was a tall fireguard around each fire. If children got wet socks then teacher dried them on the guard. Those poorly clothed were tactfully placed at the desks nearest the fire. In very cold weather we might have a break in the lesson to do five minutes 'physical jerks'. This kept the cold at bay and the blood coursing through our veins. In the afternoon the babies and early years infants had a rest break. We had to fold our arms and rest our heads on the desks. It was a kind of juvenile siesta.

One winter there was an epidemic of scarlet fever in the town. At that time, before antibiotics, this was serious. To combat the spread of infection we were requested to take large empty clean meat paste jars to school. First thing each morning these were filled with salt water by the teachers and we gargled over the sinks in the cloak room. The process was hilarious. We had competition to see who had the most musical sounding gargle. But it must have had some effect, for the fever in the town soon abated.

I cannot remember much about Miss Jeffries. But when we got to her class we all had new wooden rulers. And she handed out shiny new Geography books with lovely coloured pictures. One Saturday morning Miss Jeffries examined me for my 'House Orderly' badge in the Wolf Cubs. I must have been about eight years old at the time. My mother had gone through the procedures at home during the week before, and under her guidance I had become adept at the most difficult procedure of cracking an egg on the side of a frying pan before cooking it. Not for me the easy sensible way of putting the egg in a cup first. Told to report at Miss Jeffries's house in Wembley Avenue at 9.30 a.m., my first job was to sweep up in the hall, kitchen and living room. After that there was some dusting and polishing to do. And I was provided with polish and brushes to clean my own shoes. Then, carefully watched by the kindly teacher, I made a pot of tea for us both. I must have got bonus points for Mum had taught me to warm the pot and to take the pot to the kettle when it boiled. Tea bags were unheard of then. The measure was one teaspoonful for each person and one for the pot. And the pot had to stand for a few minutes to brew. We enjoyed our cups of tea and then for the greatest challenge – the fry-up. As I had left, Mum, bless her heart, had told me to play safe and crack the egg into a cup first. But I'd watched her so many times easily break an egg on the pan. I'll show them, I thought, surely I can do that. Sad to relate, I botched the job. The egg exploded and fell down the outside of the pan – fortunately into the grill-pan tray beneath. Miss Jeffries was amused and, advised by her, I was able to pull out the grill-pan with the egg remains and pour it into the frying pan. It cooked surprisingly well. A cross between an omelette and a fried egg, it was decently edible, according to the teacher. I was presented with the badge at the cub pack meeting a few weeks later. Trying to sew it on my green jersey was the hardest job. Mum rescued me.

Mention must be made that at Peddars Lane in those days, when infant and junior schooling ceased at eleven years, unless you were destined for the Sir John Leman or other grammar schools, you advanced into the senior section. The senior school was on the same premises but had a separate head teacher and staff. And they used other play areas, toilets and facilities. The seniors continued their elementary education at Peddars Lane until they left school at the age of fourteen years. When the 'Area' school opened in 1939 on Castle Hill the senior section closed and those pupils went there.

What other memories do I have of those early school days? In the summer Mr. Collins, a local milk-man, sold ice-cream on the Peddars Lane-Blyburgate corner. This he made nearby in a small dairy at his cottage in Frederick's Road opposite the Black Boy meadow. Houses are now built on this meadow. It was in the olden days the site for touring funfairs and circuses that came to the town. There was no sports field at the Peddars Lane school. All games and playtimes were spent on the hard surfaced playground. But on special days the school was allowed use of and access to the Black Boy meadow, notably on Empire Day when we all walked there in a long crocodile and sang patriotic hymns and waved flags. Then there was a light hearted sports day. There were sprint races, sack races plus three-legged and egg and spoon events. All good fun. The school governors and some of the town's civic dignitaries would be present. We were not formed into different 'Houses' at the Peddars Lane school, but in team games – like rounders or net-ball for the girls – we were given different coloured wide ribbons to wear across the chest. I always liked to be in the 'reds' for some obscure reason.

There was a sweet shop by the school kept by Mr. and Mrs. Mason. I did not use this much, mostly using the sweet shops near Fair Close where I got preferential treatment. But I do remember you stood on a wooden crate to survey the sweets on a sloping shelf in the front window of the shop. After making your selection you passed Mr. and Mrs. Mason by the exit door and paid them. The shop also acted as a small general store for the houses nearby. They sold potatoes plus a few groceries and provisions. Mr. Mason became a Special Constable during the war and he had a ginger moustache.

Once or twice a year the nurse came to inspect our heads for nits. She was a tall, buxom lady with silver hair that was swept back and tied. I was so sorry for one girl who after the nurse had examined her was asked to go outside. We did not see her at school for a day or so. And, poor lass, when she did arrive her hair had been cut very short like a boy's. I think this was cruel! The school dentist came each year. An inspection was made and your parents were informed if treatment was advised. This was provided free by the East Suffolk County Council whose dentist set up mobile equipment at the school. I never suffered this fate as my parents sent me to Mr. Lavelle whose dental surgery was in St. Mary's Road. He was Irish and played golf. But, sadly, he left the area soon after the National Health Service came into force after the war. Visits to him were never a source of concern. He filled and extracted teeth for me in those early years. When the Beccles Hospital Fete took place one year before the war in the grounds of Roos Hall on the Bungay Road, Mr. Lavelle was in charge of the Aunt Sally golf. I was readily conscripted by him to act as his assistant on the stall. Contestants paid six pence (two and a half pence today) a go. They had three attempts to knock a golf ball into Aunt Sally's mouth. This was a huge face painted on to a thick heavy canvas cloth suspended on a sturdy frame. My job was to hand each customer a golf club and three balls and then run to the rear of Aunt Sally to gather up the occasional prize-winning ball that did go into her mouth. Our stall was of great interest and excitement and made quite a good sum for the hospital. I walked home proudly clutching a box of very chewy chocolate toffees that Mr. Lavelle gave me as a thank you for my efforts. Mum said it was a surprising thing for a dentist to give a child. 'He must be looking for more trade'.

For good behaviour in the dentist's chair you were always rewarded with small sample packs of tooth paste or small tins of Gibbs dentifrice. This was a paste you rubbed on to your tooth brush before cleaning. One day I had to go and receive emergency treatment for toothache in the early evening. It was at the time when 'Dick Barton Special Agent', a popular spy thriller, was on the wireless. So as my tooth was filled I was soothed by the exploits of Jock, Snowy and Jack', the heroes in the story. Mr. Lavelle was a good dentist. His choice of programme much better than Radio One that some patients have to endure nowadays, I'm told. But maybe at that age I'd have settled for Radio One had it been available.

I can remember being involved in a masque or pageant that was organized at the Peddars Lane school. If my recollections are correct the seniors also were involved. The preparations took place for much of the term. With aid from teachers and older pupils from the seniors, we made costumes and weapons to dress in and carry. It must have had a medieval Round Table theme. The boys wore mock chain-mail and had white shields with red crosses. Some were knights with attendants. The girls had long frocks and stumbled as they walked, causing much mirth. Did we march to the Black Boy meadow so dressed on Empire Day one year? Maybe. Alas, there were no ponies involved.

But talking of ponies, the two Beccles Horse Sale days at Michaelmas were exciting. Many mares, with foals running beside, were led to Read Owles and Ashford's Sale-yard, a large area of about two acres on the corner of Peddars Lane and Blyburgate. Every other Friday a livestock market was held. Then, cattle, pigs, rabbits, poultry plus a few sheep were sold. There was also a sale of deadstock and some furniture. This was always of interest when we made our way home from school.

The horse sale took place on a Monday and Tuesday in mid-September. Around 200 horses were sold daily. These were all named and described in the official sale catalogue. For example: '5 year old Suffolk Mare, Beauty: – Sound, quiet in all gears. Good reliable worker.' Any claims made were proven correct, by the local vet. A buyer had a comeback if claims were false. But it was not just horses in the sale that changed hands. A number of diddy-coys – itinerant tinkers – dealers and higglers came to the town. A mini horse-fair took place. Many gathered on or around the Black Boy meadow. The pub was open all day. Heavy drinking with the subsequent bawdy behaviour was common. The horses on sale would be displayed by running them up and down either along Frederick's Road or up Ingate Street. Having seen the horses displayed, banter took place between prospective buyer and seller. And a slap of the hands indicated a deal had been struck. On these days we were advised to go to and from school by a diverse route avoiding Blyburgate where the running colts looked menacing. But I have no recall of any mishap occurring.

While I was at Peddars Lane school in 1937 the Suffolk Agricultural Show came to the town. In those days the show had no permanent base but moved around the county. The site was on the Ringsfield Road on an area now used by the Leman School as playing fields. It was the custom for the family to go and view the preparations for such an event visiting the town. And so we all strolled after evensong on the Sunday before the show. Various rails had been erected and the Grand Ring and stands were partly prepared. But, being Sunday, no work was in progress, making it an ideal time to look around. There were, however, groups of townsfolk on a similar mission. I met up with some school friends and we decided to have a race. Alas, I ran full pelt into one of the railings and knocked myself momentarily unconscious. I remember coming around with a St. John's Ambulance First Aider bending over me. I was advised always to look where I was going in future.

Another Sunday evening walk we always made together was the weekend before the Regatta. The cut by the quay was lined with visiting vessels moored close together, some two abreast. We strolled along the Suffolk side of the river almost to the Boater's Hills on the Norfolk side to view the boats arriving for the Regatta. There was a camp of the Boys' Brigade bell tents erected on the meadows of the Hills. A mast with a Union Jack was flying and bugle calls might be heard calling the Brigade lads to their supper: 'come to the cookhouse store Boys'.

Along the river wall footpath we would stop and chat to various folk some of whom the family knew and were annual visitors. It was on one of these walks that I got stung on the back of the neck by a wasp. Once I got over the initial shock I was glad to receive the care and kindness of a young lady boat owner. She gave me something to put on the sting, and to my great delight a small bar of chocolate. By the time we arrived at the quay on our way home the Salvation Army were concluding their evening act of worship. This was held by the river in August. There was always a sizeable gathering of townsfolk and river visitors to listen to the band. We paused to join them for the final hymn, 'The day thou gavest Lord is ended'. Another Sunday evening walk made in the summer holidays was to view the building site of the new Area Elementary School in the process of construction. By then war clouds were gathering and there was comment in the town that these schools (there were a few in the area) were built in such a manner they could easily be turned into military or civilian hospitals if the need arose. But they never were used for such purpose.

We all looked forward to the end of term at Peddars Lane with relish. The excitement of holidays in store was enhanced because for at least a week before we broke up normal school routines were waived. Before this we were given 'tests' so our teacher had some guide to our progress. And this was taken into account in the end of term report. I was doing quite well and was in the top five in a class of over 30. My conduct was exemplary, except I was asked to try and not 'chatter' quite so much!

At Christmas preparation began at least three weeks before the end of term. The school morning assembly was especially joyous, with the singing of carols and Christmas hymns. Even Mrs. Johnson seemed to mellow. Craft lessons took on a festive role. In the babies' class little ones were engaged in making paper chains. A variety of coloured strips were linked together using a safe, simple paste made with flour and water. And it worked. The caretaker helped the various class teachers to put them up in each room. At the end of term, maybe a week before Christmas, they were removed when the school closed and given to charitable institutions and the hospital.

One year a local benefactor paid for the children to have an end of term Christmas party. We had sausage rolls and mince pies. As we left for home we were each given an orange and a wrapped present. When I opened mine on Christmas day I was overjoyed to find one of the latest board games.

I was sad to leave Peddars Lane. When I finished there at the end of July 1941 I was not certain which school I was going to. But I did know that I would say goodbye to some of my best pals.

In the autumn of the year after your eleventh birthday you became a senior. And then, if considered clever enough and your parents wished it, you were able to sit an examination to pass the Scholarship to the Sir John Leman or similar Grammar School. For many children in spite of undoubted ability this was never an option. The reason, simple economics. Their parents could not afford to keep them at school any longer than the statutory leaving age of fourteen. The extra income a working child was able to bring into a household was often vital. But it was not just loss of earnings that played a part. It cost money even for scholarship children to attend grammar school. Uniforms, notebooks, rulers, compasses, protractors were all required and had to be purchased by the parents. Also sports gear such as shirts and shorts were needed. Sometimes these might be passed on to younger siblings or given by 'better off' neighbours whose children had left school. Such procedures were more accepted during the war when rationing of clothes and other items led to a more egalitarian outlook. But it required a very strong wish by working class parents for their children to 'get on' if they were to try for a scholarship. Sadly, the whole affair could be divisive between family and friends. It happened that people fell out because one child got to the Leman School and another had not. And it was frequently the cause of as much distress to the successful child as the one who failed.

I knew deep in my heart that my parents wanted me at the Sir John Leman School. But I failed the scholarship examinations, to their great dismay! There was another route to the school even if you failed the scholarship. This was through an entrance examination. Since it was less difficult, most children with a fair aptitude for English and Arithmetic ought to have passed this, and especially if they had some extra tuition beforehand. This was my own reluctant pathway to grammar school. But my parents had to pay a fee of three pounds a term. This may seem a trifling amount today, but my dad was paying a similar charge for my older brother, making a total of £18 a year. This would have amounted to more than a month's wages. And if you couple this with all the other equipment that had to be provided for us both, it must have come to nearer two month's wages of his regular pay. With hindsight I now realize the despair in the family I must have caused if I came home to report my glasses broken (generally once each term) or plimsolls and football boots lost.

I did not want to go to the Leman School, although later I was very pleased I did. You were a 'cissie centre' boy if you went there. That was how a lot of my Peddars Lane class-mates described them and I feared being a subject of ridicule. Why were Leman School children known as 'cissie centres'? I think because some of the teachers had gone there from the teachers' centre in Fair Close. But if it was to be the grammar school, there was one big bonus: seven weeks' holiday instead of five!

In the event, the year I started in September 1941, I did not have to sit the entrance examination. I had been stricken by a childish ailment on the day of the examination. But, although I had failed the scholarship earlier, I was considered by the headmaster, Mr. Humphreys, to have obtained enough marks to be considered as passing the entrance examination. It is quite clear in my mind being told over the tea table it was to be the Leman School for me. It was mid August and plums were ripening. I had been to the home of a friend of the family, Colonel Reginald Brooks – he was a Deputy Lieutenant and a distant relative of Grandma. Colonel Brooks had a large poultry farm on the Ellough Road at Beccles, where he kept flocks of Rhode Island Red hens. I would sometimes go and help on the farm to feed the hens and collect eggs. If I could get near a farm of any sort I was happy. On this particular day I had been helping Kenny Brooks, the Colonel's brother, gather plums. Kenny was a Down's Syndrome gentleman who lived with the family. We were deputed to gather plums growing alongside one of the chicken runs. He was always interesting company. He grew tired of carefully picking the fruit from the trees. Looking to see we were unobserved, he suddenly, with a chuckle, shook two of the heaviest laden branches. And we hastily gathered the fallen fruit from the grass. I arrived home with a bag of plums at teatime to hear I was to be a 'cissie centre boy'. But Mum was so pleased to tell me that I was going to the Leman School that I was happy just for her.

This is a good time to tell you about Kenny Brooks. Kindly cared for much of his life by Uncle Reggie and Aunt Lucy; as I knew the Colonel and his wife, he was a familiar figure in the town. It was thought beneficial to keep him busy, and he loved company and walking into Beccles. This he did several days a week, carrying a large wicker shopping basket to buy the family provisions. He had a booklet in the basket, plus a purse holding money. He had about a mile to walk, but the shopkeepers gave him a friendly greeting. Examining the list in the booklet, they would put the requirements into his basket and take money from the purse, putting any change back. They advised him where else to go until the last shop when he then returned with a basketful of household needs.

My Aunt Marge would occasionally stay for an evening with Kenny, enabling the Colonel and his wife to visit friends or go to the cinema. Kenny loved to play card games like snap or draw-the-well-dry. Snakes and Ladders or Draughts were also played to give variety to the evening. There was a break for cocoa and biscuits as Kenny's bedtime got closer. Then he and Aunt Marge would discuss recent events. One evening Kenny suddenly leaned across the table and exclaimed, 'Marge – will you marry me? But no babies, dear'. Quite shattered by this unexpected proposal and not wishing to hurt Kenny's feelings, she replied, 'We shall have to see'. As he got older Kenny's health deteriorated and his carers themselves aged. He ended his days in a colony at Little Plumstead near Norwich. He must have missed his placid home and walks into the town. The town certainly missed him.

The Sir John Leman School

How different those early days at the Leman School were from the close-knit community at Peddars Lane. There was no Miss Newson nearby in an emergency. At the junior school I knew all the boys and girls in my class and at least half of all the other children at the school. I was not the brightest by far and certainly not in sums as mathematics was called. But always I would be placed in the top five in most 'tests' as we called end of term examinations. And in composition I did very well. But after arriving at the Leman School I struggled not to be at the bottom in some subjects. It was all so different and bewildering. Our fellow classmates came from a much wider area. There were only two I recall going with me that year. They were both girls and scholarship winners: Anne Taylor and Pat Beazley. Three other scholarship children came from the National School in Ravensmere: Rex Butcher, Raymond Bartram and Stella Daines. Others had been at the Area Secondary School on Ellough Road for a year awaiting a vacancy; Dennis Pegram, June Gibbs and Colin Baker. There were also pupils who had been at the Roman Catholic School, St. Benet's. John Snowden was one who joined our class and became a friend as did Russell Pipe. These boys had to leave the class when we had Religious Instruction. A bit hard on them when we eventually took the School Certificate in this subject. It was reputed to be an easy option. It must have been as I got a 'credit'! A thought has just struck me – the terminology for subjects changed at the grammar school. Scripture became Religious Instruction. Sums became Mathematics and to my great horror this was divided into Algebra and Geometry. In English we no longer wrote compositions but had to write essays. The Literature side of things I loved and to some extent excelled in. But grammar was and still is a problem for me. In my later life I have taken great comfort in the fact that John Clare, the romantic rural poet, never used punctuation.

At Peddars Lane we did Nature Study and at one time had a tub of tadpoles in the class-room. Every autumn we took the changing leaves into school as they fell from the trees. We were also encouraged to gather hips and haws from the hedgerow. My early teachers encouraged an interest in the seasons. Mr. Esling, the newsagent in Blyburgate, had a huge mercury thermometer outside his shop. It carried an advertisement for Stephens Ink. When the weather got very hot or cold Mum and I would take a look. But at the Leman School Nature Study became Biology and this I enjoyed and kept pace with most of the others. But alas there was also Chemistry and Physics with which I never completely got to grips. There was much excitement by all of us when we had our first lessons in the chemistry laboratory and used a Bunsen burner. It was fun to heat glass tubing and bend it into animal shapes. Alas, my animals were rather deformed and out of scale. Children also joined us at the Leman School from rural areas. Many I had never met before. They came from as far afield as Southwold, Great Yarmouth, Reydon, Halesworth and Loddon and the villages around those towns. Numbered among them were Bridget Spandler, Noel Becket, David Soanes, Colin Fisk, Gwen Hopes and Molly Raven. The last, as a matter of interest, now lives in Frostenden. Now a widow, Molly Hammond works hard to promote local events for the village hall and playing fields. She is a stalwart of village activities, and in spite of poor health still helps to organize them. She used to walk daily from Frostenden to catch the Eastern Counties service bus at Stoven. Doreen Baggot was also in my class and travelled from Stoven. Some pupils cycled quite a long distance, Noel Becket and Harry Cullum from Loddon, John Baxter and Mick Powell from Westhall. The Leman School at the time had a very sensible policy concerning bicycles. I would estimate that more than half the pupils came to school on them. Some years earlier the East Suffolk Education Committee decided to provide loan cycles for senior pupils who lived more than a certain distance from their school. I believe this still maintained when I started at the Leman School. But all pupils who wished to take a cycle to school had to have a licence. This was a folded printed card with your name on. Your vehicle had to be inspected regularly to see that brakes and tyres were safe. There were also certain local school rules you had to abide by. Woe betide any child seen cycling on the pavement or the school premises or sports field. Riding more than two abreast was forbidden. You had to dismount and walk across both the junctions at the bottom of Ringsfield Road hill and St. Mary's Road near the town sign and likewise if you were riding at the bottom of Ashman's Road where it meets London Road. These rules were enforced by members of staff and the school prefects. Prefects were members of the Sixth Form. Most were preparing to take the Higher School Certificate and hoping to go on to university. Any cycling miscreant was asked to produce their licence which was suitably endorsed. After three warnings a Saturday morning detention might be given and you were banned from cycling to school for a week. It was a good scheme. I cannot recall any pupil being involved in a serious accident. I did sail over the handle bars one frosty night going down the Ringsfield Road hill and trying to race Russell Pipe. But the regular checking of pupils' cycles was commendable. Sadly, soon after I left, a young Peddars Lane boy was tragically killed on his cycle near the school.

Russell Ulph, one of the greatest and most memorable school characters, cycled in from the family farm in Weston every morning. He would be up early to help milk a herd of cows before coming to school. And he would help his father on the farm when he got home in the evening. Once when a master challenged him about arriving late he replied, 'I expect I had milked half a dozen cows before you were even out of bed!' Again, when asked what would happen if he did not make a success in life Russell quipped back, 'I shall make as good a liven' as any of 'em and certainly all I want!' And this he did. I don't think he took the school certificate but he and his brother made a success of the farm after his dad died. Not only that, he has been a stalwart of the parish and community. The local correspondent for the Beccles and Bungay Journal, he has also helped organize village hall and playing field events all his life.

Russell was to become one of the top cross country runners at the school, and was to rival Colin Baker. He had his own unique way in making it difficult to pass him in Cut Throat Lane as the finishing line got near. He continued in distance running after his school days and won several local races. One never knew what his reaction in school might be. We had read 'The Ancient Mariner' and were given special books to keep notes in and told to write the poem's title on the front cover: Russell wrote 'The Engine Driver'.

I have many memories of our exploits together. If woodwork lessons became a bit boring we pretended to be blacksmiths shoeing a horse. Remember that every village had a farrier in those days, and the procedure at the forge was familiar to us both. One of us would be the 'horse' and raise our foot between the other's legs as would a blacksmith. Then a woodwork mallet was used to hammer imaginary nails into a shoe. We tried to make the process realistic. Whoever was the farrier would cry out 'Stand still ole hoss' as the other partner in the farce moved his foot.

At the end of each term an auction for school funds took place when unclaimed confiscated plimsolls, shorts, shin guards etc. lying in the cloakroom were put up for sale. Bidding was slack when a superior pair of white cricket boots were on offer. Dismayed, Mr. Johnston-Browne, the auctioneer, appealed for a greater bid than the eighteen pence he had reached. Thinking quite good-naturedly that he ought to add a little colour to the proceedings, Russell, used to the banter around a stockmarket ring, loudly called out 'Guineas'. For this rather amusing attempt to liven proceedings, Russell unjustly received a Saturday detention. I very much doubt if he attended. His aid around the family farm at weekends was needed. I have been told recently that at this auction I challenged the auctioneer as to the legality of what he was doing without a licence, and suggested that a Dutch auction would overcome the difficulty – that is an auction in which a stated price is gradually lowered until a bidder makes a bid and thereby wins it. Johnston-Browne wisely ignored my challenge and my advice.

Sometimes I would go home after school in the summer evenings with Russell. A farmhouse kitchen tea was always a feature of these visits. A slice of home-cooked ham plus a boiled egg from their farmyard hens was our regular meal. I was reminded of these visits when I went back to the farm a few years ago. Russell had kindly allowed publicity photographs to be taken around his pet Jersey cows. It was a bitterly freezing January morning. His greeting to us all was as warm as the weather was cold. The Leman School ought to be proud that one of their ex-pupils has done so much for their local community. There is now a Russell Green in the village in his honour.

Yet another group of pupils in Form Two which I joined on arriving at the grammar school were a few that had been in Form One. This was a preparatory class of fee-paying children not yet eleven years old. Form One was under the care of Miss Jones – Lily, as we all knew her. She was also games mistress for the girls. Coupled with these duties, Lily was also in charge of the school gardens, an important item in wartime. The gardens provided some of the vegetables for the school canteen. Form One pupils at the Leman School came from the wealthier families in the town and district. They included the sons of local doctors, dentists and wealthy business people. Some of these children did not stay on at the Leman School to study for the School Certificate. They left to go to boarding school such as Framlingham College. One boy went to the Merchant Taylors School. But one or two did join us in Form Two.

Lily was a disciplinarian, and I was soon reprimanded for vigorously using a garden hoe through a cabbage patch I had been detailed to weed. I also used the same implement, to her distress, to quickly remove weeds from the paths along the various vegetable beds. 'Put the hoe back in the shed', she said, 'Then get on your hands and knees and pull the weeds out'. It seemed a laborious and time-wasting way to deal with them. But Lily pointed out to me that a weed that came up by the roots would not grow again. And she was right.

Another of the teachers I recall from those early days was Miss Barton – Granny Barton, we called her. Some of our early English grammar lessons were taken by her. I can remember her as a rather fussy old lady. But she must have been in her late fifties at the time. There was an episode when a pupil who is best nameless was perceived by Granny to be picking his nose. Such behaviour could not be tolerated and the miscreant was ordered from the classroom. As he reached the exit and was about to reach for the latch, Granny blurted out to him – 'Oh boy – don't soil the door. Take this and use it', and she handed him a piece of paper to protect the door knob as he left.

I recall to this day two items of aide-mémoire that Granny used to see that our syntax was correct. 'Never use with to end a sentence with!' My grammar leaves a lot to be desired but never since then have I succumbed to that error. And she also demanded that a sentence's meaning must not be misconstrued. Her example – 'Walking down the road in thin shoes a house appeared'. But dear old Granny retired soon after we arrived, but older friends who were her pupils throughout their school life spoke fondly of her.

Another English teacher who left for the war was 'Buckwheat Thomas'. How he got the name I know not. He was very much the academic, wearing his gown during lessons, in those days a more common practice. He was small of stature and had a gentle demeanour. But he knew his stuff. His lessons were lively and thus he kept order and our respect. He instilled a love of Dickens in us as 'David Copperfield' was the first book we read at school. My brother John had been taught by Buckwheat earlier and told me this tale. He recalled the young master's marriage. On the night the newly-weds returned from their honeymoon several of the senior boys surrounded their house in Kilbrack and beneath the bedroom window cheered and serenaded the happy couple.

I have written at length about several teachers who made a great and lasting impression on us – often because they were at the school for a long time. But there were many who touched our lives briefly in various ways. Because of the war, there was a number of staff who came to cover for teachers gone to serve in the forces. Muriel White who taught Art was deputizing for her husband Robert. I have one lasting memory of her kindness to me. My grandmother had died during the morning and the household was in turmoil when I went home for dinner. Consequently I was asked to do a few errands during the midday break. Thus I returned late for the afternoon double session of Art. The lesson was well under way when I entered the classroom and explained to Mrs. White the reason. She took me by the arm, set me at my desk and, knowing full well that my artistic talent was minimal, gently suggested 'perhaps you would like to draw me a tree in winter, just the trunk and bare branches'. Often when I see the silhouette of a tree on the sky line I am reminded of her kindness with a tinge of both sadness and contentment.

Many years later, Robert and Muriel lived in our neighbouring village of Uggeshall. Staunch workers for the local parish church, they organized Farm House Teas at their home in the summer. I still remember, as my wife and I arrived, being greeted by Mrs. White asking 'Can you cope with Miss McCarthy? Will you sit at her table?' This we did happily. Miss McCarthy was our very formidable senior mistress.

Gardening, or to give it the grammar school title, 'Horticulture', was of prime concern. After the departure of Lily Jones there were part-time instructors without formal teacher training but who had gardening expertise. Mrs. Palmer, who lived nearby, supervised some of our garden chores. There was also a Mrs. Tookay, who was keen to see we kept the front entrance of the school in order. She once detailed me and another boy to prune the laurel hedge along the school main entrance drive. She gave us secateurs and instructions as to how we were to go about the job, then left us and went to supervise other pupils. It was just before sports day, when parents, governors and local dignitaries were to visit the school and the pupils were engaged in various tidying duties. After about two hours Mrs. Tookay returned to inspect our efforts on the laurel hedge. Alas, we had completely misunderstood her instructions. We had removed what ought to have been left and left what ought to have been trimmed. From then on we were both known to her as the boys who ruined the laurel hedge. But soon – after a couple of years – it recovered, but I fear she didn't.

A local man known as Posie White in the town was the county horticultural adviser. He put in occasional appearances. My brother John told me that he arrived once to show how to lift grass turf. But it was after a very dry spell. He was not able to get his special turf cutting tool into the ground. A number of boys were detailed to retrieve buckets of water from the school cloakroom. These Posie poured on to the turf-lifting area. To the boys' amusement, most of the water just ran off the hard baked clay soil. Several bucketfuls later poor Posie still could not insert the turf-lifter and gave the job up.

A Mr. Pottenger, who held an advisory post with the War Agricultural Advisory Committee, used to spend some time at the school. He was active, as one would expect, in encouraging us to grow vegetables, particularly potatoes, which would be used in the school canteen. But he always let us stay indoors if the weather was cold and wet. Then he would put up a diagram for us to copy, showing how what he called the nitrogen cycle worked. We got on very well together as he was aware of my interest in farming. One of his indoor lessons took place just after I had been caned. The thumb on my right hand was swollen and bruised and I could not grip a pen. He expressed surprise that I had suffered in this way. 'I thought you would have been too artful for that', he said.

Father Gigon, a French Roman Catholic priest who, I think, had escaped from Europe at the start of the war, lived at the Convent near the school. He never taught me but friends said he was a great aid in helping them prepare for oral French examinations. I remember spending an evening with him and

Colin at the home of George Odam, the headmaster of the local Area School on Ellough Road. He had a droll sense of humour.

Mr. Eaton, who lived in St. Mary's Road, took us for Physical Training (PT) and also taught us to swim. His lessons were always interesting and varied. Any misdemeanours during a lesson were summarily dealt with in this manner. The culprit had to bend and touch his toes. You were given a sharp hand-slap across the backside. Dressed in thin shorts, it stung a bit but was soon forgotten with no ill will from either party. I am grateful to Mr. Eaton for teaching me to swim. Lessons took place in the town swimming pool in Puddingmoor. It was a piece of the river fenced off. Subject to the Waveney tides, swimming sports were arranged to coincide with high water. One little incident concerning Mr. Eaton took place during the summer holidays. I had gone for a ride in one of Leggett's lorries taking pigs to a slaughter house in Lowestoft. We were returning through Oulton Broad and approached the traffic lights at the end of Victoria Road. Mr. Eaton was sitting hopefully on a low chapel wall, waiting for a bus to Beccles. He pointed his thumb in good hitch-hikers' manner. 'Who's he?' said Bob, the lorry driver. 'He's one of my teachers', I said. Bob replied 'We'd better give the poor old bugger a lift then.' From then on my credit in PT lessons improved. Mr. Eaton had three daughters, all pupils at the school, each one very good hockey players. One of them, Margaret, had a lovely contralto voice and sang many solos at school concerts and in the parish church.

There were two headmasters during my time. Mr. Humphreys was there when I arrived. I seldom had any direct contact with him. He must have been a very able administrator and manager. He formed an Air Training Corps at the school. He was successful in linking boys from other schools in the town with his own pupils. Mr. Johnston-Browne and Mr. Sam Skevens, a former pupil not on active service, because of poor health, were fellow officers in Beccles ATC 759 Squadron. As members, we went to school in uniform each Friday and returned in the evening for instruction. We also went on a number of ATC camps during the summers – at RAF Mildenhall and RAF Holton, and I recall that on one occasion we flew in a Lancaster bomber. Colin was in the mid-upper gun turret and I was with the bomb aimer.

But the greatest debt the Leman School and education in the town had to Mr. Humphreys was how he coped with the aftermath of the dreadful fire which took place in April 1942. Now is a good time to write about this fire. Let me describe the event as it occurred to me. It was during the Friday afternoon when Mr. Humphreys walked, unexpectedly, into our classroom. He stood in the doorway saying calmly but emphatically 'walk quickly and quietly from the building and assemble on the playing field.' No alarms had sounded but we realized there was something unusual afoot when the headmaster quickly said as we all rose, 'All of you use the girls' stairs and exit through the girls' cloakroom', an area naturally out of bounds for boys. As we filed out and descended the stairs, talk of a fire in the school false roof was mentioned. This was at the boys' end of the school. There was then no sign of the devastation that was to follow. The stored wooden hurdles and other sports equipment made excellent kindling for the electrical fault causing the fire.

However, as we assembled on the boys' playing field, smoke and flames were soon rising through the roof. There was no panic, and form teachers were checking all pupils were present. Before long the fire brigades arrived and the school pond, which might have been thought a good supply, was quickly emptied. Hoses eventually had to go across the playing field to the water tower in South Road. Under the auspices of various staff and prefects, a human chain was formed passing books, papers and teaching materials that could be saved from the ground floor. These were stored in the homes, sheds and garages of staff and neighbours who lived in the Ringsfield Road. Only certain staff members entered the building with firemen. Prefects were also recruiting younger boys to help on various salvage duties. I was asked to help James Payne. We had to aid Mr. Pegram, the caretaker, who was moving their furniture and valuables from their living quarters on the east side of the school. Poor Jim Payne became one of the only two casualties of the fire. A piece of furniture slipped from the bedroom window as we reached to collect it. Jim, being much taller than me, bravely took the full weight and received a deep cut above the eye. Blood poured down his face. After first aid from St. John's Ambulance at the scene, he went to hospital to have the wound stitched. I'm glad his injury was not more serious. He became a clergyman and married Shirley and me at Worlingham Church in 1957. The greatest favour anyone did me.

By early evening the upper floor was a smouldering wreck and the roof beyond repair. The ground floor and much of the contents suffered tremendous damage from the water necessarily used to quell the fire. It was a sign of the affection we all had for the school that only one boy was apparently rejoicing because it looked like we were due an extra holiday. He was soon shut up.

Now, Mr. Humphreys's organizing ability and devotion of his staff and prefects was shown. On the Monday after the fire we all met at the parish church for an assembly. An arrangement had been made over the weekend that the school was for a time to share the premises of the Area School on Ellough Road.

This was a prime example of the Dunkirk spirit that prevailed in the country during the war. It was a time when everyone pulled together for the common good. Mr. Humphreys and Mr. George Odam, the Area School headmaster liaised together for the benefit and education of all children in the town. Area School children attended in the morning and we Leman School children took the afternoon shift from 1.00 p.m. until 5.00 p.m., if my memory serves correctly. Luckily, it was April and the nights had 'pulled out'. In the morning we went to the Leman School playing field for games and also to work on the school vegetable gardens and shrubberies. It was an interesting time. There were problems, no doubt, but not many learning hours were lost.

But Mr. Humphreys and his devoted team soon set to work to enable normal lessons to resume and not to impose too long on Mr. George Odam's hospitality. After a time, it was possible for some of the ground floor classrooms to be put in use. Lessons also took place in the corridors, entrance hall and even in that holy of holies the mistresses' common room. And use was made of other buildings in the town generally made available. Classes took place in the Rectory and Long Room of the parish church in Ballygate and also in the hall at the rear of the Congregational church in Hungate. There was no longer a senior school in Peddars Lane, so use was made of their former woodwork room. This became our form room and our desks were the wood-work benches. As far as possible, pupils were kept for lessons in the same place. It was the staff who relocated – a clever logistical move.

The YMCA hut in the Newmarket (now the site of the Waveney Centre for the Elderly in the town) was used for School Certificate examinations. Whenever the school met together at the beginning or end of the term we went to the parish church and to the Regal Cinema for Speech Day and Prize Giving. The school became very much a part of the town and town part of the school.

Dr. Wood was the headmaster for the last two years I was at the Leman School. I had more involvement with him. He caned me for something of a trivial offence when compared to many of my crimes. I got uncontrolled giggles one afternoon in a school assembly during a concert given by a string quartet. The harder I tried to stop, the worse it got. Not surprisingly, I was asked to leave the proceedings, and later Dr. Wood caned me – a stupid, senseless punishment that did nothing for my future conduct. In fact, by some I was seen as a bit of a hero. Few boys were caned.

But Dr. Wood and I got on very well after that. He was interested in farming because his family had an agricultural background, and Colin reminds me that his doctoral thesis was on comparative agricultural systems in Germany, the Channel Islands and Britain. He was one teacher who thought it was reasonable for a grammar school boy to pursue work in farming. He encouraged the formation of a Young Farmers' Club at the school. It was through this I met Mr. Philip Ashford on whose farm I later became a pupil. Under Dr. Wood's auspices, a small flock of leghorn chickens was kept at the school. I used to feed them at weekends. There was one little hiccup. One Monday he stopped me in the corridor and asked me if I had been to the cupboard where surplus eggs were kept. He said half a dozen were missing. He did not accuse me of taking them but implicitly questioned my honesty. Now, we got up to many pranks but would never have dreamt of robbery. I was hurt. That night after feeding the hens I somehow forgot to fasten the gate to their run. Next morning they were all over the playing field. With Dr. Wood and the other Young Farmers I spent the morning catching them. He appeared slightly amused by the whole affair. After this episode we understood each other better. He tried hard to get me a place at Sutton Bonington Agricultural College. Alas, they required School Certificate credits in Chemistry and Biology. He pleaded in vain with them to waive their ruling and accept my success in two General Science examinations. Our careers advice was negligible, however well-intentioned the teachers were.

Now that we have started talking about teachers I think it will be a good idea to go through all the teachers I can remember, subject by subject. Because of the war, there was a bigger turnover of staff than normally. Also, the school of necessity had to recruit various reliable folk to aid staffing problems.

For a short time, Mr. Sowerby taught English Literature and I can remember we read 'Lorna Doone' under his guidance. He certainly moved the characters off the page as we read and discussed the book. He always wore heavy tweed jackets. Once he had an altercation through a misunderstanding with a boy pupil who was sitting closely under his gaze in the front row of desks. Amazing us all, the boy jumped up and beneath the master's nose he threateningly asked, 'Would you like me to give you a clout, Sir?' Eventually the two had a lengthy chat at the end of the lesson and there the matter ended. There was never again any trouble between them. Although he only taught us English, Mr. Sowerby must have been a linguist of some standing. We heard later that he had eventually become one of the translators at the Nuremberg trials of the Nazi war criminals. How sad that with the passage of time we lost touch with him. How fascinating it would have been to chat with a man who would have seen Himmler, Goebbels and Goring face to face.

Eventually came Miss McCarthy who took Granny Barton's place as head of English and senior mistress. Mother Mac she was aptly nicknamed soon after her arrival. And she held sway over the whole school in her own indomitable way. Held in her early days in awe and fear by pupils and (we were told) staff alike, she nevertheless had the welfare of all her charges at heart. And she was the means of many of us increasing our knowledge and love of Shakespeare and the great English poets. If she had a fault – and boy did I suffer through it – she was obsessed by what was deemed a correct verse speak. To her, received pronunciation was the only way to declaim the lines.

One of my older friends, who eventually went to Cambridge University, was berated by her when at the end of one term they were all asked to bring their favourite poem to read. He chose a traditional Suffolk dialect poem, the 'Back'us Boy'. Miss McCarthy was not amused. She was truly heartbroken that one of her pupils had selected such a work. I felt the scourge of this narrow outlook when the school was to give a performance of the Trial Scene from 'The Merchant of Venice', at one of their wartime concerts. Eventually I lost a part in the production because I said 'Human' with a slight Waveney accent sound. Now I could have got it correct with practice. But I had witnessed some of the inept and rather wooden efforts of the other accepted members of the cast and felt my failing was trifling. To rub salt into the wound, Mother Mac asked me to continue to attend lengthy rehearsals and read in for others not able to be present. I took retribution in a way I am not proud of by removing all copies of the play. My crime was never discovered but progress was held up while replacements were found.

Mother Mac once took me to task over some boyish prank. Kept behind after the lesson, I meekly took her usual dressing down. At the end she quietly said, 'Woodward, I cannot understand it. You look angelic in the church choir as you sing 'We praise thee of Lord' and then you come to school and behave badly. What motivates you to attend church?' Honesty was not always the best policy, for I replied in truth 'Five shillings a quarter, Miss McCarthy'. And for this I received a Saturday morning detention.

Soon after Shirley and I had become sweethearts we went to watch a cricket match on the Leman School playing fields. I believe it was an evening game in June and we settled ourselves on the boundary edge on the far side of the field. No other spectators were near us so we had a splendid chance to enjoy a cuddle as much as the cricket. I was wearing a blue blazer and Shirley was in a blue frock not unlike those worn by Sixth Form girls at the time. Miss McCarthy had called in the school for some reason during the evening and on her way home she decided to look briefly at the cricket being watched by some of her older pupils, boys and girls. We watched her scanning the field to make certain everyone was behaving in a seemly manner. Then it dawned on us that we had been descried by her. In the distance she mistook us for two Sixth Formers who were becoming too amorous. Slowly she approached and we played up to the hoax, snuggling even closer together. She had got halfway round the field when the truth dawned on her, as she recognized us and her mistake. But she bravely came on and stopped to have a chat. For a few minutes we stood and talked politely to Mother Mac. She was genuinely pleased that two of her former pupils were friends and wanted to know how we were getting on. But the years rolled by and Miss McCarthy became a frail old lady. We were always pleased to see each other. And she gave me many useful tips on English Literature and what I ought to read in my retirement years. She sent me a note once on the correct use of 'lay', 'lie' and 'lies' in English grammar. She had heard of me making a mistake on the wireless. I was then a regular contributor to the BBC Local Radio Norfolk. She never wanted any of her pupils to let her, themselves or the school, down.

And finally, a little tale concerning Miss McCarthy told to me by Johnnie Youngs, a fellow pupil, many years after we had both left school. It must have been around 1947. I had left school and John was by then a Sixth Former. He was sitting at her table having school dinner. The reader must know that a member of staff sat at the head of each table and dished the food out to about a dozen children of various ages. Being the senior pupil, John was seated next to the teacher. He took up the salt cellar and liberally sprinkled a generous portion of the condiment over his meal. Aghast, not by the quantity of salt, for we had no fear of such things then, but by the manner of application, she reprimanded him thus – 'Youngs! You may have seen such practice at table on your recent school visit to France, but in England we make a delicate pyramid of salt, if required, on the rim of the plate'. Johnnie's reaction was spontaneous. Taking yet another scattering of salt, he exclaimed, 'Vive la France!'

Our English lessons took a tremendous boost when Miss Mercer arrived. Young and beautiful, she was like the breath of a cooling breeze on a hot summer's day, and her presence was felt through the school. We boys all fell a little in love with her. What was so delightful about her lessons was that she assumed we would enjoy them. Because of that, we did. I never had to receive any strong disciplinary warnings from her. If behaviour became a bit boisterous she would smile and say, 'That will do, Woodward', and when I came to heel, 'Thank you'. With her we read Tennyson's 'The Holy Grail', and the works of Keats and Wordsworth. I recall these lines from Keats:

> She was a gordian shape of dazzling hue,
> Vermilion-spotted, golden, green and blue;
> Striped like a zebra, freckled like a 'pard,
> Eyed like a peacock, and all crimson barr'd.

There was a discussion about the beat and rhythm of the romantic poets. It was explained to us that 'poetic licence' allowed Keats to make leopard 'pard'. Would that I had been granted such licence in my essays. Life just was not fair!

We read Wordsworth's 'Michael'. This appealed to me as it concerned a shepherd. But it was set in the hill farms of the Lake District and it was hard to reconcile it with the Waveney Marsh areas that I knew and loved. But, above all, Miss Mercer tutored us successfully through the School Certificate set Shakespeare play, 'Macbeth'. And I can still quote various passages from the play. I remember we had a long discussion about the use of dramatic irony. And sure enough, that was one of the questions in the examination. I got a credit grade. But I now know I failed her. If I'd worked harder I could and should have gained a distinction.

We never lost touch with each other. In later years she always came to poetry readings my wife and I were involved in. Quite a compliment, as she had earlier told me she often did not approve of amateur productions. Talking to her after a performance, I admitted that I must have been a problem in the classroom at times. She smiled impishly and replied 'You were always interesting and a challenge.'

Miss Mercer was a devout Roman Catholic, something I was not aware of at school. A few years ago Shirley and I attended the Requiem Mass of a mutual friend. Being Anglicans we remained seated whilst communion was taken. Suddenly I was aware of someone gently tickling the hair on the back of my head. It was Miss Mercer giving approval to one of her former pupils. Earlier in the service I had read John Clare's' poem 'Love Lives Beyond the Grave'. Later we met in the town. She gave me a kiss and said, 'I was given one of your books for Christmas. Well done.'

After I had left school, Miss Mercer married Lindsey Tilney, the local gunsmith, himself a former pupil. I think they first met when he came to fire his starting pistols for the races on sports day. They had three children. Robert successfully carries on the family business – the shop appears to have hardly changed since my father's childhood, although the recently renewed paintwork is a dark green rather than brown. Two daughters, Barbara and Marion, became teachers and followed their parents' interest in literature. As young Convent School girls, they both played the parts of children in Dylan Thomas's 'Under Milk Wood'. This was performed at the Public Hall in Beccles and subsequently at the Ipswich Arts Theatre. My wife got to know them as she was Polly Garter in the same production. Later in the 1960s Marion, then head teacher at Henstead School, took part in the prodigious BBC film of Ronald Blythe's 'Akenfield' directed by Peter Hall. Lindsey died some years ago. Mary's strong Christian faith sustained her, and eventually she remarried and found contentment living in the countryside at Ellingham with Mervyn Martin. In her later days she bravely battled to care for her sick husband. She herself was coping with poor health, but if we passed in the street I got a cheerful greeting. Both Mary and, later, Mervyn were cared for in their final days at All Hallows Hospice in Ditchingham.

Mary liked to have things right and proper. She prepared the order of service for the Requiem celebration of her life. I am so grateful she taught me. And I venture to write that I think she was glad to teach me. Well, most of the time!

I can remember two more teachers at the school who besides their main subject were also involved with games.

I must get a man called Benson out of my system first. Someone has said to me if you are going to write about your school life you must try to be honest – not only about your own failings and I admit to many, but also about the pedagogue's. Now, Mr. Benson was at the school for my final year. He sat in for one or two lessons in place of the other staff – I think in Geography and English. But he certainly never had any conversation with me at all. I thought of him as a snob. But I know of other ex-pupils who held him in high regard. I believe he and Colin got on very well together.

At that time in games lessons the boys who were not likely to make it into the school teams had to soldier on alone on the spare pitch. But during the war a Mr. A E Moore who was a Special Constable and also the local Beccles Town goalkeeper was recruited to help us lesser mortals for football practice. With his encouragement the afternoon sessions became well organized. But as he was not a qualified teacher he did not make an entry on our school reports. This was done in my case by Mr. Benson. I do not believe when he wrote it that he even knew or cared who I was, for he had written 'Has no ability or interest'. Even allowing for the fact that he was certainly entitled to his own opinion about my ability, to say 'no interest', the man did not know what he was saying. Had he taken the trouble to make a few enquiries before he put pen to paper he could have realized that what he had written about my lack of interest was completely untrue. But Mr. Benson did me one great favour, for I discovered at a young age that you will, alas, come across people in authority who fall short of expectations. But his remarks hurt and offended me, for I never missed a school match as a spectator at cricket or football. And I also followed both games beyond the school at local, national and international level. Of course, I ought to have challenged him on his remarks. But I do have a failing that if someone does something like that to me, as far as possible I ignore them – and this I did to Mr. Benson. I would have loved to have met him years on and chatted to him about the affair. I knew that with good reason I was not the favourite pupil of many of the staff but in later years I became a friend to many of them.

But actions of a school teacher can have a lasting effect on children's lives. I suppose in a class of 30 children there must always be at least three pupils who in the given subject at the time have potential for greater eventual grasp and understanding of the work studied than the teacher in the front of them. The great teachers have the confidence to accept this.

But around the time of the Benson report affair something happened to restore my confidence and trust in those in authority. A Mr. Greene arrived at the school to teach Geography. He also took charge of the games of us lesser mortals. And I think he liaised with Mr. Arthur Moore. Mr. Greene watched us play football with interest and decided he would form a school second eleven. Oh what joy, I made it into his team. He must have had some aptitude for football tactics for he decided that I had greater potential as a half-back rather than a flying winger. And so in my final year at school I found myself playing a few games for the school second team at right half. And it was due to Mr.

Greene's and Arthur Moore's encouragement that later, on leaving school, I played as wing-half for village teams in the area. But always I retained Pop Glover's instructions to 'come up halves' when my team was on the attack. And once or twice, with a helpful wind and a short sighted opposition goalkeeper, I even scored the odd goal or two. I do have one fond memory a year or so after I had left school of playing in a match on the Leman School pitch, by then on the other side of Ringsfield Road. We were getting a real drubbing and by midway through the second half were at least six-nil down. On the other side at centre-half was an ancient former Lowestoft town semi-professional. He gathered the ball in his own penalty area but, instead of clearing upfield to set his side on yet another goal-bound attack, he suddenly turned firing a forceful shot at his own goal. This brought a spectacular save from the goalkeeper who remonstrated at such foolhardiness. He grinned and replied, 'I wanted to keep you awake. That was a good save.'

Mathematics and Music.

I now feel very sorry for any teacher who tried to instil in me some knowledge of mathematics. They must have despaired at my efforts. If they ever wrote 'no ability or interest' on my end of term report they would have been justified.

Dear old Johnny Browne, as we called Mr. Johnston-Browne, was our mathematics teacher during our early days at the grammar school. The son of an antique dealer in Oulton Broad, he was an avuncular figure with a kindly approach to his charges. I recall him once holding a boy's head gently over a basin as he suffered a bilious attack, and then in an uncomplaining manner dealing with all the mopping up operations himself. His lessons were simpler in those early years and if I had applied myself more diligently I could have done better. One memory I have of Johnny was the large models he lifted down from the top of a cupboard in our form room of a sphere, a prism, a cube and a cone.

But later came Mr. Reginald Firth. I found his mathematics lessons hard to follow and bewildering. We never fell out in his class but he must have wondered why some of us could not grasp what to him were the most simple things.

Thankfully, as we got nearer to the School Certificate the school divided us into A and B streams. No question where I was placed. A Miss Meek, who we unkindly nicknamed 'Hecate', came to teach the B stream, but she realized how difficult her charges found the subject. She coaxed us firmly and patiently through the run up to the School Certificate examination. Woe betide us if we did not do our homework. And if we got it wrong her explanations were plain and simple. Her remarks on my final report before the examinations stated 'there has been an eleventh hour attempt to work and try, which might prove successful – if only it had come earlier!' But I did pass some of the maths examinations. I, with many others, owe her a lot, because she did bring some clarity to the fog of maths.

In these years many of the teachers covered two subjects and Mr. Firth also took us for music. Poor Solly – short for Solway Firth – must have despaired at our behaviour. Many of us did not take the subject seriously. In my case it was because at eight years of age I was made to join the choir at St. Michael's parish church in Beccles and to go at least two and sometimes three services on a Sunday plus choir practice twice a week. Small wonder I did not want another dose at school. What a pity, for later in life I discovered what joy my wife had belonging to the Leman School Choir which I opted out of.

But we did have fun in Solly's music lessons which took place in the school hall and gym where the piano had permanent residence. I retain a memory of many songs. 'Where Have You Been All The Day, Billy Boy' was one on which we could let rip, at least until Solly subdued us a bit. Billy had been walking all the day with a charming Nancy Grey, who tickled his fancy – surely the licence for us boys to find a cooperative girl to tickle our fancies. Another boisterous one was: 'Sir Eglamore that gallant knight, he took up his sword and he went for to fight.' I am quoting from memory for that is the spirit of this book. The song must have had shades of Beowulf in it. For Eglamore met a dragon who had a 'Plaguey Hard Hide' in the song. And eventually, having slain it, the gallant knight, he retired to the hostelry: 'He was so hot with fighting the dragon, that nought could quench his thirst but a flagon'. At the end of the verse came 'Fa La Lanky down dillies', which added to the fun. It was on these occasions that we sometimes got too boisterous for Mr. Firth and consequently a music lesson might be cut short for some of us. Poor Solly, his patience finally exhausted, would cry 'Out!' But we had to play our cards carefully as given 'Out!' too many times got you a detention.

We learned rhythm and rhyme and the time value of notes from a huge heavy display book that Solly set up on a blackboard easel. And from this he taught us the value of crotchets, minims and quavers. The years have diminished the complete memory of the logistics in the procedure. We had to clap the beat out and chant 'Ta Taffy Ta Taffy Ta ah ah Taffy', and so on. All good harmless fun. But, alas, I'm afraid I saw little point in it all. Music was often the last lesson of the day and the final bell never came too soon.

For all that we were all fond of Solly. He was very much an important part of school life. He was keen on cricket and played in staff and augmented school teams. He and his wife, Mary, who later became a music teacher at the school, looked after a large garden at their house on the Ringsfield Road;

like Pop Glover's, only a few yards from the school. Solly also kept bees. During the war I expect some of the honey featured as a sweetening agent in the school canteen. One afternoon towards the end of a maths lesson he suddenly came over faint. Early that day the poor chap had suffered several stings whilst collecting a swarm of bees, and suffered delayed shock. The final bell had gone and he still leaned across his desk. As we left the room I walked to him saying 'Are you alright, Sir?' And I believe I got him some water to drink. He thanked me, and I sensed his surprise that I was the one to enquire about his welfare. It must have been in 1942, for we had lessons at that time at the Area School following the school fire.

Solly was upset that I did not respond to his request to join the school choir. They met on Friday afternoons during what was termed 'Societies'. Here again this was a case where my obvious choice was the Young Farmers' Club which met at the same time, and for a lad looking to follow an agricultural career it was the most apt society for me to join. I ought to have shown more interest in his bee-keeping – it might have softened the blow. Solly had a tender heart and I suspect was amazed that anyone would not have been honoured to be asked to join his choir. He took such pride in their performance. As a concert got near, he gave up much of his own time for extra practice in the dinner hour or after normal school time. After I left, his wife Mary became the school music teacher, herself an accomplished pianist, conductor and cellist.

Both of them did so much for the local classical music scene in the town. Solly conducted the local choral society for many years. His wife was accompanist. And Mrs. Firth conducted the local Townswomen's Guild Choir and eventually became the Group Federation Choir conductor, taking the baton for concerts in Norwich and London.

Solly was a cinema fan and often attended a film show at the Regal Cinema in Ballygate or the Old Cinema on Saltgate (now Prezzo's Restaurant) depending on which film being shown most appealed to him. During the week, there were four different programmes. He was a great fan of Deanna Durbin, saying we ought to observe how she opened her mouth. He said she had wonderful tone and timbre, plus clarity in her articulation.

As Mr. and Mrs. Firth grew older, cinemas in the town closed. But they used to love watching old black and white films on the television in the afternoon. Miss Chapman, his sister-in-law, our former history teacher, lived en famille and she joined them. My wife and I were amazed on calling on them one afternoon. It was a bitterly cold January day, and Solly answered the door in his overcoat. We thought at first he was about to depart but no, they were all wrapped up to watch the TV. It was a bit like their former cinema trips. The television was kept in a separate room. And you visited it to watch films or programmes they wanted to see. The room was a bit sparse on heating, hence the overcoats on that chilly afternoon.

I spent a few evenings with him while his wife and sister-in-law had gone, collected by my wife, to a TG Choir practice or concert. He was then very frail but delighted I had gone to see him. 'You were often cheeky at school', he told me, a twinkle in his eye, but was thrilled when I asked him to play the violin for me. I felt redemption for some of my childhood failings.

Miss Chapman – Elsie – was our history teacher. In the run-up to the School Certificate examinations she made certain we knew all the 'Causes of Distress & Discontent after 1815' and about 'The Repeal of the Corn Laws'. Alas, I've forgotten them now but at the time I recalled them long enough to get a credit in the examination. Miss Chapman had an uncanny knack of guessing the examiners' questions. We could see that she was devoted to the school, her subject and all her pupils. Thus she had no problem with discipline. Well into her retirement she would travel by bus to Norwich to teach part-time at the Notre Dame School. She gave advice and tuition free of charge to anyone needing guidance in history. A school friend of my son got poorer grades in his mock A levels than expected. Miss Chapman kindly saw him and found that at his school they were only covering part of the syllabus. She tutored him successfully and he obtained the required grades. The sister-in-law of Mr. Firth, she lived with the family and was a perfect auntie to their children. My having portrayed Parson James Woodforde over the years has kept her memory alive, because I don her academic gown in each performance. I am sure she would be amused that one of her more cheeky pupils was eventually wearing her own gown.

Micah Clarke: Oh, Children, This Is Horse Work!

I only studied French for my first two years at the Leman School. When I became one of those placed in the B group I can remember Mr. Clarke, the senior French teacher, saying to me, not unkindly, 'It has been decided that we are going to have a problem getting you to fully comprehend your own language, so it would be a waste of time to try and teach you French also'. I was not sorry to stop French lessons but sad to no longer be taught by Micah, as we knew him. He, in later years, was considered by some, not to be a very good teacher. But in my time at the school he was always interesting. He followed a syllabus but we could so easily side track him on to other subjects. He had to try and get as many as possible through examinations but his aim was definitely to provide us with a full and broad education. Often deep discussions took place in the classroom about the war that was raging in Europe and the Far East. Micah quietly would tell us little facts he had gleaned. He exalted in implicitly giving the impression that he was privy to more information than the man in the street. And the truth was that he was much more informed about what was going on than most folk. He read several daily newspapers and journals. Legend has it he had these all stored and systematically logged in a huge shed in his garden. Besides discussing the war we touched on the deeper philosophical thoughts in life.

Micah lived at Geldeston just across the Waveney in Norfolk. He cycled into school most days some five miles. But he did own a car purchased in the 1930s. You can imagine how the first time he arrived at the school with the vehicle, it caused considerable interest among the pupils at the time. There were few car owners then and soon boys and girls were looking with great curiosity at this car parked on the school forecourt. Mr. Clarke observed the excitement he generated and hurried out to the parked automobile exclaiming 'It's my car, my car', proud that he had caused such a stir. And so he became 'Micah Clarke', one of the pupils supposedly being a devotee of Arthur Conan Doyle. Now, this episode may or may not be true, but I feel it is a lovely tale so let's hope it was.

My memory always pictures Micah in a brown suit. Maybe he had more than one of the same colour. He was no curmudgeon, but the sort of man who, once he had settled on a suitable and serviceable material to wear, would not want to spend his precious time looking for an alternative. But he did wear a grey suit for special occasions such as speech or sports day and the end of term services that often took place in the parish church.

His lessons commenced with the same ritual. Walking into the classroom, he addressed his pupils thus: 'Bonjour mes élèves' and the reply from the class: 'Bonjour Monsieur'. Then before the next part of the syllabus continued we had to chant out in unison: 'Un Bon Vin Blanc' (a good white wine) and then my memory fails, but the next bit was something like 'Con-Stan-Ten'. By using these few words Micah reckoned we could imitate all the sounds a pukka French person made. Mr. Clarke had a number of catch phrases and repetitive statements that flowed from his mouth automatically. He insisted that each week we must try to increase our vocabulary of French words. Often homework would be set to achieve this. 'You cannot build without bricks' he exhorted us; 'When you are learning a language words are bricks'. He then went on, 'But the foundation to build on is the grammar.'

He wrote speedily on the blackboard and of all the teachers at the school he possessed the greatest uncanny knack of knowing what was going on behind his back. He would suddenly turn to spot a boy not completely absorbed in the lesson. Girls seldom misbehaved. 'Come here, Laddie', and he would call the culprit to his desk. Then in an unvicious manner he would give the boy what he described as a gràve and acute or with both hands a circumflex. That is a gentle slap on the face on one or both cheeks. As he did this, Micah would look you straight in the eye asking you to 'stand still and turn your face towards the source of illumination'. Once or twice when his patience was tested I did see him make as if to deal a hefty blow across the ears – but, just as it looked as if he was to strike, his other hand came in as a shield, giving a resounding clap which startled the victim and the whole class. With a hint of a grin on his face Micah then informed us that '20 years ago my other hand would have stayed by my side'. The offender was then always advised to 'return to your place, face square to your front, button your jacket up and look as if you mean business'.

If during the course of a lesson or as the result of some stupid effort in homework, Micah might advise a boy or a girl that if they continued in such a vein they might find themselves on a train journey stopping five stations up the line'. This was the nearest stop on the Beccles to Ipswich train for the County Asylum at Melton.

One thing that Micah did towards the war effort and which became common practice in the school was to insist that everyone 'rule extra lines top and bottom of the page and write across the margins'. Any remarks he wished to put against your work were written in red ink in miniscule writing between the lines. Micah had two other regular cries and these might occur not only in the classroom but as he busied himself along the corridor or stairs between lessons or at dinner break. If a group of children had become too boisterous and noisy, his loud ironic call for 'Seelonce!' (silence) was heard clearly above the din. And so startled were we that it invariably had the desired effect. If there was only one miscreant involved then Micah was more specific, his call this time being 'Cease, Laddie!' But always there was a hint of whimsy in his scolding. He was never one to be feared as long as we did not push him too far.

After he had given me up as a bad job in learning French, he still had kind words if he met me on the stairs or needed to stop me running along the corridors. I can remember him calling me near the masters' staff room to tell me 'Airborn' had won the Derby at 66 to 1. Why of all the pupils in the school he wished to pass this information to me I do not know. He knew it was a popular winner, backed by many non-regular betting folk. It was a day when many bookies wept. Earlier that year Micah no doubt recalled that with another boy I had received detention for 'running a book' on the Cesarewitch. I must hasten to inform the reader that only pocket money sums were involved.

Mr. Clarke did try to make some of his lessons more relaxed. For this he often chose the last period at the end of the week but also the short spell at the end of term when examinations were over. An incident occurred that persists in my memory. There was a weekly French magazine 'La France' which was printed in this country during the war. It was full of subjects both of political and artistic interest. Included in this magazine, no doubt to encourage regular purchase, was a detective serial, 'Monsieur Stanilas Poussin Investicateur'. He can best be described as a cross between Maigret and Sherlock Holmes. But I do recall the stories were thrilling and exciting – such an alternative from the normal French lesson. To begin with Micah purchased from his own pocket enough copies for us to share one between two at our desks. As the lesson's final bell drew nearer he asked us how many in the class would be prepared to buy their own copies. Mr. Clarke knew full well there were enough affluent pupils to cover our needs. Alas, the response was negative. Poor Micah looked desolate. On reflection we all felt sorry for him. Micah kept in touch with parents who would further his cause and soon had the promise of enough copies. Thus subscribers were found and joyously our following of the exploits of Stanislas Poussin continued.

There was no such thing as parents' evenings at the school. I do not recall my mum and dad ever visiting the school during the war. This was not through the lack of interest but the lack of time. Micah did keep in touch with many parents on an ad hoc basis, and he would discuss openly in class his contact with parents. When he was summarizing our efforts, he told one lad, 'I met your father in the town during the week. And I asked him was it worth the great struggle keeping you in grammar school. He told me he is working hard and long hours so you get a good education and this is how you repay him'. His words had an impact and caused amusement, for they were addressed to the son of one of the most successful businessmen in the town. He continued, again using language in a way I only heard from him, 'Children you must remember the world is only for the fittest'.

Another of our French teacher's almost hysterical outbursts might occur when things in a lesson went totally awry. He would suddenly lift his arms in the air and plant his head on the desk for a few seconds, exclaiming, 'Oh Children, this is horse-work'. Neither pupils nor Micah took these outbursts seriously. Many of us put it down to the fact that he was French Canadian. His daughter Prudence was evacuated to Canada during the war.

Alas, I did not achieve School Certificate standard in French but I did remember enough of the language to amuse friends whom we visited for a number of years in various parts of Belgium. Once near Easter time when we were walking in the Ardenne I exclaimed: 'Au printemps les ousioux chante dans le bois'. It startled them because until then the only French had been spoken by my wife.

Another eccentricity of Micah's was that he carried on his person a walking filing cabinet. In his pockets were small booklets of details of pupils at or who had left school in the past few years. I met him at the Beccles Library some years later after leaving school and wanted to trace details of a former class-mate. To my amazement he produced from his pocket a list that enabled me to do so.

For a great number of years after I'd left school I met him in the town or elsewhere and he was always interested to keep up to date on how my wife and

I were getting on. And he liked to know what contact we had made with other pupils. One of these meetings occurred not long before he was tragically killed in a road accident near his home. He was riding his bicycle along a country lane and was struck by the rear of one of those huge articulated lorries that have no business on our small roads in the Waveney Valley.

I'm afraid, due to my lack of interest and application, I learned little French from Micah. But I did learn a lot about life, and I still cherish his memory.

Pop Glover: Geography and Games.

You can have some idea of what we thought of our teachers by the nicknames we gave them. Mr. Glover was a big man in all respects. Tall and thick set, he was held in high regard by all his pupils. And we had reason to believe he got on well with other staff members. I suspect that he considered me with mild amusement.

Except during the interregnum between the departure of one headmaster and the arrival of his successor, when he was acting head, Pop was always senior master. What a good headmaster he would have made. But he and his wife cared for a disabled son and possibly did nor want added responsibility. But he seemed to relish caring for a class full of pupils whether it was during a geography lesson or on the games field. Headmasters were even then administrators. Coupled with his role as senior master and geography teacher Pop was in charge of boys games – football (soccer) in the autumn and winter terms. No rugby was played then at the school. In the summer we played cricket. And Pop instilled a love of games to any boy who showed interest. And he was kind to anyone, like me, who did not have an immediate natural ability. He was at the hub of all school life. And he was a natural at keeping discipline. You just didn't misbehave during his lessons. His system of teaching Geography ensured that even the dullest brains got through the School Certificate examination. He went steadily through the syllabus and everyone learned by rote. His maps and diagrams were simple and effective. I soon learned how to draw a map of Ireland in the same way that we were taught our sums tables at the infants school. Pop had some colourful, simple, geographic descriptions. Rain came from 'warm air rising'. I've never forgotten how the Gulf Stream keeps part of the British Isles warmer. Years later, when we visited the Mull of Kintyre, I knew why palm trees were common and I still remember you can get a Mediterranean climate in New Zealand. Also that the sea took longer to cool than the land. So frost and snow was less persistent near the coast.

Mr. Glover always worked to a strict routine. Any maps or diagrams he would have prepared on the blackboard before each lesson. His gown held an assortment of coloured chalks. We went sedately through the work for that day. At the end of each lesson we had homework which was essentially to re-read and revise the work of that lesson. When we next met, Pop would give us a 'test' of about 20 short questions to see how well we had absorbed the facts. This took only a few minutes. He read out the answers. Then we each had to call out the marks we received. Pop was content if the average mark was around 15. If not he would sigh and say 'we'd better go through it all again'. I do not know what modern teachers would think of his methods, but I reiterate his aim was to get even the dullest brains through the School Certificate and in this he was successful. When our results came out in 1946 and he found that I'd passed and got a credit in five subjects, including geography, he came into the school cloakroom and putting his arms affectionately on my shoulder smiled and said, 'You have surprised a few of them – well done.'

One of Pop's duties as senior master was to record all the points we scored for bad behaviour. These were totalled against you personally and also your 'House'.

Now is a good time to describe the House system during my time at the Leman School. Girls were divided into Saxons, Romans, and Britons. Apart from agreeing that Saxons were sexy, Britons were brainy and Romans were rusty, the issue of the girls' Houses made little impact on us boys, except when we were allowed to cheer them on in their hockey matches. These were the only times we were allowed to venture on to the girls' playing fields. And we made the most of it during the week the matches were played. Cheering and encouragement had to be subdued. And I remember when a girl we called 'Bubbles' was loudly cheered on scoring a goal that Miss Collis, the games mistress, warned us not to use nicknames. Miss Collis insisted her girls and their supporters behaved with decorum. It was a pity she did not insist on the same behaviour from her dog. This spent most of the day in her car but when let out for exercise it often made for the boys' cloakroom where it would attempt to have its wicked way with the cloth bags holding our sports gear.

But back to Pop Glover and the House system for the boys. We were divided into Greeks and Trojans. If you were a Trojan you were trusty and the Greeks greasy. Likewise a Greek thought himself gallant and Trojans were twerpy. Trojan colour was yellow and Greek pale blue. I found this confusing as the school colours themselves were light and dark blue. When I first arrived at the school the football shirts were striped. But later they became plain dark blue.

Misconduct points could be given by all teachers for misbehaviour – one, two or even three points according to severity of offence. When you had collected a certain number you were punished by detention after school or on Saturday morning. Pop Glover recorded in a huge ledger the 'points' collected. The masters' staff common room was half way up the boys' stairs. After dinner, miscreants gathered on the landing outside. Pop would come out and, leaning the ledger on a window sill, recorded the details. He did the job with apparent detachment. I suspect he must have wondered why some pupils misbehaved. He never had a problem of discipline either in a geography lesson or on the games field.

From Pop we all learned that to win was the aim but always to win fairly. Cheating in any form was abhorrent to him. The game itself was more important than the result. But he wanted all pupils to fight for and reach their full potential. Most ex-Leman School pupils carried the same attitude into their lives and careers, both in work and sport. No one in his cricket teams would have done other than walk if they had given a genuine catch. Only the bowler or wicket keeper were allowed to appeal for LBW. And this had to be made in a polite and subdued manner. Monty Panasar would most certainly have had to curtail his antics, although Pop would have rejoiced in his bowling. Sledging of any kind was unheard of. A stylish batsman himself, he tried to school his boys in the same manner. Alas, I never made it into the school first eleven but his coaching enabled me to make it into the village cricket teams as a wicket-keeper after I left school.

During games practice Pop taught us never, as he put it, to 'run away to leg'. It distressed him to see a batsman do this. In games lessons he would stand behind the stumps and prod you with a bat if you did. He had a number of little sayings to aid your grasp of the finer points of the game. Always keen to keep the score ticking over, he liked good running between the wickets. A ball played slowly to mid-on or mid-off earned a safe single if the batsmen were alert. Hit with more speed it reached the fielder quickly and a 'run out' was likely. He gave me one piece of good wicket-keeping advice. Watch the ball from the time it leaves the bowler's hand and always get yourself in such a position that the ball comes to you and avoid having to snatch it.

We had a games lesson once a week – always the last period on a given day – and we stayed on for the length of another lesson. Two of the terms, autumn and spring, were football. I cannot remember if Pop had been a great footballer himself in his younger days but he certainly had his own set ideas how we should play. At that time all soccer teams from the most junior to internationals played with a goal-keeper, two full backs – right and left – a centre half and a right and left half back. There were five forwards: wingers on each flank plus a centre forward with two inside forwards beside him. But around that time Arsenal had established a method known as the W formation. In this formation the right and left half backs moved ahead of the centre half, and the inside left and inside right dropped back, leaving the wingers and centre forward ahead of them, to form a W shape.

Pop never let a full back come beyond the half-way line. Defenders never came up for corners and the like. But when a team was attacking he did encourage the half-backs to follow up behind the forwards to gather up loose balls and keep up the momentum of the attack. His cry 'come up halves' was often heard during training. This cry caused poor old Pop embarrassment while he was refereeing a school match against another local grammar school. Always he was neutral and fair in his ruling. If there was any question of doubt he would err in favour of the opposing team. But in the middle of the game he forgot and shouted to the Leman School boys to 'come up halves'. Realizing his error, he blew the whistle and stopping the game. Calling the opponents' captain to him, he apologized. The game was restarted with Pop rolling the ball to the opposing goalkeeper.

Pop must have spent long hours at the school after lessons had finished and also at the weekend. Quite a few of us football-crazy youngsters stayed some afternoons after school for what we called a kick-about. Some of us even arranged a mini-league of seven-a-side teams. Pop took no active part in this other than observing and seeing no great misconduct took place. At the end of the session he would stroll into the changing cloakroom to see that we left everything in order. The dressing room facilities were basic. No shower or bathroom was available. But there was a row of about eight wash-basins with hot and cold running water. Those of us who wished were able to get most clay mud from the school field off fairly easily by washing up as far as possible from the feet and then bare-chested over the sink. One boy caused some amusement when he curtailed his ablutions, remarking, 'I have a bath once a week and most of it will wear off in bed anyhow'.

During the mid-morning break in lessons a type of football match was often played in 'the yard'. This was a small wall-enclosed area that led across to the boys' toilets. These were bitterly cold in the harsh winter weather – no heating was afforded them. The game was played with a tennis ball and was unofficially between Greeks and Trojans. The idea was to keep possession of the ball. Goals did not come into it. But it kept us warm in the winter months and no doubt enhanced our ball skills. No master was in charge, but they were around in case things became boisterous.

In summer as an alternative we played what was called French cricket. Pop did not forbid the game in our free time, but he made it quite clear he thought the procedure pointless as it did nothing to improve our cricket ability. A group of boys surrounded the batsman who used the bat to protect his shins which were the wicket. You deceived by making a mock throwing of the ball. Normal bowling did not occur. The only cricket that came into the game was when you used a bat and could be out if caught. It was obvious why Pop did not like it because it went against all the style and performance he tried to instil in us boys.

He did approve of the other leisure summer activity we had. This was throwing a cricket ball as high into the air as possible by one of the older boys whilst a few others took turns in trying to catch it. One boy, Ralph Keeler, had a massive throw and would hurl the ball to skylark height. He held the school record for throwing a cricket ball in 'sports'. I do not believe it has ever been beaten. Ralph had massive hands and was a threatening fast bowler also. When he clutched the ball it would disappear from sight. I did not meet Ralph Keeler for years after we had left school. He went to Canada becoming, I understand, a skilled physiologist specializing in renal conditions. One day in the 1970's I stood in Lloyds Bank in Lowestoft waiting to be served. Suddenly I realized Ralph was ahead of me in the queue. So I made myself known to him. He was overjoyed to see me and gave me quite a hug. It appeared that he was suffering from jet-lag and feeling disorientated. He had been asked to attend at short notice an international conference at Addenbrooke's hospital in Cambridge. He told me he was to talk about a developing practice using mosquitoes to extract minute blood samples from the kidneys of patients. Ralph was a great leg-puller. I have not seen him since and wonder if the mosquito tale was a hoax. If anyone in the medical field can enlighten me I'd be most grateful. I can see the possibility, but surely the mosquito would sting the patient's kidney and do more harm. Or can you take the venom from a mosquito?

Apart from his duties at the school, Pop was also involved with other activities in the town in the pursuit of the war against 'Hitler and his Nazi Gang'. Pop held a high rank in the local Home Guard. He was a distinctive figure on all parades. I can see him now, leading his group past the saluting base. He held a vigorous salute. Longest way up, shortest way down. His broad arm and hand came up so swiftly that it seemed to vibrate for a second. His brown boots always shone like a 'shilling on a sweep's arse' as my Aunt Marge indelicately put it. What ever he did, Pop always gave a bit extra. And his men and pupils responded.

But he also used his connections and facilities at the school, organizing cricket matches against local service teams. One such team from a local searchlight battery turned up on a Saturday to play a Leman School combined eleven of senior boys, staff and a couple of ex-pupils on leave themselves. Now, this particular army group were a motley crew. Apart from the officer in charge, a sergeant and a few others, some had probably never played in a cricket match before. They had only two in white flannels in the team and from number four in the batting order played in their khaki uniforms. They had one pair of batsman pads. Pop, a gentleman as always, approached the officer to lend them some of the school equipment. The army were to field first and their wicketkeeper – who had no doubt never seen such a thing before – appeared with the white abdominal protector and 'courting tackle' shield strapped on the outside of his khaki uniform trousers like some enormous cod piece. This caused amusement to a few pupils – myself included – who were spectators at the game. Pop alerted the sergeant and after a few quick words the wicket keeper secreted the protector behind his khaki trousers. Being a searchlight operator he must have had some knowledge of the art of camouflage.

One Saturday in the winter time I was at the school as usual, looking after the chickens and hens. A team turned up from another local school expecting to play the Sir John Leman boys at soccer. A mistake had been made by someone concerning the fixture list. Pop was summoned and within 20 minutes he recruited a scratch team, and to my great joy I was instructed to get my football gear on. Of course, I was excited beyond belief. But this excitement turned to ecstasy in the dying minutes of the game which was then one goal each. A hard cross came in from the left and, playing on the right wing, I moved into the position at the far post. I have to be honest and say that the ball thundered in so fast that I could make no attempt to play it at all, but it walloped me on the chest and slowly rolled over the goal line. As he blew the final whistle and we walked to the changing rooms, Pop chuckled and said to me 'you were in the right place for once that time, Woodward'. I went home elated, telling Mum all about it. She was as overjoyed as I was. At the school assembly on the Monday morning the school captain always gave a report to everyone about the Saturday fixture. I waited for everyone to hear how I had scored the winning goal. Alas, as only three of the regular team played and ex-pupils had been recruited, it did not go down in the official records and no report was made.

I have a couple more abiding memories of Pop Glover. He tried always to continue with our football practice whatever the weather. There were two wartime winters when the school pitch became frozen hard and play would be dangerous. But one day there was a fall of about four inches of snow and so the frozen turf was cushioned. 'Out we go', said Pop, 'You will find the snow much less restrictive to good football than the heavy clay mud we are used to'. He was correct – the ball slid across the snow easily. What is more, we were soon warm even in the chill north-easter, and we left the pitch quite clean. The biggest problem was knowing when the ball had gone out of play.

I did not usually have a school dinner. Mostly I went home for the midday meal or went to the British Restaurant in the Public Hall. But I did often take a school dinner on Monday. It was helpful to the household engaged on the weekly wash – a major event. And the fact that it was cheese and potato pie on Monday, something we never had at home, made me happy to have a school dinner.

The meals were formal and very well ordered in comparison with today's cafeteria system. A member of the teaching staff sat at the head of each table at which were seated about a dozen pupils. The main item to be eaten was placed by the school cook in front of the teacher who served it out to the children. He was aided by two senior boys or girls who sat next to him or her. They would help in dishing out vegetables, gravy, etc. as required. Somehow I always managed to get a seat on Pop's table. And it was from him I discovered it was good manners to eat your meal with a fork in your right hand if you possibly could. I was surprised when I first saw him do this, but as all of us followed suit I quickly got into the habit. But peas were a problem!

The meals at school were never rushed and conversation would flow easily. When Pop saw our plates empty he would grin and say 'I think there is enough for a bit more.' Then we each had another spoonful of cheese and potato – you got the crispy bits then. Never was any food wasted. Pudding followed, generally a steamed roly-poly of some sort. But the custard in a jug was never like my mum's, for it could be lumpy. Plenty of calories – but overweight children were seldom seen. Pop's football in the snow took care of that.

Stop work, boys: Pierson Cross, our woodwork teacher

It was from my older brother John that I first heard earlier tales of Pierson Cross, the woodwork teacher at the Leman School. 'Percy', as he was known, shared his woodwork expertise between the Sir John Leman and Bungay Grammar schools. He was yet another member of staff who lived near the school, on the corner of South and Upper Grange Roads, only a few hundred yards away from the leafy, lilac tree entrance lane on the east side of the school. Brother John, with a few of his contemporaries, notably George Durrant, and a boy who lived out of town called Derek Sidlow, used to regale us youngsters with the earlier exploits of Percy. He had an eccentric motor car – if one may be allowed to describe a vehicle in such a manner. I cannot tell you what make it was but it was large and bulky. Percy used it principally to transport himself and various woodwork equipment and tools on his visits to Bungay Grammar School. One evening in the summer, the car played up – a frequent occurrence. There was a major problem in the gear box: it was stuck in reverse. Percy was certain he would be able to sort it out himself if he could get the vehicle home. And so he backed all the way home, through Mettingham, Shipmeadow and Barsham, in reverse gear. But as an expedient to safety on the somewhat hazardous journey he was escorted by five Bungay Grammar sixth form prefect cyclists. They rode before, at the side, and rear, of Percy, like destroyers round a battleship. Each boy was rewarded with a glass of home-made ginger beer and a slice of cake when they safely arrived at Beccles. I always wondered if this tale was true until the 1970s when I was watching a minor counties match at Lakenham where Norfolk were playing. I got chatting on the boundary with another spectator and it turned out he was at school in Bungay at the time and himself was one of the escorts.

Brother John told me, and I later discovered, the uncomplimentary manner Percy scolded boys who did not behave sensibly at their woodwork bench. He had great concern that the work bench was not damaged by injudicious use of chisels or saws. As he walked up and down the rows of pupils the cry 'Stop works boys – some Jackass, some noodle –'scuse my saying so – has been chiselling the bench', was frequently heard. Sometimes the culprit might have to stay behind and sweep up shavings at the end of the lesson.

If we were working steadily Percy would take the chance to sharpen chisels and plane blades. As he finished each item he'd strop the chisel backwards and forwards on the palm of his hand. We were warned never to adopt the same procedure ourselves. A prime example of do not do as I do but as I tell you. Now and again he did have a mishap and you'd see Percy's hand a bit blood stained or a piece of rag around a finger.

During the first few lessons we were given a piece of 2x2 inch of unplaned wood. This we had to plane to a smooth even surface on both sides and edges using a set square to measure the accuracy. Percy taught us to mark the wood face-side with a pencilled loop and face-edge with a pencilled V. Alas, I failed to get it even after several tries. On the first piece it was almost wafer thin before it went into the waste bin. After numerous attempts, Percy decided he would 'pass' my wood when he considered I had achieved the most successful endeavour I was ever likely to.

We then moved on to making a spade scraper, a utilitarian piece of equipment for horticultural lessons on the heavy clay Ringsfield Road gardens at the Leman School. My effort was deemed passable. On this item the accurate set square routine was not required. But I never advanced to the more complicated joinery work. Some boys were able to make small bookshelves, stools and storage boxes. I wasn't. But I did keep the school garden shed well stocked with spade scrapers. My brother John made a few useful items for the household. He was more skilled than I was by far.

Percy was a great family man. There were three children. Mary, the eldest, was a prefect when I arrived at the school and she eventually, I believe, became a teacher herself, as did Arthur, the youngest sibling, who was in the form below me. Another daughter, Betty, was a very good swimmer. As I write I can hear Percy during the school swimming sports encouraging his daughter as she gradually closed on the others to win a long distance race. This was over many lengths of the small pool. Betty had fallen behind at the start but gradually she caught them up as the race progressed and her rivals tired. All the time, unconcerned what other pupils or staff might have thought, Percy hurried along the pool edge shouting 'keep rebuilding, Betty – keep rebuilding'. This she did, winning the race and breaking the record.

Percy was devastated when, not long after, Betty died of meningitis. I fear we boys did not at the time realize what grief this must have caused all the family. Mrs. Cross and both girls had sung in the church choir at St. Michael's. The church was packed for her funeral. The whole school came, and the parish church choir, of which I was then a member, sang. The music was uplifting. I hope it gave some comfort to a family suffering such a loss. Poor old Percy, he had to start 'rebuilding' himself.

LEAVING SCHOOL

I left the Leman School officially in July 1946, but felt I gradually drifted away. I started to work on the farm at Gillingham in the holidays and at weekends from Easter 1945. And, surprisingly, when I no longer was an official pupil, for a time I kept involved with school events. It says much for the ethos of the Leman School at the time that few wished to break away completely. The Old Students membership was strong, and in my case many friends, including Rex Butcher and Colin Baker, were now sixth formers and prefects. And my wife-to-be, Shirley, was now a pupil

Certain incidents occurring in those years stand out. One was my father, to everyone's surprise, bought a dog. Poor little creature, only a few months old, he was stuck in a poultry pen at Durrant's sale-yard but had charm, and Dad purchased him on impulse, out of pity. On the day, I came home from a School Certificate examination in the YMCA hut and made my long way to the sale-yard, Father called me into the office and there, in a little cubby hole, curled up on an old raincoat, sat the dejected little creature. So we called him 'Mac'. I took him home on a piece of rope attached to his collar. He was small and had the roughest, tangled and bedraggled coat you can imagine. When you looked into his face his eyes were only partly visible as mottled sandy coloured hair hung over them like an Old English sheepdog. Was there any of that breed in the countless other types that must have gone into his pedigree? Who knows! But he was deemed surplus to requirements from a farm in Mutford. After tea he suddenly had a fit, running round the table like a bat out of hell, then he flopped panting on the floor. 'Sorry', Dad said, 'we cannot cope with such an animal. You must take him to Mr. Taylor's, the Vet, and ask for him to be put to sleep'. He gave me half a crown (12.5p). This was the standard fee for children's pets. I walked dejectedly with Mac in tow to Tee-Mor the Vets in London Road. 'What's the problem?', Mr. Taylor enquired in his loud broad Irish accent. He listened kindly as I relayed the whole episode. Mr. Taylor crushed an aspirin in a piece of strong white paper, folded it to make a funnel and poured the contents down Mac's throat. 'I'll write a note for your dad. No need to put him down. Small wonder he had a fit after what he's been through today. He'll be fine.' And so he was, remaining a lovable pet for many years. Mac was full of canine eccentricity. He hated people sneezing, and barked if anyone did. He chased every cat out of the garden. You only had to say 'Pussy' and Mac bristled. He once barked at the wireless when the announcer mentioned 'Dubussy'. But the little dog had other exceptional traits. One was a penchant for German prisoners of war. Often their transport lorries stopped in Newgate, and their attendant guards got them fish and chips. As soon as Mac spied them he would hurtle to the group and visit each prisoner in turn for affectionate coaxing. He soon got to know these fellows and they looked out for him when in the town. Was it something in the aroma of their patched prison garb the dog liked? Maybe it was just because they were pleased to have the chance to show affection. Contrary to accepted popular myth, Mac was fond of postmen. And one particular gentleman, Frank Clarke, who delivered letters to us in Fair Close, took him on his round. He would go on the complete walk and get good exercise. In later years, after Shirley and I became sweethearts, she often met Mac with the postman in Gosford Road on her way to catch the train for work. The quaint little dog soon developed an affinity with Shirley. He briefly left the postman and saw her into the railway station and then on her command would scamper off and catch up with Frank. The postman sent him home from the top of Fair Close as he finished his deliveries. Mac had a hard start in life but he gave much amusement and affection to many over the years.

The year preceding leaving school – 1945 – was a jubilant one and included the Victory in Europe, VE, celebrations. The whole town was en fête. The market square was full of relieved and joyful town and country folk, servicemen and women both British and American. Boys and girls, men and women, were dancing in the street and hugging and kissing each other. And, I was told, one particular lady was allowing all the sailors she could 'lay her hands on' in a session of petting down one of the side alleys of the market square. 'All the nice girls love a sailor', the song goes. The whole crew got loved that night. Later some of us made our way to Peddars Lane near the Drill Hall where troops and cadets were gathering. One boy had obtained a box of Thunder Flashes that the Home Guard used on exercises. Mr. Johnston-Browne was startled when we threw one that exploded close behind him. We beat a hasty tactical retreat.

Later that year the atom bombs were dropped at Hiroshima and Nagasaki. War in the Far East was over sooner than we dared hope. I was working on the farm in the harvest holidays when the VJ celebrations came in August. We had been carting barley all day. Allowed to cease harvesting early, I cycled to Beccles with the men and boys on the farm to watch a similar scene of festivities. I cannot recall if the sailors again got special treatment.

By 1946 I was working full time as a pupil on the farm at Gillingham. They were two most enjoyable years. I am so grateful to Mr. Phillip Ashford for making me so welcome on his farm. There was a plan for me to live in on a farm at Brampton, but when he heard about it Mr. Ashford said 'No, you come and be with me, Sonny. I'll pay you a bit'. Often pupils were not paid – some had to pay a premium. I was no longer at school but another education was beginning. How lucky I was to work with horses and to hand-milk cows. It was a way of life now gone forever. There must have been over twenty of us on the farm, men and boys, plus two former land girls (a bonus, that!). All had various skills and capabilities.

Everyone was in a state of euphoria because the war was over. In spite of tough times and rationing there was a lightness to life. August 1946 stands out for me for one event. Chipperfield's Circus came to town. The Big Top was erected on the Black Boy Meadow. Everyone in the area went. The marquee was packed for a week. Featured were a herd of performing bullocks. One of the men on the farm laughed when we went one evening. 'Blas bor – we can go and see performin' bullocks every Friday on Beccles sale-yard for nothin'. But we all viewed aghast as we watched the Great Blondini go across the lions den on the high-wire blindfolded and with baskets on his feet. 'Rum old way to make a living.'

I loved being on the farm and the coldest winter in years added to the adventure. For weeks the whole of the Waveney Valley was snow and ice bound. Normal farm work and cultivations ceased. We spent the day getting feed and bedding to the cattle, pigs and horses. You had to break the ice on the 'hoss-pond' morning and night so they could drink. Milk in churns had to be carted miles in a tumbril across the fields. The high freezing wind had drifted the snow so pathways were found quite bare. The ground was hard like concrete. Sugar beet, lifted earlier, was carted in a caravan of horses and loaded tumbrills to the railway station at Haddiscoe and then on to Cantley sugar beet factory. It was too cold to sit and stop for dinner. We ate our bread and cheese walking around to keep warm. But I never was miserable with cold. I could not get enough of the farm. I did relief milking on Sunday mornings. Rising at 4.30 to be there at 5 00 a.m., I got a thrill in taking Mum home a bottle of milk that had earlier held my cold tea. And I have to admit deceiving my parents who some Sundays believed I had gone to work when I left early and joined a local poacher. We only aimed to get enough pheasants or rabbits to feed family and friends. A former war veteran, he told me many tales of his exploits in the desert. No sane person could begrudge him a bird or two. The great freeze ended in March 1947. Then came the floods. I was working with the farm foreman, Arthur Rackham, on a field overlooking the Waveney Valley. He spotted the rising tide and the water surging across the Beccles marshes and on to Gillingham Dam. It was around 2.30 p.m. when he said 'you'd better get home to your mother'. By the time I had reached the Swan Hotel the water was a few inches deep on the road but only two inches on the high path. I decided it would be easy to cycle home on the path. But then tragedy struck twofold. The chain came off my bike and as I bent and attempted to put it on, my hands in the icy water, a huge lorry belonging to Mervyn Gaze, laden with milk churns drove past from Beccles. Because of the water on the road he was having to drive quickly. The wretched lorry created a huge bow wave. It soaked me from the waist down. I paddled home pushing my bike through the rising water, stopping briefly on the great Beccles bridge to decant the liquid from my rubber boots.

Next morning I found the flood had risen into the lower end of Northgate Street and was covered in a film of ice. Frost had returned in the night. No way could I get to Gillingham. I rang Mr. Ashford to say I could not get to work. 'We need you, Sonny', he said. 'Put your bicycle on the train and come to Haddiscoe station then cycle to my farm at Aldeby. I'll pay the fare'. This happily I did. I sometimes helped in the farm office or looked after pigs in a Danish Piggery. He was a good boss, if unpredictable at times. I treasure memories of the years I spent with him.

At the age of 17 I volunteered to do early National Service, hoping to join the Royal Navy. But that is another story.

Earlier Beccles schooldays: National School, Group III(a), c.1905

David and John with parents and grandmothers, 1931

David and John with parents, 1931

David with Grandmother
Woodward, 1934

David and John, 1934

Colin's parents, 1948

Colin's paternal grandparents, c.1930

Colin's maternal grandmother, c.1900

Colin's maternal grandfather, c.1905

Muriel, Cynthia, Dennis
and Colin, 1934

Muriel, Colin, Dennis
and Cynthia, 1938

David at home, 1935

Colin at Caxton Club Annual Sports, 1934

The Children's Corner, Lowestoft, 2011

'Bathing Place', Beccles Swimming Pool, 1920s

Crisp's Maltings and staff at Beccles Quay, c.1920, Edward Baker, Foreman, Colin's grandfather, centre foreground

Beccles Caxton Bowls team, c.1945. Back row, extreme right, Colin's father, and next to him is Jimmy Cutler.

School children in Station Road on their way to the Jubilee party
on College Meadow, 1935

Suffolk Show, 1938

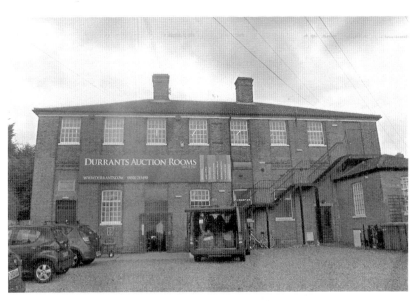

Peddars Lane School Building, now Durrants Auction Rooms, 2011

Mr. Jimmy Mason's Sweet Shop, Peddars Lane, 1930s

The 'Area School', 2011

George Odam, Headmaster of the Area School

The Sir John Leman School, 2011

Gordon Humphrys, Headmaster of
the Sir John Leman School

Sir John Leman School 1st XI Cricket team, 1946,
Colin front row left

Sir John Leman School 1st XI Football team, 1945-6, Colin back row right

Air Training Corps, 759 Squadron, Beccles, 1944, Colin, centre row fifth from left; David, foreground seated left

Entrance to Cut Throat Lane, 2011

Lower Sixth Form, 1946-47
Colin, front row left

Upper Sixth Form, 1946-47,
Front row, centre, Miss McCarthy
Front row right, J. Seago, Bruzzo's gladiatorial opponent.

Sir John Leman School after the fire, 1942

Sir John Leman School,
interior, after the fire,
1942

'Bubbles', c.1944

Colin, 1944

Mary Mercer

Frank 'Pop' Glover

Reginald, 'Solly', Firth

Arthur, 'Micah' Clarke

St.Michael's Church nave

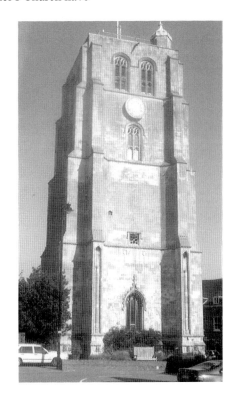

St.Michael's Church tower

St.Michael's Church
south porch

Ingate Church, north porch

War Weapons Week, Beccles, 1941

Home Guard platoon
on exercise, March
1944 with Smith gun
and commandeered cart
horse

The Maltings fire, 1912

Beccles from the air, 1970

BECCLES SCHOOLDAYS:
RECOLLECTIONS AND REFLECTIONS

Part Two
by
Colin Baker

MY FAMILY

Perhaps I should start by saying a little about my family, by way of introduction and to help me to set the scene for my recollections of my early life.

I was born on my mother's twenty-seventh birthday, 3 August 1929, in Beccles at my parents' home in Pleasant Place, an 'unadopted' cul-de-sac off St. George's Road, running north to south parallel to, and about seventy yards from, the main railway line to London. At this point the railway ran in a cutting and the trains did not unduly disturb the local residents. My parents were Doris Kathleen and Arthur Walter Baker. I was the third child and the first of two sons, and I was baptized Colin Arthur in the parish church of St. Michael, Beccles – I think by the Curate, the Rev. Verrels – the second name coming from my father. I understand that my parents had intended to call me Gerry, but friends of theirs who lived near my father's parents, the Wilsons, had a son just before I was born, and when they called him Gerry my parents changed my intended name to Colin. As a child I did not particularly like the name Colin – pronounced locally, it seemed to me, as 'Karln' – but it was infinitely preferable to Gerry with its connotations of bedroom crockery. Later in life I quite liked the name Colin and in any case one gets used to it after eighty years!

My father was the youngest of a family of six children. His father was Edward, whom we called Grandad Baker, a staunch Baptist – reckoned to be among the very best impromptu public pray-ers in the area – who worked as a foreman in one of the town's maltings by the River Waveney, close to his home. I recall him only as an old, but until the end by no means a feeble, man. He had a white, closely cropped beard – trimmed, to my amusement, by my father in his later years – and my memory of him is his wearing a striped flannel collarless shirt, thick woollen trousers, boots and a waistcoat with a silver watch chain strung from the pockets. We used to sit on his knee and he would rub his bristly beard against us, much to our enjoyment. If we larked about he would, with mock seriousness, enjoin us not to 'muck abart.' He spent his last days in bed in the front room of his home in Mill Terrace, Ravensmere, which was at the other, northern and older, end of the town from Pleasant Place. It was a common practice to move those thought to be near death, downstairs for their last days. This made caring for them easier and was eventually less of a problem for the undertaker who otherwise would have to negotiate the narrow, winding staircase. Incidentally, when a funeral procession passed in the town, everyone stood still and faced the road, and men removed their hats as the cortege approached and passed. It was also the practice to lower the blinds or close the curtains at the front of a house in which a person had just died, and so common was this practice that one judged the time of death from the moment at which the blinds were lowered – it was a sort of public announcement of the death.

My father's mother, my grandmother, Agnes, whom we called 'Granny' and whose maiden name was Turrell, was a small lady with extraordinarily Delph-blue eyes. She dressed in high-necked black long dresses and high lace-up ankle boots – laced with a silver shoe hook. I recall the way in which she would make tea with a large soot-covered kettle boiled on the living room fireplace – though the tea never tasted smoky – and standing on the armchair to reach up to get the tea and crockery from a Norfolk corner cupboard. I thought the boiling over the open fire, the lifting of the full hot kettle, and the climbing and balancing on the chair were dangerous activities for a lady of her age, though she was quite nimble and was probably quite safe.

My grandparents had on the wall over their bed a framed embroidered motto or text bearing the words 'The Lord Will Provide'. I recall an occasion when I noticed that the glass over the text was broken and I was foolish enough to say to my father that it was a pity the Lord did not provide a new glass. I became close to getting a clip over the ear and it would have been well deserved.

As a family we visited my paternal grandparents each Sunday afternoon for tea. My impression is that there were always – although I am to some extent confusing this with Christmas or other special occasions – sandwiches of tinned salmon, jelly and trifle, the latter being called by my grandfather and my father, 'superluttinquivvy', for reasons which were never apparent or explained. There was a tradition that celery was eaten with our tea at Christmas time at our grandparents' home. This always struck me as an odd tradition but a pleasant one. 'Superluttinquivvy' was not the only strange expression used by my father, for there was one other. He would often bid us goodnight as we went off to bed, or goodbye as he went off to work in the mornings, with a kiss and the words 'tushi frumshi, tissawashki, killigooly'. Again, I do not know where this came from, nor fully what it meant. It was an affectionate and charming expression, if somewhat eccentric.

My mother's maiden name was Ward and she was baptized Doris Kathleen. Her mother died when my mother was in her mid to late teens, so we never knew her, sadly, and thereafter, until she was married, my mother looked after her father and two younger sisters. When my sister Muriel died, we found among her papers a few pages from my mother's autograph book, one of which was written almost a hundred years earlier by her mother. I found reading this page an emotional experience. For the first time I felt as if, to a tiny but very important degree, I knew my grandmother. When my mother left school, she attended Gregg's Secretarial College at Putney, then worked first in a milliner's shop and later, during the latter part of the First World War, she worked in Whitehall in the Ministry of Food. I recall her telling me that she often had to run the last few yards to her office as Big Ben nearby began to strike nine o'clock. They lived at Roehampton in southwest London, having moved there from Beccles – where they lived in Denmark Road – in 1911. Her father, my grandfather, was Joshua Richard, known to others as Josh or Dick. He worked at the Caxton Press in Beccles before moving to Roehampton where he managed the Manresa Roman Catholic Press. I remember him clearly mainly as a retired man. Each year, when we were small, he took an 'excursion' train – called a 'cheap day return' in later years – from London to Great Yarmouth and he met us there on the beach to spend the day together. It puzzled me how he ever found us on that large and crowded beach. I did not guess that our location on the beach had been pre-arranged with him. I remember being fascinated at Great Yarmouth railway station when we arrived, to see dozens of low-teenage boys with hand carts touting the arriving holiday-makers for the business of carrying their heavier luggage from the station to their hotel or boarding house. Had I been one of the arriving holiday-makers I should have been deeply apprehensive when the boy I had hired to carry my luggage, raced off ahead of me and disappeared out of sight on his way to my boarding house. It was on one of these days in Great Yarmouth in the mid 1930s that I saw for the first time a huge armoured tank which I think was there on a recruiting drive for the army. Another thing which struck me was the street photographers who, without asking us, took our photographs as we walked along and gave us a piece of paper with which we could collect and pay for the developed photographs later in the day. And there was much talk about a man called Lobby Lud who would give challengers a fortune if they correctly identified and challenged him when he was wandering through the Yarmouth streets.

Grandfather Ward also visited us in Beccles and we looked forward to the visits although I have no recollection of what any of us did except that he timed one of his visits each year to coincide with the Beccles Regatta, held annually on the River Waveney. Just before he left at the end of each visit he would put his hand slowly into his trouser or waistcoat pocket and take out a brand new half crown to give to each of us. I'm afraid we too obviously looked forward to that gift and may on occasion have appeared over anxious for it. He never carried a suitcase when he came to visit us but had his razor, shaving brush, tooth brush and a clean collar in a paper bag in his jacket pocket. Very few adult shirts in those days had an attached collar and certainly none of them had a stiffened attached collar. Stiff collars, either heavily starched or 'Chinese laundered' were attached by a stud at the front and another stud, of different design, at the back of the collar band – and were kept in a shallow circular leather box. They still appear occasionally on auction programmes on television. The 'steam laundry' in Station Road did 'Chinese laundering' but it is unlikely that any Chinese worked there. Although not a tall man, Grandad Ward carried himself very erect and seemed to pull himself upright as he approached a person he knew from the past in the town. In his way he dressed dashingly, and sported galoshes – waterproof over shoes – and spats – short white or pale grey gaiters covering the ankle and the instep of the shoe. In their prime he and his five brothers had all played football for Beccles Caxton – as did my father for several years after the First World War – so he was quite well known in the town even after he had left it for Roehampton. He had lived in Beccles as a younger man but I always thought of him as a Londoner and I recall him best at Roehampton.

He and his five brothers also played cricket for Beccles Caxton team. One of the brothers was Thomas Henry Ward, my Uncle Harry, who for many years captained the Caxton cricket team. I remember either him or my Grandfather Ward – or it may have been someone else in the family – telling me about playing against Gilbert Jessop who taught at the Beccles College during the mid 1890s. He came to the College to earn his keep before going up to Cambridge at the age of 21. A protégé of W G Grace and a member of his Gloucestershire team, Jessop was a phenomenally powerful striker, was called 'The Croucher' because of his stooping stance, and used a very long handled bat. Whether or not I was influenced by this I don't know but when I played cricket at the Leman School I also used a long handled bat, but with nothing like the success of Jessop! He gained immortality locally by hitting a ball out of the Station Meadow ground – which was where the College played – clean over the railway line and station and onto the roof of the maltings on the other side, at the bottom of Fair Close. A little further and it would have landed in David's back yard! I have recently unearthed some details of the 1895 season when Jessop played for the College. He averaged 132.25 runs per innings, and scored 1058 runs, including five centuries. He took 100 wickets at 2.44 runs per wicket. In a match against a local Royal Artillery side he scored 219 not out and took eight wickets for 14 runs. He later played for Cambridge University, Gloucestershire and England. Uncle Harry and my grandfather spoke well of his ability! Perhaps one of them had bowled the ball which landed in Fair Close – gosh! How much closer could I get to fame?!

The elder of my two sisters was Muriel Olive May, born on 10 April 1926. The names Olive and May came from two of my mother's aunts. My second sister, Cynthia Doris, was born on 26 March 1928. The name Doris came from my mother. My brother, Dennis Brian, was born on 15 May 1931 and he was the only one of the four of us not to be given a relation's name, though all of us had a first name that was not a family name. Although it did not strike me when I was young – nor indeed until I was quite grown up – my mother had her four children in the short space of a few weeks over five years.

My Beccles grandparents' house was close to the Beccles gasworks, and the smell of the gas was very marked, although, whilst I am sure it offended many others, I do not recall my thinking it was particularly offensive. It was one of a terrace, and access to it was gained through an alleyway between two of the houses, which brought one to the back of them, and along a small path, with the houses on one side and the garden of each on the other – which struck me as odd but it does not now. Unlike many other smaller houses in the older part of Beccles, their lavatory was part of the house – entered from the outside – and not at the end of the garden. I recall my grandparents keeping chickens, and a mash of corn, meal of some sort and boiling water being made for them. I recall, too, my grandfather improvising the hinges on wooden boxes he made – for tools etc. – from leather straps. A good deal of home 'carpentry' was done with a pocket knife. I recall, too, my grandfather collecting his tomato seedlings from the sewage beds by the river near his house.

Thinking about my grandparents keeping chickens reminds me that one day after the war when I was visiting David and his parents I was amazed to see his father insert a pellet into the neck of a chicken. I was told this was to caponize the fowl – chemically to castrate it, fatten it and render the resulting meat more tender and less stringy. It may well have been, as I discovered later, well known to the Romans over 2000 years ago as a means of conserving grain stocks by providing an alternative to fattening the hens with corn, which was forbidden, but it was new to me! One lives and learns!

When my father was released from a German prisoner of war camp and demobilized from the army in 1919 he returned to the printing trade and completed his seven year apprenticeship. During the 1920s he played a good deal of football for the Caxton team. There are photographs of him taken with the team, and I recall him speaking of the strikers of Beccles playing against an owner's team and against a police eleven during the general strike of 1926.

Father very rarely spoke of his time in the army and scarcely ever about being a prisoner of war. Nonetheless, it is clear that his service and experiences had a lasting, though I don't think damaging, effect on him. He taught me as a child to count in German and told me the German words for left, right, attention, potatoes (which he, like many others, had stolen when he was in the prisoner of war camp and was very hungry). He taught me the various rifle drill movements – slope arms, shoulder arms, present arms, stand at ease, attention and, what is most sad, 'resting on arms reversed, a complicated movement used in military funerals. All this was done with a broom used as a rifle or, very exciting, as a drum major's mace or baton which he twirled and threw high into the air and caught on the march. When my infant son asked him about war he simply said, 'It's silly'.

The regatta to which I have referred was an annual event – discontinued during the war – held on the River Waveney in August. There were sailing events each day of the week, and a swimming gala in which races were held and water polo matches were played. From the shouts of the watching crowd we gathered that a good deal of underhand malpractice took place below the surface. Among the strong male swimmers I recall Mr. Long, Mr. Bert Moore and Tom Ward, my mother's cousin. Although there was a swimming pool higher up the river, it was not used for these races during the regatta. There was usually a fun fair, with swings and roundabouts, hoopla and coconut-shy stalls on the grass near the 'Cut', a channel cut at right angles to the river for mooring boats and, I believe, at an earlier period to enable wherries and barges to get closer to the maltings nearby. The week's activities concluded with a spectacular fireworks display that ended with a pyrotechnic portrait of the King and Queen, and signalled that it was time for us to walk our tired, weary but happy way home and go to bed.

I have mentioned the town swimming pool – known to us as 'The Bathing Place'. This was an excavated inlet at the side of the Waveney River and was approached from Puddingmoor. I am no longer sure of how big it was – perhaps ten to twelve yards wide and perhaps thirty to forty yards long. By some means the designers had managed to get the depth of the pool to vary from the low end to the deep end, even though the adjacent river bed itself must have been level. I cannot give even an estimated depth to the water in the pool, because this varied with the tides. At the shallow end at very low tides there would be only a few inches of water but at high tide even the shallow end would be up to six feet deep. The depth also varied with the tides during each day. 'Normally' there would be about three feet of water at the shallow end and at least six feet at the deep end, where the diving board was. The pool was cut off from the river by a high wooden fence beneath which was a length of wire netting to keep the weeds out and prevent adventurous swimmers diving beneath it and getting out into the river – or vice versa without paying! This length of wire netting was visible only at very low tides. There was a number of different types of changing room accommodation. There was a large communal room at the 'deep end' for boys and men to change, with a concrete floor and benches round the edge on which to sit and to leave one's clothes. There may have been 'duck boards' on which to stand. Then, at the 'shallow end' there was a number of small wooden 'family rooms' which a group could use for changing and for leaving their clothes while swimming. Between these two facilities there was a brick extension to the large single room, divided by wooden partitions into individual cubicles – though two or three could share them – with a duck board in each and a bench across the back wall on which to sit and on which to leave clothes. There were separate sets of male and female cubicles. The single communal changing room was cheaper – maybe a penny per visit – than the other types of provision. In retrospect, all this was a pretty advanced facility for the town, and was much appreciated and much used, especially in the hotter weather. We carried our swim suits rolled up in a towel – neatly as we went to bathe and significantly less neatly on our return journey home. Male swimming costumes covered the chest, and topless trunks were virtually unknown – and certainly not allowed. Similarly, two-piece bathing suits and 'bikinis' for the females were unknown. We four children went bathing quite frequently during the summers but I do not recall our parents accompanying us – neither of them could swim. I have used the word 'bathing' rather than 'swimming' because in our earlier years we simply played games in the water and enjoyed being in it. I did not learn to swim until I was about twelve years old, and for some time I could swim further under water than on the surface. The secondary schools took classes one at a time once a week in the summer term and in these we were taught to swim and to dive. Official-looking certificates were given to each pupil passing various grades – 25, 50 and 100 yards, breast stroke, crawl (known as 'over-arm'), back stroke, plunging and diving. Some people also did a side stroke, but the 'butterfly' stroke was unknown. The swimming pool was under the supervision of a council employee. This was Mr. Bert Moore before the war, when he joined the East Suffolk Police War Reserve, and his place was taken during the war, first by his brother and sister-in-law and then by Mr. Brighton. The big differences between Mr. Bert Moore and Mr. Brighton were that the former was a big man (at a time when a 'fine corporation' was considered a good thing) and an excellent swimmer whereas the latter was a small man and, more importantly given the post he occupied, could not swim. Mr. Moore taught children to swim by holding them in the water in a canvas sling at the end of a long and stout pole which he held without entering the water himself.

So these were the members of my family and the memories which writing about them has brought to the surface of my mind. But what sort of life did we– my parents, brother and sisters – live when we children were young? What was the house like in which we lived? And the road where the house was? Who else lived there? What did we do there? What games did we play? What else did we do there? What, in short, was our early life like?

Our house in Pleasant Place, later called 'Becton', a combination of Beccles, where my father lived, and Roehampton, where my mother had lived, had three bedrooms, one occupied by my mother and father, another by my sisters and the third by Dennis and me. Each room had a double bed. What the arrangements were when we had my Grandfather Ward or my mother's sister, Phyllis, staying with us, I can not remember. Somewhat surprisingly, I don't think Dennis and I ever made our own beds – I don't know about my sisters. I recall – and this is the first of many diversions to follow in my story – Dennis and me playing 'making camps' out of the bed clothes and occasionally wrestling in bed, neither of which larks could have made bed-making any easier, especially in those blanket, sheet and eiderdown days before duvets were known in England. 'Making camps' – or 'dens' – seems to have been fairly common because I remember making shelters out of old pieces of wood and tin in hollows on St. Anne's Meadow which was a piece of waste land fairly near our home. I recall a girl, younger than me, who lived close to us, finding a large discarded tin of used but still sharp and shiny razor blades on this waste land and I was asked – or volunteered – to share the contents between a number of children playing with us at the time. This girl, whose standing in my estimation plummeted and took a long time to recover, told her teacher of the find and of my leading part in distributing the spoils. I was given a telling off and made to recover all the razor blades and hand them in for disposal. In those days, many men, though not my father, still shaved with an open 'cut throat' razor – honed regularly on a conveniently placed leather belt, a 'strop'. One of the reasons why my father did not use a cut throat razor was that they were not appropriate in the trenches during the First World War and only safety razors were permitted in the 'food parcels' which the Red Cross and the families sent to the prisoners of war. Even the 'safety' razors were unlike those of later generations, for they had a replaceable blade, sharp on one side only – though later two sides – and remained sharp for only a few shaves before they had to be replaced. Various patented items were available to hone these blades, sometimes of slightly roughened glass. The safety razor was metal, plastics scarcely being known at the time. Indeed the only plastic I knew of was 'Bakelite', a black man-made substance. After experimenting – I guess clandestinely – with my father's razor when I was about thirteen, I purchased my own razor and used it for many decades. Indeed, somewhere in my 'treasures' I'm fairly certain I still have it. I certainly still have the shaving brush which I bought at the same time, its bristles worn down to so short a stubble as to be almost indistinguishable from the handle. When it was 'retired' from its intended use for lathering, it was occasionally brought into use as a paint brush for gaining access to difficult parts when painting walls. The use of lather for shaving, it inconsequentially strikes me, is a good example of multiple use. It can be used to soften the stubble on one's jaw, or facilitate the smooth gliding of the razor over that jaw, or make it clear to the shaver which parts of the jaw have already been shaven and those which still required attention – important information as one gets older!

Downstairs at home there was a front room, used, generally, only on Sundays and at Christmas time or when visitors came – which was infrequent. There was also downstairs a living room that was used as a combined lounge and dining room; and a kitchen, known as the scullery. The word 'scullery' long struck me as odd, since one did not keep skulls there, but I stopped being puzzled by this when I realized that, although one might keep butter in a buttery, one does not keep pants in a pantry. Later on, when I was in the sixth form at school and during the vacations when I was at university, I did my studying in the front room at a small black octagonal table on which plants were normally placed. The front door did not, as it did in many other, older, homes, open directly into the front room but into a corridor which led off to the front room and the living room. The front door was set back a few feet in a porch, the floor of which was regularly cleaned using a 'Bath brick' – which I guessed, wrongly, was a block of sandstone from the Bath area. I recall that at the lower end of Ingate Street, some of the houses had a front door which not only opened directly into their sitting room without the protection of a porch, but were set down a few inches from the road. To stop the dust from passing traffic entering the house through the door, they had a low wooden baffle board across the front entrance over which they had to step each time they entered or left the house.

The kitchen had a low and shallow yellow-stone sink above which was a cold water tap – there was neither central heating nor a hot water system – a Dutch oven, a gas oven, a copper and a bath. The sink was later replaced by a more modern one and I used the old one as a 'feature' in a rockery that I built in the back garden. The Dutch oven was a metal oven set in a brick surrounding with a wood or coal fire under it, in one corner of the kitchen. It was used to bake the larger, once-a-week, items – baked usually on Fridays – such as cakes, tarts, occasionally bread, and during the war a cake-cum-bread-loaf called a 'Sally Lunn'. This was new to us but was in fact the 'Bath Bun', first baked by a young French immigrant who settled in Bath over three centuries ago. Looking back on it, in Bath it may have been a luxury with all sorts of rich ingredients, but to us in war time the contents were pretty basic yet filling, enjoyable and no doubt nourishing. The daily food was cooked on or in the gas oven – a black or dark grey cast-iron contraption – or in the case of stew and soup, on the living room fire. There was an occasion, long remembered, when my Aunt Phyl, my mother's sister, who was staying with us, placed a tube of Pond's Vanishing Cream on the mantle piece above the living room fireplace, and it did indeed vanish, just disappeared, with no one knowing where it had gone, until the soup, which had been simmering on the fire beneath the mantle piece, was served up. The tube of cream had fallen into the soup saucepan! The copper in the scullery was a hemispherical cauldron – of the type, though much smaller, depicted in comics as being used by savages in which to boil missionaries – also set in a brick surrounding in another corner of the kitchen, but open at the top, where it was covered when not in use, by a circular wooden lid, with a fire under it. This was where the weekly washing was done each Monday. Father would light the fire before he left for work in the morning and fill the copper by hand – as it was also emptied with a sort of ladle in the evening – with water ready for boiling the clothes, with a handful of soda, by my mother during the morning. Father also cleared away the ashes and cinders of the previous day's fire in the living room and laid and lit the new fire each morning with newspaper, kindling wood and coal. When, as seems to have been frequently, the wind was in the wrong direction, the fire had to be 'drawn' by holding a sheet of newspaper over the whole of the fireplace but leaving a gap at the bottom through which the air was drawn and the fire encouraged to 'get going'. This was, to me, a dangerous operation, because the paper could easily, and occasionally did, catch alight, and I was later pleased when a sheet of metal, with a wooden handle, was used in place of the newspaper. During the war some Canadian soldiers stationed in the town taught us how to economize on the kindling wood by slicing it into thin slivers, thereby also getting the fire alight much more quickly. When I was in my teens, I used to enjoy sifting the ashes by hand – or rather fingers – in the morning, taking out the pieces I thought could still burn and putting them back on the fire. I used to enjoy, too, chopping the kindling into pieces about six inches long with a cross section of about an inch square. This was not a difficult operation because the kindling was delivered to the house in slab-like sections about the size of a decent slice of bread disused. I think these had been cut mechanically by the wood merchant from railway sleepers – all railway sleepers at that time were made of wood – and all I had to do was to chop them vertically into smaller strips – again an easy task because the chopping was with the grain and the wood split easily.

The kitchen copper – which was not made of copper but of a lead-coloured metal – was also used to heat the water for the bath which was under a table top at one end of the kitchen. On Friday nights the table top was removed so that the bath could be used. The bath was not plumbed and had to be filled and emptied by hand. I think the whole family bathed that evening each week, though I recall only my own baths, and I think my parents must have bathed after we had gone to bed. These were fairly rapid affairs, because the amount of hot water was limited and there was no time for a leisurely soak. Drying was finished off in front of the living room fire, for the kitchen was unheated, though the fires from the Dutch oven and the copper must have given some warmth. The lavatory, called 'the double yew' – the 'W' part of 'WC', water closet – was a few yards along the 'steps' outside the, kitchen door. It was part of the house, but entered from the outside. Later, after I had left home, and after my parents had bought the house, the lavatory and the coal shed next to it and also part of the house, were incorporated into a bathroom and lavatory that led off from the end of the kitchen, so that no longer did one have to go outside to the lavatory and no longer did one bathe in an unplumbed bath under the kitchen table. The lavatory pan was ceramic but encased in a wooden 'box' that was kept scrupulously clean by daily scrubbing. Toilet paper, of the type used today, was unknown to us, and consisted of cut-up sheets of newspaper. It may be that the British compulsion to buy newspapers daily, whether they are read or not, stems from this earlier practice and from the needs to have paper to light and to 'draw' the fires, and in which to wrap fish and chips!

Although I have referred to 'the steps' outside the back door, there were in fact no steps there. The word was used to describe the paved area just at the back of the house and probably came from Holland because that area just outside the house is known as 'stoep' in South Africa. Today one might more grandly use the word 'patio'.

All the decorating of the house, both internally and externally was done by my father, as was the practice of our neighbours. The internal redecorating was both with wall paper in the main rooms and with distemper in the hall and on the stairs and landing. Distemper was powdered chalk or lime mixed in a bucket with water and with a coloured powder added to it. When used as a medium by artists to paint pictures it is mixed with size or glue – but that is a different type of painting! The powders were bought at Clatworthy's, Gunn and Hill's or Skevens' hardware shops. I remember the colours pink and pale green being used in the house and the difficult job my father had to mix just the right quantity of coloured powder to get a good match. The wall paper was bought in rolls with an unpatterned strip or border or selvage down the sides which had to be cut off to make the strips butt well onto each other. I can't properly remember, but maybe the plain strip was down one side only and this would have been overlapped by the adjoining strip – but I think not, because I recall Mother helping Father to cut the strip off with great care. He also did the re-glazing and puttying of windows when this was necessary as, for example, when we broke a window with a cricket ball or catapult.

Just about the only job not done by Father in maintaining the house was sweeping the chimneys. This was done by a professional chimney sweep who would place sacking over the fire place – no fire was lit that day – and then shove his broom up the chimney, making sure that he twisted each additional rod the right way so that they did not come undone in the chimney. In removing the brush rods he unwound them the same way. Allowing the rods to unwind half way up the chimney was a calamity to be avoided at all costs. As children we were asked to go outside and shout when we saw the brush-head appear through the chimney top. This was great fun and there was keen competition to be the first to shout 'It's out!' even though I am sure the sweep knew when it had emerged and the need to push his brush hard, stopped. Occasionally the chimney of a nearby house would catch fire as the accumulated soot caught alight. My mother was always alarmed when she saw the smoke of a burning chimney – sufficiently alarmed to ensure that our own chimney was regularly swept, perhaps once a year. Cleaning the windows, dusting the furniture and shaking the rugs was a weekly chore for my mother, and there was an additional annual 'spring clean' in which a particularly thorough dusting and shaking and polishing and rubbing took place and curtains and blankets were washed. I always admired, and was alarmed by, the way the housewives in Pleasant Place clean the upstairs sash windows, without the use of a ladder, by sitting on the window ledge with their legs inside the house and the rest of their body outside as, skilfully balanced, they rubbed and polished the glass panes.

OUR ROAD

Our house was at the end of a terrace of three houses, built just before my parents were married on 20 June 1925, which they rented – and continued to do so for at least as long as I stayed at home. It was near the far end of the cul-de-sac, called Pleasant Place, though strictly speaking this name applied to a terrace of six houses on the opposite side of the road, built in the 1890s. On 'our' side of the road, the western side, there was an adjacent terrace of four houses with a further four behind them, known as Gladstone Terrace, also built in the 1890s. The rear four always struck me as strange, since their front door was at the back and was rarely used, because it led nowhere. Later, after I had left home, the three houses of which ours was one were sold, and I think my parents paid three hundred and twenty pounds for ours and even then had to take out a mortgage for it. It was only after the war, when new houses were built on the meadow at the top, southern end, of the road, and Pleasant Place was no longer a cul-de-sac, that our house was given a number: eighteen. How this number was arrived at I do not know, because the sequence was interrupted by having the eight houses of Gladstone Terrance numbered separately.

Being at that time a cul-de-sac ending with a wooden gate which, with a smaller 'passenger' gate at its side, led onto a grass meadow owned by Mr. Crickmore, Pleasant Place had a feeling of cohesion, a piece of territory to which the inhabitants, especially the children, could have a sense of belonging. For the children it was in a sense cosily cut off and secure, safe and protected, though not too isolated.

There were a dozen or so children in total living in the road who regularly joined together to play and go for walks and whose ages covered a range of only four or five years, though rarely if ever did they play as a whole group. The active group at any one time and in any one activity was fluid and fluctuated in size and membership, but the 'core' at least for part of the time was Cynthia, Dennis, Joyce Simper, Minnie and Peter Adams, Derek Day, John Porter and me, though even this core varied in size and composition depending on what it was we were doing.

There were at least another dozen 'children' living in the road but they were either younger or older, some of them much older, than the 'core' of 5-11 year olds. Of the 22 houses in Pleasant Place, 11 of them, during my time, were occupied by widows or childless couples. Including the grown-up offspring who were out at work or who had left home, the size of the families varied a good deal. Mrs. Fisher had one child; Mrs. Day, Mrs. Freeman, Mrs. Godfrey and Mrs. Porter each had two children; Mrs. Robinson and Mrs. Simper had three, my mother had four, Mrs. Adams had five and Mrs. Keable had eight. Incidentally, it was one of these ladies who in reprimanding one of her daughters for answering her back told her, 'Shut your mouth when you are talking to me!'

Mrs. Keable lived next door to us and she played a quiet, informal, but important part in our early life. She was considerably older than my mother, already had a large family, and must have been a great help to her when my parents were first married. She was an ever-willing helper with advice and she was always there to help us if we children got into any trouble. I recall two occasions when I cut myself – not badly – playing while Mother was out shopping and Mrs. Keable helped to dress my wounds. There was a small gate in the fence between their property and ours and if ever we needed help, we could easily go to see her. She was good company for my mother and they enjoyed a quiet chat in the infrequent gaps in their daily work. Some times when I was very small I used to think that maybe Mother was spending more time chatting than she – or more likely I – wished, and I am told that occasionally I resorted to disreputable devices of my own to get her back into the house. These devices included telling her that the dog had brought a dead bird into the house, and saying that the cushions had fallen onto the fire. She probably knew that these were not true but she could not take the risk of ignoring them. Some children can be unbelievably devious on occasions! The Keables were a nice family and good neighbours. Mr Keable taught me how much easier it was to pull a wheel barrow rather than push it – he drove a horse and wagon in his daily work. He always referred to being 'on the land' when he was on his allotment. He habitually tied a piece of string round the bottom of his trouser legs as a precaution, he said, against rats running up inside them in the grain mill where he worked. He also tied string round his waist to keep his trousers up, in addition to a stout leather belt and a pair of braces – Suffolk men are cautious! And when he involuntarily broke wind he would explain with a serious smile, 'Brown bread, Colin, brown bread!'

We played a variety of games in the road or nearby, and it is strange, looking back, how very rarely we visited each other's homes. Even when it rained we would not go into each other's homes but returned individually to our own to continue playing. Playing marbles was a favourite game at certain times of the year, I guess in the drier weather when the playing surface was not muddy. The marbles were very cheap to buy – most of us owned six to ten of them – and they were made of baked clay with only very rarely a coloured or plain glass marble, known as an 'alley'. We kept them in small cloth bags made for the purpose. There were two versions of the game which was played, mainly but not exclusively by boys. Either there was a straight competition to see if one could so aim his marbles as to hit his opponent's. The other was seeing how many marbles one could pitch and roll into a small depression scooped into the road surface, known as a 'bibby' hole – and consequently this version could not be played on tarmac! There was also skipping with a rope held either by oneself or by friends standing at each end of the rope. Occasionally two or more children would skip with the same rope at a time. Skipping was more a girls' game than a boys' and I never mastered the technique. Boys, but rarely girls, played conkers when those nuts were in season, and there were the usual stories of how some disreputable boys soaked or even boiled their conkers in vinegar or other – sometimes more personal – liquid to harden them. There were arguments, too, about the optimum length of the string used: length increased the power of the blow, but shortness increased the accuracy. A conker which had broken and triumphed over – or conquered – two other conkers was known as a 'two-er', three a 'three-er' and so on. Although one occasionally had a sore knuckle where a competitor's conker had hit it, I do not recall any other injuries being caused. We, especially the girls, played hopscotch with the lines drawn in the soil surface of the road with a stick – elsewhere, on tarmac, chalk was used. We rolled hoops made from the rims of old cycle wheels. We had go-carts made of a plank, fixed onto old pram wheels and axels and steered with a piece of rope attached to the front axel. These vehicles required an adult to do most of the making. We ran races. We played leap-frog. We swatted 'billywitches' – large flying insects – with tennis racquets in the harvest season. We, boys and girls, played in a den hollowed into the hedge at the bottom of the road; and we walked over the bridge to St. Anne's Meadow to play and make dens or camps, and on other occasions we took much longer walks into the countryside. The hedge at the bottom of the road which I have mentioned surrounded Green's apple orchard which was between Pleasant Place and the railway line. I have no recollection of our ever having been tempted to enter the orchard and take any apples from it. When we were small my father used to tell us that the flour from Green's Castle Flour Mill just across St. George's Road was blown onto the apples in the orchard and when it rained and the sun shone they would turn into baked apple dumplings. Although there may have been a good deal of traffic, originally horse-drawn carts and later lorries, taking grain to the mill and flour from it, I have very little recollection of there being many vehicles.

We also occasionally played a game in which we flicked a cigarette card from between our first and second fingers as far as we could. Success depended on flicking the card briskly and horizontally. Packets of cigarettes each contained a small card, perhaps an inch and a half by three inches, with a picture on the front and a description of the picture on the back. These cards were printed in sets of, I guess, 25, and the intention and attraction was to collect a full set and then move on to further sets. With a full set one could acquire an album into which to place the cards. The cards and the albums were usually attractively presented. Sets of cards covered a very wide range of interesting topics: regimental uniforms, film stars, sportsmen, railway engines, ships, kings and queens, flowers, birds, and many others. Workers at the Caxton printing works were not allowed to smoke while on the factory premises and as a consequence they 'lit up' the moment they walked out of the front gate. Just outside that gate a group of boys would be waiting asking for the men – women smoked much more rarely – for their cards as they opened the packets and took out a fag. They were a rich source of cards, and woe betide any youngster who tried to muscle in on the preserve of the group of boys habitually waiting there. These boys invariably asked the hurriedly departing men for the cards in a sentence which was reduced to what sounded like a rapidly repeated single word: 'cigarettecardsplease-cigatettecardsplease-cigarettecardsplease'. We, not being members of the factory gate select collecting fraternity, and living at the other end of the town, relied on our fathers and neighbours giving us their cards. Members of the factory gate group were not themselves collectors but entrepreneurs who sold on their cards to avid collectors who were missing a number of cards from their collections. The rarer the card, the higher the price demanded. There was a brisk internal market in which the factory gate boys exchanged cards between themselves. Today and in a fast declining tobacco market, there are few if any cigarette packets with cards in them, and collections from the past command significant sums on E-Bay and at Collectors' Fairs. Incidentally, in those days of heavy smoking a man would never start up a cigarette without offering others with him a cigarette. Not to have done so would have been considered the depths of parsimony.

We also made a number of 'weapons of combat', though we did not fight with them. First, we made bows from saplings taken from the hedgerows, often ash, with string tied as tightly as we could without breaking the wood or the string. The arrows were any straightish piece of thin wood we could find.

Most attempts to fletch the arrows failed and we just did without any feathers at the ends. The bows and arrows did not always work well but we enjoyed making them. Second, we made swords by again taking a thin straight branch from the hedgerows or a thin bamboo from the garden shed and at one end attaching a hand-guard made from an opened-up tin with two holes cut in it through which the handle end of the sword was pushed. Our enthusiasm for making bows and arrows was at its peak immediately after our having seen a Robin Hood-type film at the cinema, and our enthusiasm for making swords was at its peak just after watching a Three Musketeers-type film – in all of which Errol Flynn seemed to be the star actor and Olivia de Havilland his partner. Third, and not connected to any film-watching, there was the pièce de résistance, the most technologically advanced of all our weapons – the 'pop-gun'. The barrel of this piece of artillery was a straight length of wood cut from a branch of the elder tree, varying from about six inches in length with a diameter of about an inch, to the very much rarer blunderbusses, the Big Berthas – today they might be called the 'Exocets' – eighteen inches in length and two inches in diameter. The pithy centre wood of the branch was then removed, usually with a red-hot poker. Another length of wood of about the same diameter but of harder wood was fashioned by shaving it down so that it just fitted into the round hole, the bore, running through the barrel, but a handle was left by not shaving down the whole length but leaving two or three inches of the original wood. We finished up with what looked rather like the handle and inner rod of a bicycle pump. The non-handle end was then made into a sort of brush by spitting on it and pounding it on a brick so that it looked like a miniature chimney sweep's brush. The rod was then inserted into the barrel, withdrawn to its fullest extent without actually removing it. A hulled acorn was then pushed firmly into the other end of the barrel, fully blocking the exit. The pop-gun was fired by pushing in the handle so that the brush end increased the air pressure until 'Pop' and the acorn was fired out of the far end of the barrel. In the case of a really good gun – not necessarily a whopper – the 'pop' was often a loud 'bang' which delighted the proud owner. All this sounds very complicated but in fact it was quite simple to make and fire a pop-gun. My young grandsons today think this is just another of Grandad's stories!

As an aside, when we were playing football at school and a throw-in was to be taken, the word 'hull' instead of 'throw' was often used. It was also used generally to mean throw, for example a cricket ball or a stone. It is not a word I have heard used in this sense since leaving school.

There was a degree of seasonality about our games and pastimes. Using an earth surface for marbles and hopscotch depended on the road being dry and not too wet as in winter. Conkers, together with the acorns and pithy elder wood used in our muzzle-loading pop-guns, were available only at certain seasons of the year. Billywitches briefly appeared only at the harvest season. Country walks were usually taken, tadpoles were collected and newts were caught in the summer, and so on.

I have taken some time to write about the games we played and where we played them, because when we were not in school they took up a good deal of the rest of our time and were an important part of our lives as children. Apart from the country walks, with one exception, they all took place in our road with friends drawn from neighbouring families. The exception was a friendship I formed with Maurice Rix in the latter years of our junior school and first year of our secondary school. He lived at the old brick fields at the far end of Darby Road-Wash Lane, near the railway crossing on the London Road. He and I would go for fairly long walks, for example to Weston where, he has recently reminded me, he had a 'secret' place for hiding money – I think two pence – in a hollow in a tree trunk near the church. We also walked through the fields near his home and I particularly remember our finding bee orchids there. His mother, who was very kind to me, told me about the old brick fields and brick making, including showing me the circular trough cut in the ground where the clay was 'puddled' by a horse walking round and round the trough.

Looking back on our road, maybe Pleasant Place was too confined a society but we were small and our mothers could discreetly keep an eye on us – partly to see if we were safe and partly to check up on any untoward mischief we might be getting up to. We had lots of time ahead of us to grow up and become part of a wider society, and there were other aspects of our early life.

OUR EARLY LIFE

I guess like all childhood memories of home life, my recollections are disjointed. They are certainly gravely incomplete. My earliest memory is of my mother nursing baby brother Dennis in bed – I have a strong impression that it was a Sunday morning though I cannot imagine why I should think so. I recall little more of it, save that Mother was anxious that I should not feel neglected, left out or resentful about the new baby being nursed. I don't think she need have been concerned, but it would have been typical of her to be sensitive to the possibility and guard against it. I could not have been more than two years and a very few months old at the time.

Another very early memory is of being taken up to bed by my father, carrying me on his shoulders and with a candle in a holder in his hand because there was no gas or electricity upstairs, and both of us having to 'duck down' as we reached the low part of the stairs ceiling. Given these circumstances, I think I could not have been more than three years old at the most.

Yet another very early memory is of a Sunday morning when we children were out for a walk with our parents. We went specifically to see the new traffic lights at the junction of London Road, St. Mary's Road and Peddars Lane, which had just been installed. We were walking up Peddars Lane towards the lights. There was a rubber pad on the road some yards from the lights which, when depressed by a vehicle passing over it, changed the lights. I recall thinking that if a vehicle could do this, maybe I could, so I jumped on the rubber strip and, hey presto, the lights changed! My father gently told me not to do it again, 'because a policeman is coming' – I could see no policeman but the possibility was enough to dissuade me from jumping on the rubber strip again. In those days, though we did not fear policemen, the thought that one might discover us in even a mild anti-social act, as it might be called today, was enough to dissuade us. I have learned recently that the traffic lights – which remained the only ones in Beccles while I lived there – were installed in 1934, so I would have been between four and five years old at the time.

A further early memory concerns the annual athletic sports at the Caxton Grounds. Part of the memory derives from a photograph showing me at the age of five or six, winning a handicap sprint race, taken just before I reached the finishing line, a piece of string held across the tracks. I have no recollection of the race itself but I do remember that I was awarded, as a prize, a pocket watch which had a black dial and green luminous hands and numbers. Just as clearly, I remember the criticism of some adults who voiced their opinion, which I heard, that it was ludicrous and unfair that I had been given such a generous advantage in the handicapping – which was probably true but which was not of my doing. The following year I also won and this time I was awarded a small table-clock. Maybe the handicappers had made a mistake two years running but I heard no criticism the second year.

I think it must have been well before the war, probably in 1936 or 1937, because I was quite small, that a plague of caterpillars attacked the willow trees on the 'fens' by the river, across the 'Cut', near the gas works and my grandparents' home. These caused great consternation in the town, I guess because they were eating the leaves of the willows and threatened to destroy the trees. I was told that many solutions were attempted to get rid of the caterpillars, such as trying to smoke or burn them out with fires placed at the base of the trees, but all to no avail, until someone suggested an unusual solution. I had been taken to see these caterpillars attacking the trees – there were dense, thick, whitish-grey shroud-like webs covering the trees and nearby grass, with the caterpillars eating among them. It looked very eerie and frightening to a child. Then I was taken to see the final solution in operation. A brass band was brought to the area and settled themselves among the willow trees where they played loudly for quite a long time – and it worked! The caterpillars stopped their devastation, the 'gunge' was eventually cleared away, and all was well.

It is one of those events which those who saw it do not expect all others to believe. But I saw it!

While it must have been a struggle for my mother to feed a family with four children, especially during the war, I don't think we were ever hungry, though like all growing children we were, or at least I was, always ready for the next meal. For breakfast during the week we would have porridge or bread and milk – thickish slices of bread soaked in hot milk and eaten with sugar (by the children) or salt and pepper (by my father). I recall a cereal breakfast food, called 'Force', first becoming readily available in the grocery shops – or maybe this was the first time my parents bought it for us – when I was, I guess, about five or six years old. It seemed to cause great excitement in the family and I remember the packets clearly with their 'Sunny Jim' character on them. These corn flakes did not replace the porridge and bread and milk but added a nice variety to our breakfasts which also included bread, butter and jam. On Sundays we had a fried breakfast, prepared, I think, by my father, of bacon or sausage, fried egg and sometimes fried tomato or fried cheese. Occasionally we also had fried mushrooms which Father and I collected in a field towards Barsham – one near the Leman School cross-country course which I came later to know well – and on a number of our early morning mushrooming trips we saw Mr. Glover from that school also gathering mushrooms. Intent on their mushroom-collecting, he and my father simply said good day cheerily and carried on gathering, no doubt hoping that neither would reveal to others this particularly rewarding mushrooming field.

What we called 'lunch' – later and elsewhere called 'elevenses', 'break' or 'snack' – was usually a rusk or a biscuit, maybe with a soft drink, taken as a short break mid-morning. 'Proper' lunches, which we called 'dinner', varied with the day of the week. On Sunday Mother would roast a beef joint and this would be served with gravy, Yorkshire pudding – called 'batter pudding' – boiled potatoes, cabbage and, when in season, carrots, beans and peas. Monday lunches were invariably cold beef, potatoes and cabbage – not requiring too much preparation time on a busy morning taken up in washing the bed linen, towels and clothes. Lunches during the remainder of the week included baked liver, 'pigs fry' which I think was something like tripe with onions, sausages, steak and kidney pudding, egg and bacon tart, meat pasties, pea soup, Irish stew, cottage pie and macaroni cheese bake – macaroni was the only pasta we knew of. We also had a number of different fish meals, usually on Friday but, as I recall, usually at tea time when Father came home from work, rather than at lunch time. I think my mother did not really like preparing and cooking fish – with their open eyes, their slimy scales, their slippery skin and their nauseating 'innards'. There were no 'Bird's Eye'-type pre-packaged frozen fish meals or any other such meals. The fish most often were fried herring, but there were also sprats, soused herring, kippers, bloaters, shrimps and winkles, these last being 'winkled' out of their snail-like shell with a pin. There were also cod's roes, some of which were 'soft' and others 'hard' – we children preferred the latter. We were told, correctly, that the hard roe is an unprocessed form of caviar, which sounds very nice, but what we were not told was that it is the egg-filled fish ovary, and the soft roe is – swallow hard! – the sperm-filled fish reproductive gland. Sometimes it's best not to know! Crab at a certain time of the year was a great favourite with my father and my sister Cynthia. The second course – which was the term we always used to mean sweet, pudding dessert or 'afters' – varied and included suet pudding eaten with jam, golden syrup or custard; dried fruit pudding; apple crumble; rice pudding; macaroni pudding; tapioca pudding; semolina pudding; sliced banana and custard; apple dumplings and egg custard. Tinned fruit – sliced peaches, pineapples and pears – jelly and trifle, sometimes with condensed or evaporated milk or custard, were 'treats' reserved for tea time on Sundays, birthdays and Christmas time, rather than being a staple part of our diet. In summer, especially when fruit was plentiful, Mother made 'Malvern Puddings' – now called 'Summer Puddings', I think – in which a basin was well lined with slices of bread with the crusts cut off, and then filled with mixed fruit – blackberries, black currants, gooseberries, raspberries, loganberries and sliced apples. After a topping of more slices of bread had been put in place, the pudding was pressed down by placing a weighted plate on the top. After a day or two the fruit juices soaked through the bread and was ready to be turned over – now fairly solid – and eaten with custard – excellent!

'Tea', which was the meal taken at about six o'clock when Father came home from work, was often of toast – huge piles of it, toasted on a long wire 'fork' by the children in front of the sitting room fire – with baked beans, or peanut butter, or Marmite, or beef dripping, or Welsh rarebit, or fish paste, or meat paste, or toasted cheese, or scrambled eggs, or poached eggs. Alternatively, tea might be bread, butter and jam, with a slice of cake. Fairly regularly, perhaps once a fortnight, we would buy fish and chips from one or other of the half dozen or so fish and chip shops in town – Bond's, Fitt's, Whisker's, Peck's. These would be bought wrapped in a sheet of greaseproof paper and then two or more layers of newspaper, brought home, put on plates and eaten at the table – always with fish knives and fish forks which are so rarely seen today. The order in the shop was, for example, for 'two and one' meaning two penny worth of chips and one piece of fish. There were no other items sold in the fish and chip shops – no sausages, pies, mushy peas, pickled eggs, samosas, curry sauce, etc., as one finds today. Some people, however, did buy – or were often given gratis – the tiny pieces of batter and maybe the odd flake of fish which had fallen to the bottom of the frying cauldron. Incidentally, in the winter, eggs were preserved in a large bucket of isinglass because the hens did not lay in winter – or so I was told. And during the war, powdered egg was a frequent substitute for real eggs and became a normal ingredient of many dishes. There was powdered potato, too – not particularly palatable – and powdered chocolate – excellent! Preserved food, in addition to the eggs in isinglass, and the jams, included chutneys, picked red cabbage and pickled onions. Recently, in a tidying-up session, my wife came across my mother's recipe for pickled onions. Most meals were accompanied by a cup of tea. I do not recall ever having coffee in the house but there was the distinctively labelled liquid 'Camp Coffee with Chicory Essence', which we had sometimes, though I have forgotten at which meals – probably mid-morning breaks and not 'supper'. This traditional label showed a splendidly attired, standing, Indian serving a seated and kilted army officer with Camp Coffee from a silver tray. Under pressure from equality groups in the last few years, Camp first removed the tray, and now the Indian and the army officer are seated side by side, enjoying a Camp Coffee together. 'Supper' was a late evening snack of home-made rusks or bought dry biscuits, often with cheese –I recall no other types of cheese than cheddar – and a cup of cocoa. And so to bed.

Our diet was fairly well balanced and regularly included a variety of vegetables and fruit. My father grew the vegetables in the garden at home: potatoes, carrots, cabbages, broccoli, sprouts, peas, runner beans, broad beans, celery, parsnips, lettuce and tomatoes. All of these, as was the practice at the time, were planted in straight lines, using two pegs or sticks and a length of thick string to ensure straightness. The pegs were cut to a length which was used to mark the spaces between each line of plants. It was a very precise affair. When not in use, the string was wound round the pegs in figures of eight to stop it getting tangled. I still use these figures of eight to wind the cables of lawn mowers and other electrical equipment. Seed potatoes were placed in trays and kept in the dark under my parents' bed so that they could begin to sprout, ready to be planted out, traditionally on Good Friday, when they were 'dibbled' into the soil with a hand-made tool, known as a 'dibbler' and resembling a thick spade handle sharpened at the lower end. The carrots were preserved during the winter in saw dust in a barrel kept in the coal shed. Potatoes also lasted some time without going rotten but the green vegetables were available only seasonally, there being no refrigerators or freezers. The small pantry in which most foodstuffs, especially the perishable items, were stored, which led off the sitting-cum-dining room, was usually a cool room, and a sheet of perforated galvanized zinc instead of window glass allowed in air from outside. Even so, in hot and especially thundery weather, for reasons I do not fully understand, butter went rancid and milk 'went off' unless it was scalded – a job which had to be done watchfully lest the milk boiled and 'caught' on the base of the saucepan, which made it difficult to clean.

Our diet also routinely included meat, though not in large quantities, usually beef and occasionally lamb – though I do not recall pork – and fish. A special treat, enjoyed particularly by my father, who saw to it, was 'salt beef,' a personally selected joint of beef immersed at the butcher's shop in a tub of brine for, I think, a week. I am not sure whether the salt beef was cooked – probably – or eaten uncooked. In any case I think we usually ate it cold in slices. There was an occasion, which must have been before the war, when there was a glut of herrings landed at Lowestoft. This fish was so plentiful on that occasion that it was given away by the basketful. My father took me to Lowestoft by train early one summer evening with mother's shopping basket, which was filled at the harbour quayside and brought back home. The quantity of shining silvery herring in that basket was such as to last several large meals for a family of six, but I do not remember how it was cooked. I am certain that none of it was thrown away. I remember that towards the very end of the war, North Sea fishermen predicted another glut of herring because they saw huge shoals swimming southwards towards Great Yarmouth and Lowestoft. Royal Navy minesweepers cleared a channel down the North Sea to enable the fishing boats to catch the fish safely as they moved southwards. Chicken graced our table only at Christmas time, and turkey, goose and duck were out of the question. There was one exception to the generality that chicken was eaten only at Christmas and that was the occasion when our dog, Rip, who accompanied us, the children, on one of our walks, chased one of Mr. Spratt's chickens on his vegetable small holding at Swine's Green. I was deeply worried about this unfortunate incident, feeling, I guess, in some way responsible, and I told my father about it. He went to see Mr. Spratt, who claimed – probably correctly – that the dog had killed his chicken and he insisted on compensation. A sum of sixpence was eventually agreed and then my father demanded that he be given the chicken. A recently killed chicken was produced and Father was quite 'chuffed' with the way he so successfully conducted this intricate negotiation. The chicken, roasted to perfection and accompanied by fresh vegetables, was produced at the next Sunday lunch! Pancakes – which we were taught to 'toss' when we were old enough to risk catastrophe – were always made on Shrove Tuesday and eaten rolled up with freshly squeezed lemon juice and sugar. Salads of lettuce, tomato, spring onions and cucumber, were a regular meal during the summer, either by themselves or accompanying other food. Lettuce was often eaten with a dressing of vinegar and brown sugar

As children before the war we had the usual types of fruit – oranges, apples, pears, bananas, black currants, gooseberries, blackberries and very occasionally strawberries. Each year we went as a family blackberry picking, often in hedgerows two or three miles from home and usually in the Ellough or Weston area. I guess each family had its favourite places to pick the fruit. These were expeditions lasting several hours and were treated very much as a family affair. We took our own small baskets in which to collect the berries, and my father took Mother's shopping basket – what a multi-purpose and commodious receptacle that was! – which we filled before returning home. The higher branches of the hedgerows, where the plumper and riper fruit was often found, were reached by a long stick with a hook at the end, and sometimes we children used an ordinary walking stick. At home the fruit was used partly stewed with apples for immediate use but mainly to make blackberry and apple jam or bramble jelly.

There was, too, a year early in the war when there was a glut of plums. These were sold very cheaply and the Ministry of Food gave extra rations of sugar that year so that people could make plum jam as a means of adding to the food supply, not wasting the fruit, and turning it to good use, especially since as jam it was preserved and its benefits could be enjoyed over an extended period. The local newspaper reported in April 1941 that 2460 lbs of fruit jam had been made with 16.5 cwt. of fruit and12 cwt. of sugar by volunteers working at the Area School. It may also have been the same year, but I think probably not, when a Mr. 'Bumpy' Harvey – so called because of his nodulated face – who had a soft fruit garden in St. George's Road, had a huge crop of red and black -and the rarer white – currants, and he invited my father to pick as many as he could carry. I went with him and spent several hours picking the fruit and being encouraged by Mr. Harvey to 'walk into 'em, Boy', that is eat as much fruit as I liked. At home Mother, whose ample shopping basket had once again been brought into service, made jam with the large quantities of currants we had collected.

It must have been during some of the wartime harvests that we went as a family to glean in the stubble of the wheat fields near Beccles and collect grains of wheat from the ground with which to feed the chickens which my parents kept at the time. One summer – probably 1943 or 1944 – I cycled with one or two others daily for a week or so to Westhall to work on Mr. Powell's farm, helping to bring in the harvest. Mr. Powell was the father of Mick Powell a friend, and good cricketer, at the Leman School. The work was mainly picking up sheaves of wheat with a pitchfork and lifting or throwing them onto a horse-drawn cart. It was hard work but the weather was beautiful, we took piles of sandwiches with us from home each day, we were young – and we were being paid for the work! I bought a small suitcase with the proceeds, which I used in place of a satchel for my school books and which I still have. Again I am not sure of the date except that it was during the war, when for several evenings a week I joined Maurice Rix and a few other boys, to hoe between the rows of flax plants being grown in a large field at Weston, just beyond the Duke of Marlborough pub, I think on land owned by Mr. Seppings, the butcher. Owners of land had no choice in the matter since they were ordered by the Government to grow specified acres of flax. I am not sure to what purpose the flax was put, whether for making linen or, as some claimed, to make ropes to hold the barrage balloons in place, but in any case it reduced the country's dependence on imported material, and increased my otherwise virtually non-existent income – the proceeds went on buying gramophone records.

There were inevitably shortages of many items, primarily foodstuffs, during the war, and when news of a consignment of a scarce item became known, news of it passed quickly from mouth to mouth and, in next to no time at all, queues formed outside the shops in which the items were to be sold. The queues were very orderly and no one dare break the line, for even the normally long-suffering and reticent Suffolk folk would not put up with such outrageously unfair and unsocial behaviour.

There was a number of small cafes in the town and although I do not recall going to any of them with my parents I do recall with pleasure the many occasions when I was in about the fourth form at the Leman School and I went with a few friends – I recall most clearly Johnny Hopes, the son of the Police Superintendent at Halesworth who had previously been the Inspector at Beccles – to have beans on toast after school, at Took's café. Johnny had to wait to catch his train home and went to the café to pass the time. He often treated me. He was a dangerously amusing fellow, full of larking about and sometimes wandering perilously close to getting into real trouble. He, unlike the rest of us, had a legitimate excuse for smoking cigarettes – I had given up smoking two years earlier! – because he had asthma and was allowed to smoke herbal cigarettes, though he did not by any means confine himself to herbal fags. Heaven knows what mischief he would create today with 'grass' and 'weed' being more readily available. One of his more amusing and less damaging larks was to dress in his Sunday suit, put a carnation in his jacket lapel and stand in the archway of the main door of the parish church, arm in arm with one of the girls in our class – June Gibbs – also nicely dressed and carrying a bouquet of locally acquired flowers. They then got one of us to take a photograph of the happy couple. Momentarily those to whom they showed the photograph believed that they had gone off and got married! A copy was sent anonymously to the local newspaper but not published. Sounds daft now but it was vastly amusing at the time and damaged no one. Johnny's sister, Gwen, became head girl at the Leman School, and many years later his younger brother, Eric, joined the Colonial Police and prosecuted cases in my court in Nyasaland. Although as a family we did not go to cafés or restaurants in Beccles, I recall later on, towards the end of the war, going with my parents to Palmer's Restaurant in Yarmouth where we had tea and cakes of the sort always then referred to as 'fancies' or 'pastries'.

On the whole we were a healthy family. We, or at least I, had our fair share of grazes, cuts and bruises resulting from playing or larking about. Cuts were treated either with 'Germolene' antiseptic ointment and a light bandage or, if they were deeper, with a hot poultice of pink lint immersed in boiling water and kept in place with a longer and more secure bandage. At home bandages were made from strips of old sheets. Even more serious cuts, usually to the knee, were treated by a visit to the doctors' surgery, and on occasions the cut would be treated by cauterizing with a dark blue 'pencil', rather like a stick of sealing wax, and painfully-stinging iodine, and again covered with boiling hot lint which was covered with a thin sheet of rubberized material to keep the heat in and 'draw out' any infections, and then securely bandaged with professional, not home-made, bandages. I received this treatment when I seriously cut my knee when I fell over in the road because, in order to protect a new pair of plimsolls, I covered them with dusters which came undone and I came a cropper. Father made a box, with a red cross painted on it on a white background, in which bandages, plasters, antiseptic ointment, Dettol, boracic powder and other simple medicaments were kept. Bouts of diarrhoea were treated with a day at home and doses of arrowroot – and an occasional morale-boosting bar of chocolate from Mr. Sam Culley's 'shop' – really a shed, but a nice one – across the road from our house. I guess like most children, each of us had measles, mumps and chicken pox but I have no recollection of them. Dennis later, as an adult, had scarlet fever. Parents were always worried about poliomyelitis, diphtheria and meningitis because they were fatal, but I recall only one case of each occurring in Beccles when I was being brought up. We had very few days off school because of illness, and decisions to keep us at home were not taken lightly. There was a council 'truancy officer' – a Mr. Carter, I think, who lived in Frederick's Road – but I do not know how fully occupied he was because I do not recall a single case of a child playing truant. Friday evenings were marked by a spoonful of jet black California syrup of figs to keep the family 'regular'. This and other medicaments were bought at 'Putty' Watson's, one of the few chemists' shops in town. Why he was called 'Putty' I do not know. I recall quite clearly the shape of the syrup of figs bottle and its distinctive label. I gather that most people did not like syrup of figs but I enjoyed its taste. The chemist's shop had huge, broad-bodied, narrow-necked, glass containers of red, yellow or green liquid in their windows – symbols of their trade, I imagine. The only other trade symbol I remember was the red, white and blue staff outside the barbers' shops. I don't think there was a pawnbroker's shop in Beccles which would have had three balls as its trade symbol.

If we were ill enough to require a doctor but could walk to the surgery in town, we did so and sat – it always seemed silently – until it was our turn to go in to see the doctor, each patient being summoned by the loud ringing of a bell. There were several doctors on the 'panel' but we always, if we could, saw Dr. William Maclaren – a large, hearty, jovially bluff Scotsman, deeply respected for his medical and surgical ability and his confident, kind and reassuring manner. If, on the other hand, we were not well enough to go to the surgery but required a home visit, Dr. Maclaren called on us, entered the house without knocking on the door – a practice which caused no offence whatsoever – made his diagnosis, wrote his prescription, asked how other members of the family were getting on – he had delivered at least one and probably more than one of us – and strode out. I suppose he might have had a car to drive on his house visits but I do not recall seeing one. No money ever exchanged hands on either a visit to the surgery or a house visit, nor were any bills sent, and I am quite clear that the question of whether we could afford medical attention never arose. It must have been paid for somehow – probably through my father's membership of a friendly society, maybe the Foresters, to which he belonged. The surgery had a small but well stocked dispensary on the premises, run by Mr. Button, and access to this reduced the number of occasions on which we would need to visit a commercial pharmacist – always known as 'the chemist'. The prescribed medication was dispensed by Mr. Button as we left the surgery. Again, no money changed hands.

Shopping was a very different matter from what later became the norm. There were no super-stores and no self-service stores, no shopping malls and no out of town shopping centres. Rather, one was always served by a shop assistant from behind the counter and one never served oneself. Indeed, one could not serve oneself because there were no open shelves, all the goods except a few bulk items being kept on shelves behind the counter or at the back of the shop. Today, serving counters are very rare, having been replaced by stacked shelves and check-out points. There were relatively few pre-packed items, save for branded goods such as tinned food, jams, bottled goods and – though not always – tea and cocoa. Even black treacle was poured into jars, vinegar was poured into bottles, soap was cut and wrapped in paper, and such items as sugar and flour were weighed and wrapped in paper bags as one waited. Bacon and ham were sliced on the counter and wrapped in paper. Butter and cheese were cut into the required weight portions – often precisely the correct weight at first cut – before being wrapped and handed over to the customer. The skill, speed and neatness with which the assistants made and secured these packages was remarkable. A weekly delivery of groceries was made to the house by the Co-op in accordance with a list Mother wrote in a small note book. I recall, possibly incorrectly, the order of the regular items: butter, marg, lard, cheese, sugar, bacon, vinegar. The reason I think this may not be fully correct is that as very small children there was no margarine. Certainly, before the war we would never have been given margarine, instead of butter, on our bread. I recall with sadness and shame how when, during the war, we were required to have margarine instead of butter, I inadvertently called it lard, which distressed my mother greatly. I feel badly about it even now. For a while margarine was not rationed, and using it enabled my mother to supplement the butter, which was rationed.

There was a number of nation-wide grocery stores – the Cooperative Wholesale Society, the International, the Home and Colonial Stores and others.

In Beccles there were the first two of these. The Beccles Cooperative Society was a very go-ahead business, and over the years grew to consist of a full range of departments – fruit and vegetables, grocery, butchers, men's outfitters, ladies' outfitters and millinery, footwear, chemist, coal merchant and, later, a pasteurizing milk plant. They even opened a branch store in Ingate and a number of small shops in nearby villages. I do not recall many people complaining that the Co-op was driving out the smaller retailer, though they may have done so. On the other hand, smaller retailers continued to flourish in the town even as the Co-op expanded. Some idea of its size can be judged by the fact, which I learned recently, that by the end of 1940 sixty members of its staff had joined the forces. Every retail sale was accompanied by a receipt, a small slip of pale green paper, showing the amount spent and the membership number of the customer. Annually these slips were collated by the company and a dividend awarded to each member, proportionate to the amount spent. This 'divi' was eagerly looked forward to by the customers and it made a valuable addition to the family's spending power. So important was it to remember one's Co-op number in order to claim every penny of dividend that it became indelibly printed on our minds – I still remember it clearly.

As an aside, I recall my first home leave from Africa in 1958 and my visit to a Co-op shop in south-east London to buy a loaf of bread. Simple enough task, you might think, but not so. I had been accustomed for four years to bread being home made in an old petrol tin oven and an open wood fire with the dough leavened in the sun with dried hops rather than yeast. So I was looking forward to the easy task of simply buying a loaf. When I asked for a loaf of bread the assistant asked, 'Brown or white, Sir?' Easy. I said, 'White, please'. Then she asked, 'Large or small?' 'Mmm. I had become used to only one size of loaf and I did not know how small 'small' was so I replied, 'Large, please'. 'Wrapped or unwrapped?' Oh dear! 'Wrapped. please.' But still the questioning went on. 'Sliced or unsliced?' I thought of fleeing from the shop but persevered. Never having bought, or even heard of, sliced bread, I thought I would try it. 'Sliced, please'. Still she was sweetly relentless, anxious to please: 'Thick or thin, Sir?' Indifferent to its thickness I plumbed for thin. Surely that must be the end of the inquisition and I could now receive the loaf and run off with it, but again, no, for there was just one more question – 'What's your Co-op number, Sir?' And when, finally and I thought triumphantly I told her my mother's number she delivered the coup de grace: 'That's not a London number, Sir!' The point of this story, in addition to emphasizing the persistent importance of the Co-op number, is that there had been significant changes even to the sale of such an everyday item as a loaf of bread in the few years I had been away, and we sometimes forget how lucky we are in Britain to have such a wide and varied a choice as we do have even in small matters. Much of Africa considers itself fortunate to share a loaf of bread – never mind whether it is white or brown, large or small, wrapped or unwrapped, sliced or unsliced, thick or thin – though they would cherish their divi if they got one!

Other shopping was done locally. The Misses Smart had a small grocery and general store 'over the bridge', that is on the other side of the railway line that ran under St. George's Road away from the town, at Swine's Green – probably originally 'Swain's Green'. We generally bought only sweets here and did not otherwise frequently visit the place save during the war when we bought certain items with ration points, such as cheese, corned beef, sardines, etc. Father bought some of his cigarettes, 'Players' or 'Craven A', from the Misses Smart – others he bought at shops nearer the place where he worked. The Misses Smart's shop was really just the front room of their house, with maybe a small space further inside for storing goods. There was a number of examples of such 'cottage industry retail outlets' close by at the time – small scale, one person businesses – run from front rooms or more frequently garden sheds at people's homes.

Mr. Sam Culley, opposite our house, ran a fruit and vegetable business, with a few items of confectionery, from his shed. He also delivered his wares from a small, nicely painted hand cart. He was a Salvationist and regularly accompanied the local Salvation Army Band as it played in various parts of the town. He constantly and quietly hummed marching hymn tunes as he slowly walked down the road or pushed his cart – slowly because he had either bad feet or bad boots or possibly both. If we ran short of copper coins to put in the gas meter in the front room we were sent with a silver coin to Mr. Culley who always had change. There were two other Culleys in the road, brothers I believe. A little lower down Pleasant Place from our house was Mr. George's house. He was a greengrocer and peddled his wares from a horse drawn cart. The fruit and vegetables were stored in his shed and the horse was kept, I think, in the garden at the side of his house. We did not often buy from him, my mother preferring to deal with Mr. Culley. Next to him was Mr. Cole, who used his large shed to repair and renovate mangles, lawn mowers and similar cast iron items. He painted the metal work in a traditional dark green paint with red 'piping' and placed them on his well trimmed lawn close to the road to attract customers. There were three other Cole families in the road but I am not sure they were related. At the bottom of the road, just at the corner with St. George's Road, was Mrs. Stammers's house at the back of which was a small shed that she used as a shop. Here we bought paraffin, washing soap, candles and matches. She sold vinegar, too, for I was once sent to get some vinegar from her and boldly set off with a basket to buy it, only to discover to my fury when I got there that I had not brought a bottle in which to put the vinegar. I recall clearly, as for many years did the rest of my much amused family, demanding to know on my return how I was expected to carry vinegar in a basket. I did not receive, then at the age of five or six or subsequently, a satisfactory answer to this quite reasonable question. I was not amused then though I am now.

Nearer the Peddars Lane School, Mr. Club plied his trade as a cobbler from a shed at the end of his garden. He was an interesting, gentle and helpful man who soled and heeled shoes and boots, cut laces with a well worn and incredibly sharp knife from larger pieces of leather, sold 'Segs' and 'Blaikies' – metal pieces to protect the heels of shoes and reduce the wear and tear on them. He placed a large number of tacks or small nails in his mouth and took them out singly and with extraordinary speed, held them to the soles of the shoes he was repairing on his last and hammered them in – all in one movement so that my father, when I was very young, was able to convince me that he actually spat the nails into the soles! Mr. Club also sold dog collars and leads and mended handbags and school satchels. The school satchel which all grammar school pupils carried is another item no longer used. Strangely, he also sold light canes of the sort which school teachers might use to chastise their errant pupils. My mother bought one of these canes, I think as a warning or a deterrent to us –at least to me – but she never once hit us with it and it is inconceivable that she ever would.

The cane was used at secondary school but not often, though I recall having to be present when I was teaching for a short time at the Leman School, when the headmaster caned one of the boys. The boy was made to bend over a chair while the headmaster gave him six strokes of the cane. I recall the look on his face as he lifted the cane and then struck it heavily and quickly across the boy's buttocks. The screwed up, grimacing look on his face, the gritting of his teeth and the measured pause between each stroke was disturbing, though I did not know, nor do I know now, whether he was sadistically enjoying thrashing the boy or steeling himself in a job he found grossly distasteful.

Another, but very different, form of business conducted from a shed or other wooden building in the garden of domestic premises, was the Little Home School in Kemps Lane run by Miss Dunt. I know about this school only because Miss Dunt lived in Kemps Lane and her garden at the bottom of which her school, a wooden structure, was located, stretched down to Crickmore's meadow which was the meadow at the end of our road. Even then I would not have known about it had I not heard the children at singing lessons. I guess there were perhaps a couple of dozen infant and primary school children there and they wore a pale grey uniform with red and white piping. All rather elitist.

Kemps Lane was an odd road. It was a road which went nowhere although clearly it had been intended to go somewhere in the past. It began at the Butcher's Arms on the London Road, went up a short incline and then continued across a bridge over the railway line to join up with Darby Road, but permanent barriers closed off the bridge from both Kemps Lane and Darby Road, even though the bridge was a vehicular bridge wide enough to take at least single line traffic.

Pedestrians and cyclists used the bridge but vehicles could not. The bridge looked strong enough and I never discovered why, at that time, vehicles were not allowed to use it.

Other tradesmen and women carried out their business from a room in their house. One I have in mind is Mr. Youell, who had been a full-time tailor before being employed at the printing works. When required, he continued his tailoring part-time in the evenings and at the weekends from his house in Bridge Street. I had dealings with him after I left school and started to wear suits regularly. I bought suits, one at a time, from such shops as 'The Fifty Shilling Tailors' or from other outfitters during their sales. None of the suits cost me more than three or four pounds. So long as they were roughly my size they would do, and I took them to Mr. Youell at his house and asked him to tailor them to fit me and to bring them, if necessary, into a more current style – otherwise Mr. Jack Woodward would describe them, as he once did when I wore an untailored jacket, as being of 'a comical cut'. Mr. Youell sat cross-legged on a high bench in his front room and, with the work placed on his knees, sewed by hand and later ironing the restyled suit with a small flatiron, sitting in the same position. I think he enjoyed this work and felt that he was in some way repaying my father for having helped in securing for him the position in the printing works. We shared much amusement when, the suit being almost completed, he would run a thread around the edge of the lapels and pull it vey slightly tight, saying as he did so, 'There, young man, that makes it look just as if it was bespoke and hand made' – which, of course, it now was!

There were several people who called at the house to sell their wares. Mr. Bean, tall and lanky, dressed in black, came weekly to collect the insurance money – just a few pence – and enter the transaction in a little book which my mother kept. I think she took out death, fire and accident insurance cover. I recall only one claim being made and that was when a piece of coal fell out of the front room fire and burned the wood of the 'fender' in front of it. The insurance company insisted on the fender being repaired rather than being replaced, which turned out to be a long, fiddly, and almost certainly more costly, job, done by a Mr. Martin from Peddars Lane.

Another trader who peddled his wares in our road was Mr. Squires – I think there may have been two of them, brothers, who had, in addition to their permanent premises in, I think, Northgate, a black, covered van, pulled by a very patient-looking horse. Mr. Squires sold paraffin, soap, and other domestic materials. His horse had a nose-bag – a hessian bag hung from its neck – containing fodder which it ate as it stood waiting to move on to the next customer. My mother rarely bought from him, preferring to support Mrs. Stammers who sold virtually identical wares. Mr. Squires is an illustration of from how wide an area street tradesmen, especially those who used horse drawn carts, drew their customers. He came from the northern end of the town and sold his wares in the southern part – and areas in between – whereas Mr. Spratt and Mr. Bloomfield, whom David has mentioned, came from the southern end but delivered in the northern parts – and areas in between. They did not confine their trade to only one part of the town.

Milk was brought each morning except Sunday to the house by Mr. Ulph, a dairy farmer who drove his pony and 'float', as the nicely painted two-wheeled milk vehicle was called, carrying two or three large metal cylinder-shaped containers called 'churns' from which he poured his milk – always full-cream in those days – into a smaller churn which he carried to the house. From this smaller churn he lifted the milk in jug-shaped metal ladles measuring half and full pints which he poured into the waiting crockery milk jug at the back door of the house. He sold milk in this way to many, possibly all, our neighbours.

Other 'delivery men' also called at the house. Newspapers were delivered – thrust through the letter box – each morning including Sundays. In pre-e-mail days the telegram was the way messages were conveyed quickly. These were transcribed by hand and in pencil by a clerk in the post office and then delivered in sealed envelopes at all hours of the day by a uniformed telegram boy on a red bicycle. I recall one of our neighbours receiving a telegram from a young soldier she had met, and her mother approving of the young man, whom she had not yet met, because he had 'such beautiful handwriting'!

Others also called at the house, including the 'Clean Easy' man who periodically came with his large suitcase packed with a wide range of domestic cleaning items such as dusters, brushes and polish. The housewives reckoned these to be good value. On the other hand, there were some, probably only a few, unwelcome door-to-door salesmen who pressed housewives to buy their goods. I recall my mother's distress, eventually bordering on terror, of one of these unscrupulous scoundrels who bullied her into accepting a set of saucepans. They were probably good saucepans, though maybe over-priced, but my mother just did not want them. She refused them time and time again, but eventually he just left them with her. Then, for what seemed like several weeks, at times when he knew my father was at work, he returned and demanded the money. In the end, on my father's advice, she just left the saucepans on the door step and refused to answer the door, cowering inside, and hiding so as not to be seen. He eventually took them away. Though a rare incident, it was deeply disturbing and affected the whole family, particularly my mother, for many weeks, for we did not know when he might return without warning and start all over again.

I did not notice the significance at the time, but the most frequently used sweet shops were located near the schools. They were examples of what geographers call the factors affecting the location of industry, though I never heard a school teacher refer to the existence of this splendid example on their very doorstep. The nearest to Peddars Lane school was Jimmy Mason's shop which was immediately adjacent to the school and did a roaring trade. Certainly, he was the recipient of most of our one penny a week Wednesday pocket money. Our Saturday pocket money was spent at a shop cunningly located – though, again, it did not so strike me at the time – almost opposite the Regal. Mason's shop was peculiarly but cleverly laid out with the counter holding the sweets sloping down towards, and visible from the outside of, the front window. Inside, we stood on a box or raised platform to view and select the sweets – which we had spotted from the outside – and then paid for them as we passed Mr. Mason on the way out. There was no way in which anyone could have passed him without paying, though I honestly do not think it would have crossed many, if any, children's minds to have attempted to avoid payment. There was a great variety of sweets from which to choose but I do not recall potato crisps being sold there although my parents did buy us an occasional packet of Smith's crisps, the only variety then on sale, each packet containing a small blue paper sachet of salt. There was a similar shop, Parker's, across the road from the National School, but I recall visiting it very rarely and only when we visited Aunt Aggie, my father's sister, who lived nearby in Denmark Road. Parker's was the only place I knew that sold 'locust beans' – carob beans – which I enjoyed, but which passed out of my life until many decades later when I came across them again in Turkey. The Leman School was in a residential, somewhat superior, area of the town, in which sweet shops would probably have been prohibited. The nearest was Mr. Harvey's, later Mr. Harris's, shop, perhaps a quarter of a mile away, but located where many pupils passed it on their way home and close to a bus stop used by pupils travelling to and from places like Southwold.

There were several men's hairdressers in Beccles, and an informal but well recognized hierarchy was attached to them. In the middle of the range, charging four pence a time, were Mr. Forster in Blyburgate, who cut my father's hair and for a long time my own – invariably short back and sides, military in style – and Stanley White in Hungate, who could be persuaded to be a little less strict in style and to whom I later turned, though I was never quite at ease with his regularly singing the hair with a burning taper. At the 'lower' end of the hierarchy, charging two pence and some said one penny a visit, was Sammy Crisp who owned a barber's shop in the Old Market. Members of my family did not visit his shop. At the top end of the hierarchy was Mr. Barber – yes, his name really was Barber – whose premises in Smallgate were rather different from the others. First, his hairdressing room was approached through a well stocked tobacconist shop which he owned. Other barbers also sold cigarettes and other male requirements but Mr. Barber had a 'proper' tobacconist shop. Second, his was not a one-man business, since his son worked alongside him and he had an apprentice hairdresser with him. Third, he and his staff did not wear the workmanlike aprons of the other barbers in town but a short white tunic, rather like those worn by dentists and male nurses in hospitals today. And finally – this was the big difference and symbolized Mr. Barber the barber's peak position in the hierarchy – there was a private cubicle for the cutting of the hair and the shaving of the faces of those few men of social standing and affluence within the community who could afford this elite service, away from the gaze of lesser mortals. In my teens I turned to Mr. Barber and he became my regular hairdresser, mainly because he and his colleagues purported to pay close attention to the individual wishes of their clients to a degree which the others did not, although I never had the audacity, courage or funding to seek seclusion in the private cubicle! I suspect that had I asked I should have been refused. My father remained loyal to Mr. Forster throughout his life. All the barbers in town – though I am unsure of Sammy Crisp – also shaved their customers if they wished, using 'cut throat' razors – stropped dashingly on a leather strap – and lashings of frothing, thick, bubbling lather, and wielding both razor and brush with professional aplomb and occasional apparent indifference.

Sammy Crisp had a brother, Billy, who had, in modern parlance, learning difficulties. Although he was well known in the town as being rather odd, and although people may have poked fun at him when he was not present, no one so far as I know ever teased him, was unkind to him or bullied him. Similarly, there was a lady who also was seen as a little odd, and many tales were told of her behind her back. For example, it was said that when she went to the doctor's with a stomach ache and she was asked if she had passed anything that morning, she replied, 'Only a horse and cart on my way to the surgery.' Unkind things were said, but rarely done, and bullying in a physical sense and overly strong teasing did not occur – or perhaps I did not know of it. This does not mean that there was not an occasional scrap between two boys, but overt picking on a person because of some personal characteristic of theirs did not happen.

At the Leman School I think there had been some sort of initiation ritual, which had ceased before I went there, of chucking new boys into the school pond or ducking their heads under the cold water tap in the cloak room. The pond is now fenced off from the rest of the premises – as if disowned by the school – and is not as well cared for as once it was, and today lacks its former attractiveness, which is a pity.

There was, however, another form of male initiation and that was the change from having worn short trousers to wearing long trousers. It took place as an inevitable matter of course and seems strange and worthy of comment only in retrospect. This was a significant point in a young man's life and somehow marked a stage in growing up. Boys wore short trousers, men wore long trousers – I recall how one young man, returning from military service in the Middle East, wore shorts in the town during the summer, and was roundly ridiculed. The change usually took place on a Sunday when one donned the brand new long grey flannel trousers for the first time and went, deeply embarrassed but mildly proud, to church or at least for a walk in the town with one's parents. Then it was all over and done with save that there might be a tincture of twitting from older boys the next day when one went to school with legs fully covered for the first time. It was no big deal, as one might say today, but what fun the academic social anthropologists would have in explaining the phenomenon were they to study it with its coincidence with puberty, its maleness, the imagined significance of covering the lower limbs, the religious significance of the ritual of the attendance at church or the walk through the town with their parents – the elders of the tribe!

As small children, we were given a penny to buy sweets on Wednesdays and four pence on Saturdays: a penny for sweets and three pence to go to the cinema in the afternoon. There was also a penny, later three pence, for church collection on Sundays. In retrospect, this was quite a lot of money to spend on each of four children every week. Some friends suggested that if we went into the two-penny seats at the cinema we would have two pence instead of a penny for sweets. In addition, we would be able to creep back from the two-penny seats to the three-penny seats when the lights went out and the film started. This matter of two-penny and three-penny seats is interesting. It was somehow felt that the offspring of families of slightly higher social standing, aspiration or pretence paid three pence for seats that were a little further back, away from the screen, though, so far as I recall there was no great difference in the style or comfort of the seats. For them to sit in the two penny seats was considered mildly infra dignitatem. There were also, at least at the Regal cinema, nine-penny seats further back still, some of them, on the very back row, 'doubles', that is seats for two with no arm rest between them, useful, some said, when accompanying a friend of the opposite sex, and – I was told, and later discovered for myself – were well worth the additional investment! I think those double seats must have been rather cold, because some couples occupying them occasionally seemed to need an overcoat over their knees to keep warm.

There were two cinemas in the town, the Regal and the Cinema. Again, there was a social difference, for the Regal – which I can remember being officially opened, I guess during the mid-1930s – was reckoned to be somewhat higher up the social scale than the Cinema. The Regal was a newer, larger, more modern, purpose-built cinema with private boxes and a balcony. The Cinema was older and less well appointed and did not have a balcony or boxes or maybe the double seats, nor the fancily uniformed commissionaires and usherettes of its smarter competitor. This social difference did not matter to the children and I do not recall any reluctance on my parents' part to allow us to go to the Cinema. The children of the town attended whichever cinema had the film they most wished to see, but I think it unlikely that, for example, many aldermen of the borough and their spouses would have been happy to be seen at the Cinema, rather than the Regal, whatever the film. I do not recall either of my parents going to either of the cinemas. Every performance at both cinemas ended with the national anthem, during which the audience stood, and frowned mightily on any one who had the temerity and lack of patriotism to leave before the last dying note of the anthem. This was not just an expression of wartime nationalism, for it preceded the war and remained the custom for some time after it. Indeed, the radio programmes and later the television programmes habitually ended each evening with the National Anthem. The cinema programmes followed a set pattern. First there were advertisements followed by a 'trailer', that is brief excerpts of films shortly to be screened. Then there was the 'supporting' film, usually a comical one – 'The Three Stooges', Charlie Chaplin, Buster Keeton, Abbot and Costello or 'The Marx Brothers' – or a 'Perils of Pauline', or a Cowboy and Indian Western film, We particularly enjoyed the films of Will Hay, with his 'side kicks', Graham Moffatt and Moore Marriott who were side-splittingly funny whether in a short supporting film or in a longer production such as 'Oh, Mr. Porter', 'The Ghost of St. Michael's', 'Where's that Fire?' and 'Old Bones of the River'. There was also a news film – either Pathé News or Gaumont British News – bringing us up to date in pictorial form with what was going on in the world. And then there would be the main film. The whole show, with an interval – an 'intermission' – when the stage curtains were lowered, lasted about two hours. At the Regal there was at one side of the stage a clock which was ignored by most but was used by others to say to themselves, for example, ' Goodness! How much more of this drivel do I have to put up with?' or 'If I'm going to kiss this girl, I have only twenty minutes left to make a start on it!'

At both the local cinemas the programme for Thursday, Friday and Saturday, with a matinee on the Saturday afternoon, was different from the programme for Monday, Tuesday and Wednesday with a matinee on the Wednesday afternoon. Additionally, there were two viewings or sittings on some evenings. This was a surprisingly full provision of a dozen performances a week at each cinema – and I may be under-estimating the number. There was no cinema on Sundays until the Second World War. When we were small – perhaps Dennis was 4 or 5 and I was 6 or 7 – the two of us would climb into my mother's bed first thing on Sunday morning and, while our father was downstairs lighting the fire and reading 'Reynold's News', tell mother all about the films we had seen the previous afternoon, often in great detail! She always feigned great interest – she was a very patient person. I suppose it could be argued that the reason my parents did not go to the cinema was that Mother was regularly told all about the films by her sons! Today I can't remember the details, particularly the ending, of a film I have seen on television only an hour or so earlier! Many years later, in 1980, when I was a member of the ceasefire and election commissions in Rhodesia-Zimbabwe and had to wear distinctive headgear – a bright red band round my bush hat – so that I would not too readily be shot at by one side or the other – I remember thinking how much easier it was in our Western film days when you could always tell the 'goodies' from the 'badies' by the colour of their hats and their horses – good, white; bad, black – though even they got shot at by mistake occasionally, and who could decide in Rhodesia-Zimbabwe if the whites or the blacks were 'goodies' – or 'badies'?

Many of the names of the cowboys in the Western films remain clear in my memory. Many of them were handsome men, others more rugged and some were singers as well: Gene Autry, Hopalong Cassidy, Tom Mix, Roy Rogers, John Wayne, Buck Jones, Tim McCoy, William Boyd, Harry Carie, Gary Cooper and Randolph Scott. Just as important and often more amusing were our favourite 'side kicks' to the main stars. These men were usually older, were often toothless, had funnier faces, were generally scruffy, were bearded or badly shaven, but were indispensible assistants to the more flashily dressed cowboy stars. Those I remember best were Randy Waller, Fuzzy Knight, Gabby Hayes, and a splendid old chap, the greatest of them all, called 'Windy'. There were, too, 'girl cowboys' – stunning beauties who rode horses fantastically well, wore jodhpurs and low-necked check shirts. Like their male counterparts, they always 'got their man', in their case not a 'baddie' but the star himself – and they did it by means other than shooting the poor guy!

On bank holidays we went for a family walk in the country. We walked quite long distances, for I remember on at least one occasion catching a bus back from Toft Monks which must be three or four miles from home. On that occasion I recall thinking how very lucky we were that quite by chance a bus came by at just the right time to take us home. It did not occur to me until very much later that my father had probably looked up the bus schedules in a timetable and had timed our return accordingly. On these walks we were encouraged to look at and collect the leaves and flowers of the various plants which we found in the hedgerows and then look them up in a small 'Observer's' book when we got home. We had a collection of these very good books dealing with flowers, trees, ferns, butterflies, moths, insects, birds, dragonflies, pond life, spiders, etc., but we were often too tired when we got back from our walks to do justice to them.

On sunny summer afternoons from when I was about three or four years old my mother took us to the Common, Dennis in a push chair – which we called a 'trolley' – and the others of us walking. I remember helping Mother to push the trolley from the bottom of Station Road, up the slope to the bridge over the railway line at the railway station and helping to hold it back so that it did not run away downhill on the far side of the bridge, and the gentle walk down the Avenue, stopping to feed the ducks on a little rivulet part way down that lovely tree-lined road to which no vehicles had, or could have had, access. Although it led to the Common, it came from nowhere and must have been created in connection with building the railway in the mid 1800s. Just inside the cast-iron gates separating the Avenue from the Common there was an enclosed children's playground with swings and a see-saw on which we enjoyed playing. When Father left work he joined us for a picnic tea on the grass. A little later, we walked home, sometimes through the town, as we had come, and sometimes along Common Lane and Grove Road. They were happy outings.

Most of our visits to the Common were confined to the children's playground area, but occasionally we would walk further into the Common – across to Boney's Island – to us a mysterious place, a woodland island, surrounded by a shallow depression, on the highest, though not noticeably so, part of the Common, so named because of the huge bonfire which was lit there in 1814 to celebrate the defeat of Napoleon and the return of peace after the Napoleonic wars. And further over, to the east, Father pointed out the 'butts', a disused firing range, with its man-made hill of sand where the targets had been used, and the shallow trench-like firing positions facing it at intervals of 100, 200 and 500 yards. On the way over to the butts there were harebells to see and admire – tiny, delicate, pale blue bells growing close to the ground. I do not recall seeing them anywhere else.

As children we were regularly taken to church by our parents. My father had been brought up as a Baptist but had not been baptized. Neither of these facts seemed at all important to us, for he invariably accompanied us to church when we went as a family. It was inconceivable that he would not do so. It was a matter of course. A little later on it seemed a mild regret that he did not take communion with us. I think he did seriously consider being baptized and confirmed, but he never was. I think, too, my mother would have been pleased if he had, though it was not an issue in the family.

When we attended church as a family we did so at the parish church of Saint Michael each Sunday morning for matins – known as 'morning service'. For many years we sat in the same pew, in the right hand aisle, half way forward – or back – and I remember the place because it was by a memorial tablet to Lieutenant-Colonel Cuthbert Caruthers Phillips of whom I knew nothing except that his memorial tablet helped me find our usual pew in church. When we were quite small we were encouraged to keep quiet during the sermon by being given blank paper and crayons with which, crouched down below the level of the pew, we drew pictures, which were more likely to be of characters we had seen at the cinema the previous day than of religious characters. We were also induced to keep quiet by my mother separating Dennis and me by sitting between us! The girls did not need to be separated and my father always sat next to my mother with my sisters next to him. When, as occasionally happened, the bishop preached at the parish church my mother would suggest in advance that when we saw him at matins we should look out for special features of his garb, particularly the red bands holding the pleated cuffs of his surplice, his large pectoral cross, his episcopal ring and his ornate shepherd's crook. This ensured that we paid close attention to what was going on in church that morning, and we also learned new words such as episcopal and pectoral. I do not recall His Grace wearing a mitre, which was a pity – we would have liked that and would have learned another word.

I enjoyed the singing, and the choir of boys, men and women – but not girls so far as I recall – seemed to be a very much more powerful part of the singing than it does in many churches nowadays. They really sang! On a recent visit to the church I was told that St. Michael's now has no choir and it is difficult to gather even a few singers together to form a small choir for special occasions. Of the clergy I remember Rev. Harold Birch who had a stutter when he sang – and sometimes when he talked – and seemed to have constant difficulty in swallowing between his words I recall, too, Rev. Harper, a curate, and particularly the occasion when, as he passed us, walking up the aisle for the recessional hymn, there was, to me, an appalling smell, and for very many years I secretly blamed him for having broken wind in public – and in the Lord's House to boot! I recall confiding in my mother this accusation. It is only in recent years that I have realized that if indeed there was a breaking of wind it might have been by a nearby member of the congregation rather than by the curate himself. There was also the Rev. Miller, a curate, who on the occasion of visiting us at our house was told by my mother of my apparent interest in the church. This she deduced from the fact that I – now to my embarrassment – dressed in one of my sisters' black skirts as a cassock and a white vest as a surplice, and arrange for myself, in the front room, a small altar at which I used to officiate, cleric-like. I am not sure whether this worried my parents but I know it would have worried me as a parent. I guess I must have been quite small – I hope! Anyway, the Rev. Miller suggested that I join a church choir. This I did and joined the Ingate Church choir at I think the age of seven. Each Sunday evening, just before leaving the house to go to church, my father dressed my hair with a dollop of Brylcreem to 'spruce' me up, and then at the last moment ceremoniously gave me a pinch of the budgerigar's bird seed to eat, and told me that it would help me sing like a canary! Similarly at the last moment before we ran off to Sunday School at the Ingate church on Sunday afternoons we would belatedly remember that we had been asked to bring a 'text' to the school and, having forgotten it, we asked Father for one. Invariably, week after week, he would say, 'Love one another', and off we would happily run. As an aside, it has always interested me the way in which Church of England clerics traditionally introduce hymns by repeating the number in Hymns Ancient and Modern (which were printed in very large numbers at the Caxton Press), for example: 'Hymn 234, the two hundred and thirty fourth hymn', followed by the opening line. I suppose this gave the congregation an extra moment or so to fumble through the pages and find the right hymn. Then the organist played the first line or so as an introduction and as a reminder to the congregation of the tune, and this gave yet a few more moments in which to fumble – and surreptitiously glance sideways to see if their neighbour had found the right place!

I cannot remember when it was, except that I was quite small at the time, when an evangelical, revivalist, week of ardent exhortation, joyous hymn singing, and stepping up to the platform took place in a large marquee on St. Anne's meadow. We attended one evening or maybe two when the marquee was full of folk praying aloud and singing enthusiastically. I vaguely recall Mother holding the sleeve of my jacket to restrain me from going up to the platform with others, confessing my sins and being 'saved'.

A year or so after I joined the Ingate choir I was invited to be 'auditioned' by the organist and choirmaster, Mr. W Storeton-West, at the parish church at one of their twice or thrice weekly choir practices. I recall with fear even today Mr. W Storeton-West as an elderly, shortish man with an off-white loose surplice and an orange-yellow stained moustache, dyed by years of cigarette smoking. This audition was well before the war because Mr. W Storeton-West retired from being the organist early in 1940. I recall the utter loss, embarrassment and terror at being presented with a hymn book of music and told to sing a couple of verses by myself. Not an unreasonable request under the circumstances, save that I could not read music – I still can't – and I had no idea of what to do. If I had known which hymn it was, I could possibly have had a go at it but as it was I was clearly taken to be an unprincipled, impudent and incompetent impostor, an irresponsible and irreligious scoundrel attending under false pretences and wasting the choir master's time. All this in God's house. I am not sure whether or not I was asked to leave, but I have the feeling I was bawled out. In any case, I fled and had nightmares for days afterwards being pursued by an organist with grubby surplice flowing behind him, waving sheets of music at me, hissing nicotine stained venom at me and threatening me with eternal damnation. I was terror-struck and I do not recall ever being so utterly lost and not knowing any way out since then. A number of my infrequent but recurring dreams over the years and into adult life have contained an element of being completely out of my depth, utterly unprepared for, and totally unable to get out of, an important public occasion, like conducting the Royal Philharmonic at Wigmore Hall, or playing Dvorak's cello concerto at the Royal Albert Hall, or giving a public lecture on Himalayan mountaineering at the Royal Geographical Society, or opening the batting for England at the Oval. A mixture of delusions of grandeur, imminent doom and incomparable terror. Another dream-cum-nightmare has been being in a large city, confident that I knew my way back, taking the turning I thought was the correct one only to find that I had never seen the place before, and the more I tried to retrace my steps the more unfamiliar the surroundings became and the more I was lost. In both these types of dream, mercifully, I awake just before being led to the gallows or going insane with confusion and despair. Whether it was as a result of the terrorizing audition at the parish church I do not know. Mercifully, Mr. W Storeton-West did not appear in any of these dreams, though I know he was watching from behind a nearby curtain!

I suppose at the most there were fifteen members of the Ingate choir, all boy sopranos, but whilst there were no girl or men singers in the choir, the Misses Watson were staunch supporters and reinforced our singing from a pew behind the choir, one of them playing the harmonium. I recall them making the pleated and starched white linen collar ruffs which we wore as an innovation in the choir – Staunch support to the singing, and to the Ingate church generally, also came from Mr. and Mrs. Honeywood who lived in London Road. They were a particularly well dressed couple and he was quite 'dashing' in an Errol Flynn sort of way – certainly 'the ladies of the church' seemed to flutter round him. He was the cashier at Read, Owles and Ashford, the auctioneers, and just a week or so before war was declared, on August Bank Holiday, he took his wife and daughter, Mary, to Great Yarmouth for a day on the beach. One of the national daily newspapers was running a competition to boost its sales in which, if a member of the public was carrying a current copy of the newspaper and correctly identified and challenged a Mr. Lobby Lud in the street he would receive a prize of £10. Mr. Honeywood did this and, since the previous week's prize had not been claimed, he won an extra £10. He was the only person I ever heard of who won the prize, though many made the attempt.

I enjoyed singing at Ingate – there was no music in our hymn books to read and the organist was the gentle Miss Watson and not the frightening Mr. W Storeton-West! We had a choir practice every week when we rehearsed the hymns, the psalms and occasionally an anthem in which I was from time to time asked to sing a solo. The notation in the psalm book interested me with its oblique marks between which one must neither take a breath nor pause no matter how breathless one became or how quickly one gabbled the words between them. An oblique mark is known in our modern computer times as a 'forward slash' – in my youth the term 'forward slash' would have meant something quite different. The Misses Watson, rather than the curate, took these practices. It was the curate who officiated at Ingate, and very rarely the rector. There was a hierarchy in the choir: one rose through long service, rather than ability, from choir boy to book boy to head choir boy. In the fullness of time I was fortunate to rise to this last dizzy height. The book boy's task was to set out the psalm and prayer books in the choir stalls and make sure they were all ready before we entered in procession from the vestry for the first hymn. The churchwarden at Ingate was Mr. Herbert Watson, brother of the Misses

Watson, a kind man who worked, as did most men employed in Beccles, at the Clowes Caxton printing works. Of the curates at Ingate I recall only two: the Rev. Charles Hulbert and the Rev. William Richard, 'Dickie', Barnes. Hulbert was noticeably under the influence of his wife who was very ambitious for her husband and who clearly, and probably correctly, believed herself to be a much better curate than he was. She was sufficiently keen on him looking well groomed in the pulpit that she obliged him to wear a hair grip to keep his hair out of his eyes, something no other man would think of putting up with at the time. After a year or so at Beccles, the Hulberts moved on to Halesworth where, no doubt to his wife's great satisfaction, he became the rector. A decade later, when I was an undergraduate at Birmingham, I went to a lunchtime organ recital in the City Hall given by Dr. George Thalben Ball, a well known pianist and organist, and choir master and organist at the Temple Church in London. In speaking to him after the recital, I was asked where I came from, and when I told him Beccles he said, with a twinkle beneath his bushy eyebrows, 'Ah. That's near Halesworth where I play from time to time and where Mrs. Hulbert is the Rector!' I recall an occasion – I think it must have been at a choir practice for the patronal festival – at the parish church, when Mrs. Hulbert was rehearsing the joint Ingate-Ravensmere-St. Michael's choir. She was keen that part of one of the hymns or anthems should be hummed rather than sung – quite a good idea which, as Puccini shows in 'Madame Butterfly', can be very effective, indeed moving. However, she had the utmost difficulty with Mr. Sammy White, a septuagenarian or maybe even an octogenarian, who had spent all his adult life as a chorister in the parish church choir. Mr. White purported to have no idea what the good woman was talking about and insisted that he just did not know how to, nor was he physically able to, hum. 'Hum? Hum? I can't hum! I don't know how to hum!' Mrs. Hulbert failed – a rare occurrence!

During the early part of the war, when the Ellough airfield was being built, four Welshmen who were engaged on the construction came regularly for several weeks to Evensong at Ingate and they asked if we could sing the hymn 'Guide me O thou Great Redeemer' to the tune 'Cwm Rhondda'. They sang so lustily, melodiously and joyfully – bellowing the 'Bread of Heaven' piece and repeating the lines – that we sang it again the following Sunday, and the next Sunday, and the next for several weeks until they left the area. It was great singing which we all, Welshmen, choir and congregation enjoyed heartily. Living in Cardiff in recent years, we have heard that hymn sung many times and at many different functions, and I rarely hear it without wondering what happened to the four Welshmen who sang with us at Ingate seventy years ago.

Despite my worrying experience at the Parish Church audition at the hands of Mr. W Storeton-West, I enjoy church and organ music. My father would

163

read in the Parish Magazine about any anthems to be sung or a special piece of music to be played at matins, and he encouraged us to enjoy them. Father sang the bass part of each hymn and this seemed to come naturally to him. Mother, who sang in choirs – though not church choirs – in London before she was married, had a soft soprano voice. I guess we four children all sang soprano. At the end of the services, we sat still in the pew for a few minutes while most others went out, and we listened to at least part of the organ music being played as the congregation departed. It is a habit which I follow even today, for it has often struck me how, when each Sunday morning throughout the length and breadth of Britain, beautiful music is played in wonderfully attractive churches, on magnificent organs by skilled and dedicated organist musicians, and what does the congregation do? Walk out!

More important, to me, than earlier curates was the Rev. Barnes, a young unmarried cleric who, when the Rev. Hulbert moved on to Halesworth, took over the Ingate Mission Church in June 1941 immediately after being ordained. He took me under his wing in a way which to later generations might have appeared dubious but which at the time was seen – and now is still seen – to be simple, though unusual, kindness and thoughtfulness. He took me to places that I would otherwise not have visited and, in a way, introduced me to sections of society of which I would otherwise have had no experience. He took me to a garden party at Staithe House down Northgate owned by Dr. Wood-Hill's family, where we had tea by the river and swung from a rope tied to the branch of a tree leaning over the water. He took me to Cambridge for the day, showed me round, visited his old college, Downing, and the huge university library. He took me to plays at the Norwich theatre, to lunch before the show and to tea at the Bell Hotel afterwards. At lunch I recall him eating several bread rolls with, or before, the soup – there were limitations on the amount of food available during the war but one could eat as many bread rolls as one wished. At tea the cast of 'Worm's Eye View', which we had just seen, were staying there, also having tea, and Ronald Shiner and others of the cast signed my copy of the programme. When eventually my voice broke and I had to leave the choir, the Rev. Barnes and Mr. Watson gave me a small prayer book on the fly leaf of which they thanked me for my loyal service, as they saw it, to Ingate: this was in 1944. The Rev. Barnes, with the Misses Watson, who seemed to flutter around him, put on a play at Ingate in the church, in which I played the part of the archangel Gabriel, dressed – embarrassingly now – simply in a white and gold pleated Grecian skirt, and had, among few other words, to say 'Jesus of Nazareth' which I feared would come out as 'Nesus of Jazareth' – I don't think it did! After I left the choir I became a sidesman, seeing people to their pews and taking and counting the collection, for a few years. Dickie Barnes left Beccles for Halifax in June 1945. My last memory of him was towards the end of the war when it was decided that the sand bags round the small observation post on the top of the parish church tower should be removed. His solution was pragmatic – to have them chucked off the top of the tower, me doing the chucking and he making sure a hundred feet below that no members of the public got in the way of the descending bags. Dangerous, but how else to do it?

I have mentioned that it was the Curate rather than the Rector who took the services – always the evening service – at Ingate. But there was also a number of lay preachers who took the service when the Curate could not do so. I remember these lay preachers because in one way or another they all seemed to me to be eccentric. There was Mr. Johnson Hindes, who was an active local politician involved in Town Council affairs. On reflection, I think 'active' is too strong a word, for he was elderly and slow of movement and possibly of wit. We did not like him, and we were sorely tempted to dodge going to church on the evenings when we knew he was to take the service. The problem was that we usually did not know in advance who was to take the service in the absence of the Curate, and by the time he entered the vestry it was too late for us to do a bunk as we would have called it then. Today I think young people would call him 'boring' though that is a word I gravely dislike and one which we used very much less frequently than it is used today, largely because when we found ourselves at a loose end or uninterested in what was going on we quickly found other things to do and did not rely so heavily on other people to entertain us. Then there was Mr. George Odam, the headmaster of the Area School. He was quite entertaining but occasionally ferocious in his delivery. I recall an evening when, just before we entered the church singing the processional hymn, he asked if he could borrow my watch because he had forgotten his and did not want to give too long a sermon. It was the watch which I had won in the Caxton races several years earlier and I was very happy to help him restrict the length of his sermon. When he was some way into his address, but not yet reaching the peroration, he took out my watch from his pocket beneath his surplice, looked intently at it, shook it vigorously, and loudly pronounced, 'This watch has stopped, Boy!' It had not previously stopped and it did not stop again for several years after that. I guess he was looking for an excuse to bring his sermon to an end – the Lord works in mysterious ways His wonders to perform. Then there was Mr. Fowler, a local coal merchant – called by himself a coal and coke factor – who seemed to enjoy, relish and delight in the sermons which he delivered. I recall one such sermon, a long-winded, convoluted and rambling, but quite interesting, disquisition, in which, after he had got a considerable way into it, he suddenly stopped, looked puzzled and said words to the effect: 'Please forgive me. What I have been saying so far, I said was about Saint Paul. I now realize that I should have said it was about St. Peter. I am sorry about this. I will start again.' And so he did – from the beginning!

But the visiting preacher I most vividly and joyously remember was a man who had worked as a missionary in one of the Middle East countries. He spoke in fascinating detail about life in the desert, the highlight of which came when he told us about the practical difficulties of trying to drink condensed milk from a tin in the middle of a sand storm. His seriously delivered demonstration was unforgettable. Having struggled to open the imaginary tin with a recalcitrant imaginary tin opener, he stepped aside from the lectern and crouched in front of the altar, protecting himself from the howling, grit-swirling gale. With his trembling left hand he pulled his surplice part way over his bowed head to shield his grimacing face; then, cupping his writhing right hand, he wrestled to get the imaginary tin of condensed milk to his quivering lips, all the while hissing and snorting, sucking and puffing, groaning and blowing in a most convincing representation of a blistering sand storm. It was magical! Those to whom he ministered in the Middle East were fortunate to have him! A great man who I hope gained as much satisfaction from his life and vocation as a missionary as he gave lasting pleasure to at least one young choir boy.

He was the only missionary I met who worked in the Middle East. Most of the other missionaries we heard of – but did not meet – worked in Africa and we learned much about David Livingstone at Sunday School, but the missionaries I remember visiting Beccles when I was young came from China. I recall one wizened lady missionary, recently returned from China, who gave a lantern slide show in the Rectory Hall. I remember little of the evening except that she showed us some tiny shoes which the upper class Chinese women wore to cover their feet which had been tightly bound since birth to keep them small. She also showed us some beautiful, long silver sheaths which were used to protect the finger nails of high class Chinese who, for reasons which I have forgotten, did not cut them.

I was confirmed at the parish church when I was, I guess, about thirteen years old. The confirmation classes were conducted by the Rev. Barnes and for reasons which I do not recall took place at the home of Mr. Odam – maybe he lodged with the Odam family. I was the only one taking those classes though more young people were confirmed at the time – probably from neighbouring parishes – otherwise it would hardly have been worth the bishop's time to visit Beccles for a confirmation. I remember nothing of the instructions, save that I should recognize the point at which the collection was to be taken by the words, 'Let your light so shine before men that they may see your good works and glorify your Father who is in heaven.' Lest I should forget this I was advised to think of the light shining on the bright new three penny piece which I had in my pocket ready to place in the collection bag. Pavlovian-like I still reach for my pocket whenever I hear the words 'Let your light so shine …' My mother told me subsequently that she was nervous at the confirmation service that I would duck out of the commitment and disappear through the side door of the Lady Chapel. I do not think I was in fact in any doubt about being confirmed, though I do remember going to the cinema that evening with a young lady known as 'Bubbles' and wondering if this was quite the right thing to do so soon after being confirmed. Between us we decided it would be OK but, just in case, we agreed for that evening not to use the double seats on the back row.

Perhaps I should say a little more at this point about Bubbles. Her proper name was Barbara Olive Brown, and for a very short period these initials formed her nickname, 'Bobby', but soon everyone was calling her Bubbles – which fitted her personality. She was a few months younger than me and we were in the same class at the Leman School. She was dark-haired and strikingly good looking, very popular, athletic, good at games, an excellent swimmer, and an accomplished leading member of the local dancing school. We had a close, though not exclusive, friendship for the whole of our time at the Leman School, even after she left at the end of the fifth form and became a hairdresser and I stayed on until the end of the sixth form. It was not really a teenage romance but we enjoyed each other's company and liked being together. She was a 'fun girl'. We saw lots of each other, mainly out of school hours, until I left Beccles and she married and had a family – her two daughters were also strikingly good looking and excellent swimmers. Sadly, she died of a cerebral haemorrhage when she was in her mid-fifties – by that time I had not seen her for many years. Just one anecdote. I ran my first cross country race in the spring term of our second year at the Leman School, and there were two clandestine attempts in advance to influence its outcome, one sordid, dishonourable and unsuccessful, the other, more highly motivated, charming and successful. Just before the race one of the boys asked me to let him win and in exchange he said he would give me, without commitment, some chewing gum as a down payment and then fourpence after the race. I don't think I accepted the chewing gum but I know I did not agree to let him win the race because although I could, if I wished, have agreed to let him beat me, I could not commit others to let him beat them – unless he bribed us all, which at a groat a time with up to fifty runners would have been expensive. Much more importantly, also just before that first race Bubbles handed me a small, neatly folded, handkerchief in which were a photograph of herself and a tiny silver charm. She asked me to carry the handkerchief, photograph and charm with me on the race as good luck tokens. She smiled, discreetly blew me a kiss, and disappeared with her friends. I took the handkerchief and its contents with me. – and won the race, breaking the record. I carried it in every annual cross country race for the remainder of my seven years at the school, won every time and broke the record three times. Bubbles was delighted. She was a remarkable young lady.

To return to the question of church-going – for some weeks when we were in our mid-teens, David and I fairly regularly attended the Spiritualist church in Beccles on Sunday evenings. My recollection, though I may be mistaken, is that this was at David's instigation and I have often wondered what his father, for many years a churchwarden and a leading chorister at the parish church, thought of it. My mother was mildly amused and my father thought that, whilst there might be some validity in Spiritualism, it was unwise to treat it as a religion. The church still exists though I am not sure whether it has functioned uninterruptedly since our day, and it now meets in the St. John's Ambulance Hall in Blyburgate. When we attended, the church was run by a Mr. and Mrs. Payne who lived next to the Institute, fairly close to David's home. The meetings were held in a room in a house on the south side of the Old Market and were invariably opened by Mr. Payne with the words, 'Good evening, friends, and a hearty welcome to you all.' We went partly out of curiosity and partly as a lark. I do not remember if there were prayers and hymns – I expect there were – but we were more interested in the séance which was held every week. The mediums – why not 'media', I wonder – were almost without exception women in their middle years, often sporting a fur wrap or stole, although there was an occasional male medium. Some were 'billed' as being of national reputation and standing. I recall only two specific things about these séances. The first is that one evening the medium said she was 'drawn to a young man on the back row' – which is where David and I usually sat. It turned out that the message 'coming through' was for me and it was to the effect that whoever the anonymous caller was they knew I was having trouble with a book I was reading – one with a brown paper cover, as nearly all my school books were – but that I should not worry; all would be well, dear. I was indeed having some difficulty with a brown paper covered book which was part of the French course I was taking, and indeed all was well at least in the sense that I passed the examinations in French. The other memory concerned two local ladies, both I suspect widows, one of whom received a message from the other side which greatly excited her. The medium asked if she had been brought up in the country – yes, she had. Had she lived in a cottage? Yes, she had. The medium gradually took her through a description of her family home, the lady, somewhat hard of hearing as it turned out, agreeing with each point as she went along. Were there flowers in the garden, she was asked. Yes there were. 'It's a little hazy and the picture is fading – hold on, dear, I'm still listening – but were some of them sweet peas?' 'Yes', came the prompt and excited reply, 'we did have pigs in the garden', whereupon her exasperated companion nudged her and loudly said. 'Sweet peas, you fool!'

My parents encouraged us to join the Young People's Union, a club held once a week in the evening at the Rectory Room, under church auspices. There was a prayer at the beginning and at the end of each evening's activities and most of the time was devoted to handiwork of some sort or another: needle work for the girls and fret-work for the boys of which making jig saw puzzles was a popular example. This was another and valuable way in which we met young people – not necessarily church-goers – from other local schools whom we might not otherwise have met. I recall Edgar Brown, who lived next door to my aunt in Denmark Road, as one of the leaders who taught us fret work.

Muriel and Cynthia went to Brownies and Guides, Muriel becoming a Lieutenant, but I – and I think Dennis – did not go to Cubs and Scouts. I'm not sure why. Instead, Dennis may have joined the Boys' Brigade, and I, while at the Area School, joined the St. John's Ambulance Brigade. This was at the beginning of the war, in 1939 or 1940. I recall how thoroughly we were taught to make and tie bandages on the most difficult parts of the body, for example the chin and the shoulder blades; to make, fold and apply slings; to make and attach splints to broken bones; to recognize and treat accordingly the different types of bone fractures; to stop bleeding by the use of pressure points and tourniquets; and to scrape limewash off ceilings to give to people to swallow as an antidote to ingested poisons. What one does nowadays when ceilings are no longer limewashed, I do not know. We learned the bones of the body – all 206 of them – and their functions, and the vascular system, in a way that has kept them familiar in my mind ever since, though I do sometimes get metacarpals and metatarsals muddled! I was fascinated, and a little frightened, to be shown – and then to practice – how to remove a 'foreign body' from beneath the upper eyelid, by rolling it up and backwards over a match stick. An important aspect of the St. John's Ambulance Brigade, though one of which we did not notice the significance at the time, was that it included both girls and boys, working and learning together – unlike the single sex Cubs and Scouts, Brownies and Guides, Boys' Brigade and Girls' Brigade, the Air Training Corps and the Army Cadet Force. We went on a number of simulated exercises, including a large one at Lowestoft involving all the emergency services, where the ground was strewn with mock corpses and pretending casualties covered in red ink 'blood', wailing, moaning, cursing the enemy, groaning and telling us just how many bones of their body were broken, smashed and mangled, in a most realistic way. There were 'umpires' to judge how well or badly we had done. I have often thought how much more valuable, indeed essential, tuition in first aid is than some of the matters taught at school then and now. Our tutors were not trained teachers or professional medics but extraordinary 'ordinary' people from a variety of occupations who were enthusiastic, thorough and keen to hand their knowledge and skill to others, especially young people. Our meetings were held in a hall in Blyburgate and I recall the names of Mr. Crisp and Mr. Piper, though there were others, including women, all of whom gave up their spare time not simply to practice first aid when needed but also to teach others. They added greatly to my education and personal development. I am grateful to them.

Later, both Dennis and I joined the Air Training Corps, which met once a week in the evening at the Leman School. We learned how to drill, use the morse code, recognize different aeroplanes and the various parts of them and the principles of how an aeroplane flies and is steered. More of the ATC shortly.

There was also a sports side to the Air Training Corps. We played soccer and cricket against the Army Cadet Force and competed in cross country races with them. A good deal of my own athletics was with the ATC, and I ran in cross country races at Kettering and Purley, and in flat meetings at the University ground, Fenners, in Cambridge and the White City in London. In nearly all of these events away from home I was outclassed by much better or better trained athletes, and looking back on them I think I was somewhat overawed by them – a country boy in a large city. My father arranged for me to have a chat with Mr. Lindsey Tilney, a local athlete with an outstanding record as a sprinter. He was very helpful in talking to me about what I might expect at Fenners and the White City. He also had the great good fortune to marry Mary Mercer – of whom more later. At Fenners one ran clockwise rather than anticlockwise, on a black cinder track instead of the grass to which I had been exclusively accustomed, and a third of a mile per lap, instead of a quarter. At the White City, things were even more daunting. The place was huge, one was called from the changing rooms, through a tunnel, to re-appear above ground by the side of the track which was made of red marl. It was built for the 1908 Summer Olympic Games and was later used for the British Empire Games in 1934. Father, who came down to London to see the running, said that when the starting pistol was fired, I jumped backwards!

Until then I had run in plimsolls which were usually fine for running on grass, but now, so I was told, they would not do for running on cinder or marl tracks. But where did one buy spiked running shoes, even if one could afford them, especially during and shortly after the war? Certainly no shop in Beccles or nearby would have dreamed of stocking spiked shoes. Through my father, we acquired a pair of heel-less, soft leather cycling shoes from Stanley Keable, who was a keen cyclist and lived next door to us. These, so far as we could judge, looked very much like spiked running shoes, except that they had no spikes! We got some broad headed clout nails, used for fixing roofing felt on sheds, and Father somehow got three holes drilled through the head of a dozen of the nails. We then tacked them on to the soles of the cycling shoes to act as spikes. Disappointingly, but not surprisingly, the tacks did not hold, the nails bent almost immediately, and the spikes fell off. Next I tried to find some real spikes to put on the shoes. I tried various places and lastly went to a second-hand, bric à brac shop at the Old Market end of Northgate, run by a grumpy, scruffy and rather fearsome old man. When I asked if by any chance he had any spikes for running shoes, he virtually went berserk, waved his arms and shouted at me, saying that I was a snob, because only snobs wore spiked running shoes. He advanced menacingly towards me and ordered me out of his shop immediately and, bewildered and scared, I fled his premises. I am still mystified by this outburst. He was, to me, a latter-day W Storeton-West who threatened to throw bric à brac at my head in my dreams! Somehow, we did indeed obtain some spikes – solid steel broad headed spikes – though I can not remember from where. These we took to Mr. Club, the cobbler, and he pushed them through a thin leather sole and then attached the new sole, spikes and all, to the old sole of Stanley Keable's cycling shoes. Apart now from being very much heavier than they ought to have been, these were the shoes I used for track athletics thereafter. After the war one or two boys at school wore proper spiked shoes, mainly for sprint races but I retained my home-made spiked shoes. I wonder what happened to them.

I do not remember much about the cross country race at Purley, save that I have a visual impression of snow covered downs with lots of colourfully dressed athletes a long way in front of me toiling up the slopes. Of the Kettering cross country race, I recall two things. First, the weather was bad during the week preceding the race and there was grave doubt about whether the race would be held because of the heavy falls of snow, and whether, if it was, I would wish to go. I was desperately anxious to go and I recall the meeting at the Leman School one evening a few days before the race, at which Johnston Brown, maths master and Flight Lieutenant of the ATC, tentatively asking me if I felt able to go. When, promptly, I said 'Yes', he thumped me on the back and shouted 'Stout fellow! Stout fellow!' He had no idea how very keen I was to go, and he seemed to treat my acceptance as an act of great courage, loyalty and self-sacrifice and as a personal favour to himself. The other thing I remember is the home at which I stayed overnight at Kettering. The family of one of the local ATC cadets looked after me extremely well, were kind and even warmed my pyjamas in the oven! Of the race itself I remember nothing.

Many families in Beccles, as elsewhere, kept a domestic pet. Among our pets at home was a brown dog of no great pedigree, known as 'Rip' – he the chicken-chaser and provider of our out-of-season chicken dinner which I mentioned earlier. I must have written about him to an aunt because it became quite a saying in the family, 'Rip, the dog, has a kennel.' Several families owned a dog when I was small – rarely more than one at a time – which was kept, like most other family dogs, in a kennel outside the house and chained. Dogs were allowed in the house but not overnight or when there was no one at home. To some extent they were looked upon as guard dogs. The Robinsons and the Keables, our next door neighbours, had dogs and I recall that Mr. George also had a dog, because when I was quite small I was running down the road past his house when his dog leapt over the gate and knocked me down

– frightened but unhurt. I am not sure where one acquired dogs but none of them was of any recognizable breed or outstanding parentage.

We also occasionally had goldfish which were acquired by taking rags and old woollens to a rag and bone man who from time to time came to the town and plied his dubious trade near the school. The goldfish never survived long but I do not think I was too upset when they died and were found floating upside-down in the jar – we came to expect it. I always thought I was cheated by this rag and bone man and his likes, and he never gave me more than one fish no matter how much cloth I handed him. I felt the same – in this case disappointed rather than cheated – with the price received for the rabbits which on a few occasions I sold at the Friday stock auctions in the town. We had a number of rabbits and when they were little I liked carrying them inside the front of my shirt where they gave a nice cuddly warm feeling. They used to scratch as well, and I remember my father being none too pleased – or appearing displeased – when they ate the aster flowers in the front garden. Three or four of these were wild rabbits which I found in a hole at Shadingfield when they were very tiny. One of these – my favourite – was named Felix. They were sweet and I think survived for quite some time. Another of them died, and I long attributed its demise to Cynthia having dropped it, though she claimed – I guess correctly – that the one she dropped was not the one that died. Incidentally, Shadingfield was four miles from Beccles and I went with friends of my own age, one of whom, Derek Day, had a grandmother living at Shadingfield. We must have been under ten years of age and we were unaccompanied by adults, which shows both how far we walked – eight miles there and back – and how 'un-dangerous' being out by ourselves without grown-ups was considered to be. We – I – also had two very different kinds of 'birds' as pets: a budgerigar and a bat.

The budgerigar's acquisition astonished me at the time and for many years thereafter. I very much wanted a budgerigar as a pet, and one day I discovered one trapped between the two panes of glass in the bedroom sash window. I believed this was a direct answer to the prayers I had been making for a budgerigar. I guess it had escaped from its owner and got caught between the panes of our window. I was quite small at the time and do not recall the bird's fate. The family had a number of budgerigars in succession after that – my mother in particular liked them.

The bat's acquisition was equally surprising although not the result of prayer. I found this tiny, jet-black, furry, velvety little creature in the space between an outside door and the door frame. It could easily have been squashed if the door had been shut before I found it. I think the rest of the family was not anywhere nearly as fond of the baby bat as I was. I called it 'Bimbo' and kept it in a blue wooden box, with leather hinges – made, though not for the purpose, by my grandfather Baker – and have no recollection of how it was fed – I think with milk. As with the budgerigar, I do not recall how long I kept it or what its eventual fate was.

Although much of our 'entertainment' took place outside the home – school, church, playing in the road with friends – an important part also took place within the home: playing with board games such as Snakes and Ladders and, later, Monopoly, or with toys such as Meccano and bagatelle, or with small lead model animals or soldiers, or with card games such as 'Sevens' and 'Muggins'. But a particular influence on us was the radio. From as far back as I remember as a small child we had a radio – a 'wireless set' – which, to start with, was powered by an acid battery (charged at a garage-cycle repairers in town) and connected to the radio with a number of red or black terminals which we called 'red men' and 'black men', and outside the house it had a wire sunk into the soil to earth it, and a high wire to act as an aerial. In those days, and indeed until 1971, a licence had to be taken out for every radio set owned, as, too, it did for each dog until 1987. Father was the only one who knew how to make it work. Later we had a more up-to-date radio, powered by mains electricity. In the absence of television, and despite the news and entertainment programmes at the cinema, the radio had an extraordinary influence on us, notwithstanding the fact that there was only one British radio station (though we also listened to Radio Luxembourg for children's programmes) and only one programme provider, the BBC. Broadcasting was from 7.00 a.m. until midnight. It started and finished with the news and ended with the national anthem.

One of the early programmes I remember listening to or hearing about on the radio was the boxing match between Joe Louis and Max Schmeling in 1938. There was great public interest in this match and it seemed that everyone in Britain wanted Louis, the 'Brown Bomber', to win, largely if not entirely because Schmeling was a German and already there was a growing – or renewed – dislike of the Germans and their belligerent activities. I think many people had been a little disappointed when Welshman Tommy Farr, the 'Tonypandy Terror' was beaten by Louis, but Schmeling was different. Whilst in other countries it may have been seen as a racial conflict, to many in Britain it was a nationalistic, anti-German, bout and folk rooted for Joe and were delighted when he won.

Each Sunday evening during the war, at about six o'clock, the national anthems of each of Britain's allies was broadcast and the list got longer as the war went on. We learned the tunes of many national anthems this way. To us, even as children, the broadcast speeches of Winston Churchill were a delight, with his unparalleled use of the English language, his ability to rouse the spirit of patriotism in the British people, and his ridicule of Hitler – 'Mr. Schikelgruber'. Many of us, well over half a century later, can mimic his way of speaking and remember the famous expressions: 'Never before in the field of human conflict ...'; 'Some chicken, some neck'; 'From Settin in the Baltic to Trieste in the

Adriatic, an iron curtain has descended across the continent …'; 'Advance Britannia, Long live the cause of freedom, God save the King'. Incidentally, there was great joy in our part of Beccles when it was announced that Churchill had succeeded Chamberlain as Prime Minister, and the expression 'Good old Winnie' was on all lips. A few years earlier there had been great support and sympathy for King Edward at the time of his abdication.

To return to the radio, the names and some of the details of the various regular programmes remain indelibly printed on our minds. For example, there was 'Monday Night at Eight' which was introduced with the jingle, 'It's Monday Night at Eight O'clock, Oh can't you hear the chimes? They're telling you to take an easy chair, so draw up by the fire side and take out the Radio Times, 'cos Monday Night at Eight is on the air.' And there was Saturday evening's 'In Town Tonight' which, accompanied by 'sounds off', was introduced with the words, 'Once more we stop the mighty roar of London's traffic and, from the great crowds, we bring you some of the interesting people who have come by land, sea and air to be In Town Tonight', followed by Eric Coates's march, 'Knightsbridge'.

Important and memorable, too, were the comedy programmes. Most comics or comedians appeared in pairs – Arthur Askey and Richard Murdoch, Richard Murdock and Kenneth Horne, Murray and Mooney, the Weston Brothers, Naughton and Gold, Flanagan and Allan, Flotsam and Jetsam, Nervo and Knox, Nosmo King and Howard, Elsie and Doris Waters – though there were several single comedians – Tommy Trinder, Jimmy James, Rob Wilton, Stainless Stephen, Gillie Potter, and others. All of these added a good deal of humour and pleasure to our lives, and enabled us to sit down together as a family and enjoy the programmes. Amazingly, there were ventriloquists – on radio! I recall my parents turning off the radio and hurrying us off to bed when Max Miller came on the radio; his was a 'rude' type of humour, I gathered, though it was meaningless to me until I was a little older. I recall, too, listening to two other broadcasts during the war, of which my father did not approve – or pretended not to approve – though they were something of a giggle for my mother. One was 'Lord Haw Haw's fascist, pro-German broadcasts which attempted to undermine the resolve of the British people, but which in fact were the source of much amusement and ridicule, and the other was an anonymous communistic broadcaster who tried to undermine our war effort by attacking 'the bloody bosses'. I picked up the radio frequency of this latter broadcast when by chance I overheard it in Mr. Forster's barber's shop. Both programmes were broadcast in the evening and when my father returned from work – at times he worked until nine or ten at night – we had to switch off the radio quickly before he came in – this listening and the quick turning off was really a game played between us, my mother and my father, played with semi-mock seriousness.

The most memorable of all radio comedy programmes must have been 'Itma', short for 'It's That Man Again', the man being Tommy Handley, who seemed to go on enjoyably for ever and who became a real part of British life during the war. He was 'Minister of Aggravation and Mysteries at the Office of Twerps', and he had a vast collection of personalities with him: the dipsomaniac Colonel Chinstrap, Mrs. Mopp the charlady, Funf the German spy, the Diver, Sir Short Supply, Norman the Doorman, and Sam and Lefty, two gun-shooting gangsters. Two of the boys in our class – John Snowden and Rex Butcher – were named Sam and Lefty after them, though in Rex's case it was partly because he was a left-footed football player. The catch phrases were so numerous that there must be a dictionary of them somewhere. That these programmes and their catch phrases should stay so long and so clearly in the memory, ridiculous and trivial as they may sound today – though no more so than those of modern times – indicates what a great influence they had on us.

But it was not only the radio which played an important part in our family's life, for the gramophone also played its part. We did not have a wind-up gramophone, or indeed any other gramophone, when we were small, and it must have been in the mid to late 1930s that the family acquired its first record player. This was simply a turntable powered by mains electricity and using the radio as a loud speaker. Simple but effective. It made a great difference to our lives and played an important part in our listening to and learning to appreciate and love music. Unlike the radio, on which a good deal of music was also played, we could choose which music we wished to listen to. I recall very clearly the first set of records my father bought to use on the new record player. No doubt my mother played a full part in selecting them, but it always seemed that it was left in Father's hands. These first records included organ music – Bach's great Toccata and Fugue in D minor – a boy soprano, Ernest Lough, singing 'I know that My Redeemer Liveth' and 'Oh for the Wings of a Dove'; a tenor, Heddle Nash, singing Arthur Sullivan's 'The Lost Chord', Tosti's 'Parted', and Alfred Joyce Kilmer's 'Trees'; Strauss waltzes – Vienna Blood and Blue Danube; JS Bach's Choral Prelude, 'Sheep may Safely Graze' and, on the other side, Handel's 'Arrival of the Queen of Sheba'; and Mendelssohn's violin concerto played by Fritz Kriesler. Many years later, the first concert which my future wife and I attended together, included this concerto, played by Campoli. After a few years, I began to add my own records to the family collection, saving up my weekly pocket money of five shillings a week (when I was I guess 15 or 16 years of age) until I could afford a new record at about a pound each – purchased from Morlings music shop in the New Market. That I can remember the composers, the singers, the soloists, the tunes and the words of at least the opening verses of the songs shows just what a profound effect the gramophone had on my appreciation, albeit a layman's appreciation – deep personal enjoyment really – of music.

I have used the expression 'layman's appreciation' for I cannot read music and I have never played an instrument, except for occasionally as a boy playing the 'Jew's harp' and much later mastering a simple tune on the recorder which my children were learning to play. As a child, like my siblings, I was given piano lessons, and serious attempts were made to teach me to play. My two sisters and I were taught by a Mrs. Stimpson in Ballygate, in a dark room of her house. I recall none of the tuition save that she beat the tempo with a hefty wooden knitting needle. This would have been fine had she not also repeatedly corrected my many errors by beating not simply the tempo but more seriously my knuckles with the knitting needle. Whether it was a consequence of this primitive teaching technique, or not, I don't know, but I took a profound dislike to being taught to play and I took the greatest exception to the daily half hour practice sessions – Czerny's exercises – which my mother insisted on. Eventually, disappointed and weary of my appalling tantrums at the keyboard, my mother allowed me to give up the piano lessons. Dennis was sent to a different piano teacher. Nonetheless, I love listening to music, including piano music, and I especially enjoy orchestral music and opera. I am, too, a compulsive conductor, using a slender, non-Stimpson, knitting needle as a baton in my teens, and I find it difficult not to conduct music which I hear on the radio or on the gramophone, though I am able to resist the compulsion in concert halls and at the opera. Similarly, I have strengthened myself against conducting vigorous symphonies when driving a car, though recently I had to be restrained from conducting an imaginary orchestra with a chop stick in a Chinese restaurant!

The part played by school in the development of a liking for music was important. I have already written of the hymns we sang each morning at the Peddars Lane School, and there were also assembly hymns at the Area School, but my clearest memory is of music at the Sir John Leman School. This was not confined to hymns at assembly although these were a regular part of starting each day. Mr. Firth – known as 'Solly' either because he taught the 'tonic sol-fa' or more likely because of the Solway Firth – would often introduce and play on a gramophone pieces of music at assembly, possibly once a week, and I recall particularly Richard Strauss's tone poem, 'Till Eulenspiegel's Merry Pranks', with Solly telling us the story and showing how the music related to the different parts of it, all the while pensively sharpening the thorn gramophone needles he preferred to use. He also taught music in class for an hour or so a week, when he tried to instil in us some of the elements of singing – 'do, ray, me, far, so, la, tee, do', and the tempo, 'ta tay te ta, taffy taffy tar', or so it seemed. Much more important and much longer lasting in its effect was his teaching and encouragement of singing. By no means an inspiring teacher – though rather better at music than at mathematics – he managed to enthuse even the most wayward of us boys such as Dennis Pegram, Ralph Keeler,

Frank Wilkins and myself – I think the girls were easier to encourage – who willingly joined the school choir. I recall us singing 'Hiawatha's Wedding' at a public performance, and the gentle, soft, carefully paced 'Matthew, Mark, Luke and John, Bless the bed that I lie on', at a big competition. Privately the words 'Bless the bed that I lie on' became' 'Hold this horse while I get on', or 'Went to bed with their trousers on', but we did take the singing very seriously, largely because we enjoyed it. Another long-remembered piece of singing was not at school nor at the instigation of or under the guidance of Solly Firth but – extraordinarily – 'Micah' Clarke, the French master. It must have been in the spring of 1948. Micah lived at Kirby Cane and it was either at the Kirby Cane or more likely the Geldeston church, that the anthem, 'In my Father's House are many mansions. If it were not so, I should have told you', was to be sung on Whit Sunday. The choir was a small one of perhaps three ladies and, so far as we could judge, one man – Micah lui-même. For whatever reason he asked Dick Cannon and me to join the choir to sing the anthem. Dick was a rather studious-looking fellow and a great mimic, particularly in his assuming the walking characteristics of members of the staff. We went, cycled, to the church for two or three practices, and then sang at the morning service on Whit Sunday. Dick, singing tenor, and I, singing bass, enjoyed it immensely though neither of us could puzzle out why Micah had asked us and not others. Agreed, he was short of male voices but this could not have been new and there were many others whom he could have asked. He had never spoken to us previously about singing and he never mentioned it again. I'm glad he asked us; it was a happy and enjoyable – unique – occasion. Whitsuntide and 'In my Father's House' never pass without my recalling Geldeston church, Micah and Dick.

The importance and effect of this singing at school and in church is profound, in many ways more profound than any other part of my school education and I suspect of many others. If I take just Hiawatha's Wedding Feast, it is hearing and singing the music which makes me remember the words, not seeing and reading the text. Save for learning them to sing at school I do not think I ever read the words as a poem except for once reading it to my mother-in-law. Yet many passages are as clear in my mind today as they were sixty odd years ago:

You shall hear how Pau-Puk-Keewis, how the handsome Yennadizzi, danced at Hiawatha's wedding. How the gentle Chibiabos, he the sweetest of musicians, sang his songs of love and longing. How Iagoo the great boaster, he the marvellous story-teller, told his tales of strange adventure, that the feast might be more joyous, that the time might pass more gaily and the guests be more contented …….
Onaway, awake beloved, thou the wild flower of the forest, thou the wild bird of the prairie, thou with eyes so soft and fawn-like, if thou only lookest at me, I am happy, I am happy.

Frequently over the years I have awakened my wife in the morning with 'Onaway, awake beloved', and address her as 'thou the wild flower of the forest, thou the wild bird of the prairie.' And if asked by her how I am I not infrequently sing in reply 'I am happy, I am happy.' All this is a gentle joke between us and I accept is, to say the least, 'quaint'. The point I am trying to make is that in at least the case of Hiawatha's Wedding Feast, it is the singing, the sound, which is the source and retentive mechanism of these memories, memories which, unlike so many others, fade far too quickly and disappear into the distance as we look backwards in the rear-view mirror of history. Additionally, these examples of music and singing illustrate, I believe, just how broad, varied and good an education was provided, whether by design or by chance, at the Sir John Leman School at that time.

To return to our home life, I mentioned earlier that Monday lunch was always cold meat and vegetables so as to relieve my mother of cooking a meal on a day devoted to laundry. Many of her days were taken up in hard work but Monday must have been the worst of them. Father would have lit the fire under the kitchen copper before he went to work. Then, having given the children breakfast and got them off to school, she had to strip the sheets off the beds – bottom ones only – and pillow slips ready to be washed. There were no fitted sheets in those days. This linen and much of the clothing was washed by hand with hard washing soap – no detergents then, though there was a flaked soap product called 'Lux' which was used for 'delicates' – then boiled in the copper, with a handful of soda, and periodically pummelled with a wooden stick kept for the purpose. Then they had to be rinsed in cold water into which, for the white items, a squeeze of 'Reckitt's Blue' was put to make them look whiter. Thereafter, the washed items had to be mangled to squeeze out as much water as possible. The mangle was a heavy cast iron affair with large wooden rollers, and the pressure on the rollers was altered by turning a large screw at the top. Items with buttons on them had to be carefully lined up between and at one end of the rollers so that they would not be crushed and broken. Turning the handle on a large wheel at the side of the mangle to send the clothing through the rotating rollers was a heavy task. The tighter the screw the more water was squeezed out but the harder the effort required to turn the handle. The squeezed-out water ran into a large zinc bath under the mangle and had to be emptied. Then the items were taken in a large 'linen basket' down the garden and pegged individually – with 'dolly' pegs, often bought from door-to-door gypsy saleswomen – to the rope 'linen line' suspended from tall poles. The rope was then hauled to the top of the poles – with the heavy washing pegged to it – secured and left there to dry in the wind. There might not be any wind, it might rain, the linen line might – and periodically did – break in too strong a wind, throwing the linen onto the garden so that the whole operation from rinsing onwards had to be repeated – and completed by the time we and my father arrived home for lunch, for which at some time during the morning Mother had at least to peel and cook the potatoes and lay the table. In the meantime she re-made the beds with clean sheets and pillowslips, putting last week's top sheets on the bottom of the bed. When the washing was dry or nearly dry it had to be un-pegged, folded into the basket, taken indoors and ironed, sometimes the following day, with a flatiron – and later an electric iron – before being aired in front of the sitting room fire on a 'clothes horse'. It could then be put away in a warm cupboard ready to be used the following week when the whole operation was repeated. If rain started to fall and threatened to wet the linen drying on the linen line, it was the custom for the first woman noticing the threatening rain to shout loudly to her neighbours to warn them.

My mother was not unusual, for this arduous clothes washing routine was the lot of nearly every housewife, yet I never once heard her – or any of our neighbours – complain, except when the linen line broke, the clothing fell onto the ground and had to be re-washed. It must have been heart-breaking when that happened. Yet one of the nicest photographs in the family collection is a small, unmounted, snap taken in 1926 soon after Muriel was born. It shows my mother hanging out the nappies on the linen line at the back of the house. She had been married a year; she was living in her own newly built house with its inside bath and its lavatory part of the house; she had nice, helpful neighbours; she had recently had her first baby; her husband had a good job; the ten day general strike was just over; the war was fast fading into the past; and she looked so completely contented and happy – and it was wash day! It is a tiny but, to me, a striking and lovely picture.

I have spent some time writing about wash day because of the immense burden it relentlessly placed on almost all mothers and housewives. How times change – mercifully. Perhaps when next we kneel down to put our quick-dry clothes or light weight duvet cover in the shiny white washing machine or to take them out of the fast whirling tumble dryer, we should dwell on our knees a moment longer and remember those who toiled before the coppers, wrestled with the mangles, prayed the linen lines would not break, wielded the heavy flatirons and knew nothing of the ever changing and frequently renamed pink, green, blue or yellow brands of powders, liquids and tablets which, always 'new and improved', increase 'freshness' by 65% – what rot! – and which make life so much easier today.

HOLIDAYS

With two exceptions, we did not go away on holiday. There were holiday periods when school was closed for I think six weeks in the summer and a week or perhaps two at Christmas and Easter. Half term holidays were so short that I had forgotten they existed until I was reminded recently that there was a day off at Peddars Lane and probably the Area School, and two days at the Leman School – quite a contrast with the present day's full week or more.

The 'real' school holiday was in the summer and this was normally spent playing in the road and going for walks with friends locally. There were breaks, too, on Good Friday – always a misnomer it seemed to me – Easter Monday, Whit Monday, the August Bank Holiday, Christmas Day and Boxing Day, when my father was free to join the rest of the family and, apart from the last two holidays mentioned, go with us for long walks in the countryside.

The two exceptions to the generalization that we did not go away on holiday were both the result of particular family circumstances. Without those circumstances I believe we would never have gone away on holiday. The first was when I was about three or four years old. My mother was not well – not ill but just not well after having four children in a fairly short period, having had jaundice and having had all her teeth extracted. I think my father decided, probably on the advice of our doctor, that the family, especially my mother, should 'get away' for a while, enjoy some open air and recuperate. This was done by going on a 'camping' holiday at Gorleston. A lorry was hired, with driver, to take us and our goods from Beccles to near Links Road on the southern outskirts of Gorleston, where we lived for a week in a tent and a horse-box shaped caravan. Mum, baby Dennis and the girls slept in the caravan while Dad and I slept in the tent joined to it. I remember the setting quite well – the field we were camped in, the caravan and the tent, but nothing about what we did, what we ate, nor how the cooking was done or what we did for lighting, for there were no facilities there. We were the only campers there and I am sure it was not a regular site for camping but just an available field fairly near the sea, one which somehow my father had learned about. I remember that the lorry belonged to Hawes, the greengrocers in Beccles, and I recall thinking I was told that on our way to Gorleston, we would have to cross the Waveney River – which was correct – and also that we would be going under the river, I guessed in a tunnel – which was not correct! Whether I confuse over with under and therefore bridge with tunnel, I do not know but I was certainly mistaken by it all. I think the whole family felt better after that holiday. It was never repeated.

The second exception to our not going away from home on holiday was also the result of special circumstance, that is, my Grandfather Ward lived in London, and going to stay with him both enabled my mother to visit him and her sisters and also enabled us all to enjoy a holiday. My mother and we four children went by train to London where we took a bus or busses to Roehampton. For the second week, my father, who, like most people at that time, had only a week's holiday from work, joined us and then a week later we all returned to Beccles. This happened once and possibly twice. The one, probably the second, I remember was in 1937 – my Aunt Phyllis, who lived with my grandfather, was already married but her son, my cousin Tony, had not yet been born – he was born in 1938 – and Dennis was quite small.

Some, but naturally not many, memories of that Roehampton holiday have remained fairly clear in my mind. All I recall of the steam train journey there and back was going through the tunnel just outside Ipswich station when we had to close the windows to keep the smoke out, and hope that the lights in the carriage would come on in time so that we would not get too frightened in the dark. The tunnel seemed to me as a child to be immensely long although as an adult I realized it was quite short. Another memory is the fun we had playing on Wimbledon Common across the road from Grandfather's house, 83 Medfield Street, and particularly climbing the silver birch trees there. I recall, too, going to the ponds on the common, called Kingsmere and Queensmere, seeing the ducks and swans there, watching adults and children sailing small model yachts on the sailing pool, and attending a cricket match. I thought Grandfather's house was a great place. It seemed very large to me although when I revisited it as an adult it looked much smaller. Part of its attraction was that it faced Wimbledon Common just across the road, and whilst it had two floors at the front there were three at the back, the house being on a slope. The fact of a house having more floors at the back than at the front astonished me, perhaps because being brought up in Suffolk one is not used to such slopes on which to build a house. As an aside, I recall that when my wife first visited Beccles and had Boaters' Hills pointed out to her by my father, she searched the horizon in vain for some 'real' hills. At Roehampton, I recall going each morning to the local baker's shop with my sisters – Dennis was too small, I guess – and buying fresh crunchy bread rolls which we then ate with bananas for breakfast. I recall, too, buying pear drop sweets and enjoying the flavour, and my father buying a film for his small box camera, a film which required him to pull what seemed yards of paper from it before it could be used.

Elements of a visit, or visits, to nearby Putney also remain in my mind, such as the unhappy smell from the brewery which has stayed with me to the extent that I never smell a brewery today without recalling Putney. We also went to the cinema in Putney to see Sabu in 'The Elephant Boy' – which was released in 1937 – and another film, also released in 1937, called 'Makushla' which for years I believed was about Irish immigrants to America, but which later I learned was about an American cop who fell in love with a girl whose father and brother were notorious gunmen and cattle rustlers. I particularly recall that the cop and the girl sang a song, 'Makushla'. We were prevented from walking over Putney Bridge on one occasion because the IRA had, we were told, placed a bomb on it – this at the latest was 1937. I saw for the first time a 'cut price' sweet shop – which I mistakenly thought was a 'cut throat' shop – and I bought a tube of Rolo chocolate sweets there at a low price. We paid a visit to schoolteacher Aunt Evelyn, my mother's other sister, who lived in an upstairs flat at Richmond. I had never heard of, and most certainly had never been in, a flat before. Everything seemed very quiet there and I remember only three other things about the visit. One was the gold star-shaped wall clock on the sitting room wall, which I thought was beautiful and looked very expensive. Another was being told to be very quiet because other people lived in the flat below and should not be disturbed. The idea of anyone living underneath the place where one lived was novel to me. The other memory of the visit was hearing the ringing of a hand bell in the street outside the block of flats and being told that it was a muffin man coming to sell his wares – also a novel experience. My first visit to the London Zoo was during one of these holidays at Roehampton. My last memory of my grandfather Ward, many years after our pre-war visit, was having been to watch a cricket match on Wimbledon Common and saying goodbye to him there, kissing him on the forehead and then walking away. He was sitting on a bench and I turned to look at him from behind as I walked away, wondering if he would turn round. He didn't and I think I was a little disappointed – at least I am now. I liked him. He died in May 1956 when I was already in Africa.

I have written of the various train journeys which we took – always with great excitement. In those days, before diesel and electric trains were common and the overwhelming majority of trains were steam trains fuelled on coal endlessly shovelled into the furnace by the 'fireman', there was always the danger during the drier summer months of grass fires being started by sparks and hot cinders flying from the engines. The danger was acute in areas with hay fields or ripening grain crops close to the railway line, as was the case with Crickmore's meadow, close to our home. There was the danger, too, of the fires spreading to and damaging local dwellings though I never knew of such a calamity occurring. Adults were always on the look-out in the drier weather, ready to help fight and extinguish the fires. They were not frequent but were sufficient of a concern for me to remember them, and the worries about them, many years later.

Our other holidays – day trips – were usually to the beach at Lowestoft and occasionally to Gorleston. We caught the train from Beccles station to Lowestoft and walked to the 'children's corner' on the beach, carrying – or rather my parents carrying – swim suits, towels, spades and pails and a sandwich lunch. My earliest memory of this must have been not later than about 1934, when I was at the most five years old, because my parents wheeled Dennis in a push chair – a laborious task over the soft sand of the beach. No sooner were we settled on the beach than we thought it was lunch time, and Mother and Father had to be fairly firm in making us wait until it was nearer mid-day. I only once remember seeing my father in a swim suit and my mother never. Neither of them could swim. My mother, in particular, was afraid of the water. She said her father, however, would never drown because he was 'born with a veil over his face'. This must have been a reference to an old belief in the protective power of being born without the birth sac being ruptured – not that I knew anything about such matters until very much later. I was twelve years old and at secondary school before I could swim. We played in the sand – digging holes, scooping out channels to let the water flow in, making sand castles, and paddling in the water with my father, who rolled his trouser legs up to his knees, and my mother, who tucked her skirt up just above her knees. Although we spent many hours in the sun and often got nicely sun tanned, I don't think we often got sunburned – or at least not very much. We were always told that the sea air was full of ozone and this was healthy for us. I often wonder if this was the same ozone as that which today is so vilified by those who worry about climate change. Sometimes we brought a bunch of sea weed home with us, and over the following weeks would, we thought, be able to forecast the weather by noticing how damp or dry the sea weed was. Also we brought home with us prized collections of tiny shells and an occasional stone with a hole through it. When we were a little older, we were taken from the beach to Kensington Gardens at the south end of Lowestoft and had rides in small boats on the lake there. These trips to the seaside came to an end when the war began because mines were laid on the beach and coils of barbed wire were stretched across it. The Lowestoft beach was opened a few months before the end of the war but by that time we were too old for family beach trips though I do recall two of us from school spending a pleasant Sunday afternoon in the relative seclusion and peacefulness of Kensington Gardens with a shared girl-friend – shared for the day! – also from school.

My parents had a soft spot for Gorleston since this was where, in Bell's Road, they had spent their honeymoon in 1925. Our visits to Gorleston were fewer as a family but more in the course of Sunday School annual outings – called 'treats'. Unlike a trip to Lowestoft, that to Gorleston and Great Yarmouth involved a change of trains, I think at Haddiscoe. Parts of the Sunday School outings are very clear in my mind but I guess other parts are muddled. I do not know how we foregathered, or where, but we travelled to Gorleston by train, and the highlights were tea at Matthe's restuarant, and a trip by steamship up the river from Gorleston to Great Yarmouth. Maybe we returned to Beccles directly from Yarmouth railway station rather than coming back via Gorleston. We were given special pocket money for these trips and I recall buying for a few pence a tortoise at Yarmouth on one of these occasions and taking it home, somewhat to my parents' consternation. I don't think it survived the following winter, and my potential anguish was assuaged, quite easily, by being told that it had hibernated. By the following spring I expect I had forgotten all about it.

There were also occasional day trips to Norwich to visit my father's sisters, my aunts Lucy and Amy. I have only one clear memory of those visits and that is my father helping us to make kites out of a frame of thin bamboos tied with string and covered with brown paper which was glued over the frame. The tails of the kites particularly impressed me because they consisted of a long piece of string trailing from the bottom end of the kite frame and having old bus tickets – thin card about two to three inches long by an inch wide – tied into the string at intervals of about ten inches. They worked very well and we enjoyed flying the kites – not always successfully – on Mousehold, a grassy, sandy area above the city. It was at the army barracks on Mousehold that my father enlisted during the First World War. I learned during our childhood visits to Norwich, and later, that the simpler the kite, the more likely it is to fly easily. I enjoy kite-flying and am more content and successful with a simple kite than with the fancy kites which kind members of the family have from time to time given to me as presents. The longer the string and the higher the kite, the better. It is an enjoyment so personal and profound as not readily to be shared with others – just me, the kite and the wind. I should have done much more of it over the years. One of my most enjoyable and memorable experiences in kite-flying was many years later as a grown-up, travelling down the Mississippi on a stern wheel paddle steamer and flying a kite from the stern of the steamer as it travelled gently along – Heaven!

I wrote just now of bus tickets. These little pieces of card were spring-clipped on a small board held by the bus conductor – different coloured tickets for differently priced fares. The conductor removed the relevant ticket from the holder, placed it in a slot in a machine he held round his neck, and by depressing a handle, which sounded a bell, punched a hole in it to cancel it. I was given a toy bus conductor's outfit as a present when I was small – cap, ticket holder, tickets and the cancelling machine, complete with bell. I remember very clearly that after using the kit for a while I decided to take the cancelling machine to pieces to see how it was made. I guess it was quite simple but what really surprised me was that when I opened up the bright, shiny metal machine I discovered that the metal was a recycled Tate and Lyle Golden Syrup tin – green and gold painted on one side and bright and shiny on the other. Whether they were reused tins or unused tins put out for scrap I know not but I was pretty impressed with the ingenuity at the time. Who says the Green Movement is new?!

An innovation during the war was 'Holidays at Home' when the local community organized special events such as talent competitions, music hall-type shows, concert parties, fashion parades, athletics matches and beauty competitions – 'Miss Beccles', or 'Miss Waveney', or 'Miss War Savings' for example. The Dagenham Girl Pipers performed in the town on at least one occasion. I guess the object was to maintain morale during a period when there was much to worry people and when other forms of holiday – such as trips to the sea-side – were not available.

It may have been during one of these holidays at home weeks, though I think not but later in or just after the war, that Arturo Stephani and his 21 Silver Songsters visited Beccles as part of a wider tour and performed on the stage at the Regal cinema. Stephani, whose real name was Frederick William Whisker, was an impresario who enjoyed considerable success in Britain in the 1930s, and toured European countries and America. He had a brother living in Beccles – Nick Whisker, the fish and chip shop man. Among the gifted youngsters in Stephani's troupe was Ronnie Ronalde who sang popular songs and danced on the stage – in clogs and also a pair of extremely long-toed shoes, and who was a remarkable whistler. He later enjoyed international fame and did a good deal of recording.

It may well have been during one of these week-long holidays at home that the only public boxing match I recall seeing in Beccles was staged. This was in the New Market and the ring was set up near the green grocers' shop owned by the Tills family. I recall the name of 'Sonny Tills' being high on the list of favourites to win. I remember the way the boxers snorted as they manoeuvred round each other waiting for an opening to knock the living daylights out of their opponent. And I was fascinated, too, by the way the 'seconds' flapped a towel vigorously, first to the right and then to the left, in front of each boxer and poured water over his head to cool him down as he rested, breathing heavily through a bloody and twisted nose, between rounds. It all looked very professional to me. Incidentally, the only boxing I ever did was for just one session at the Leman School when the boys were taught how to box, the rules and techniques – which was interesting, but it was followed by a few minutes actual boxing with gloves on which was less enjoyable. I hated it then and I still think it is an odd way for anyone to take exercise. Georgie Adams, who lived in Pleasant Place and who was the younger brother of the friends, Minnie and Peter, with whom I played as a child, later became a very successful, and scarcely ever defeated – and then only narrowly – boxer, both amateur and later professional.

One other, very different, type of holiday ought to be mentioned though I did not know much about it. I think it was before the war rather than in the early days of the war that Jewish schoolboys were taken into a few Beccles family homes for a holiday from where they lived in London. Who they were and where they lived in London was something of a mystery. I did not meet any of them although two were taken in by families in St. George's Road quite near to our home. My recollection is that they were well dressed – caps and school blazers – well behaved, quiet, boys of maybe about seven years of age. They may have been refugee children of families fleeing from the Germans.

When I was about sixteen I accompanied the family of a girl friend to the Isle of Wight. The parents, my friend and her brother were keen members of the Boy Scouts and Girl Guides Associations and they were taking a fairly large number of Scouts and Guides for a camping holiday on the Isle. I went along as an extra helping hand. I remember little of what we did except that I found the Isle a scenically fascinating place. But I do recall that while I was there I received a letter from my father telling me that I had received an invitation from Sidney Wooderson, known as 'the Mighty Atom', one of Britain's best athletes ever, then the world one mile record holder, to join three other teenagers in a team to compete in a four by one mile race which Wooderson was arranging. My father offered to pay my rail fare to get back to Beccles and then join the team. I do not recall my reasons but I made what now is very clearly the wrong decision – a huge mistake – and did not return home to join the team. It was a fantastic invitation and I turned it down. Unbelievable!

It is odd how once one starts to remember specific incidents about one's earlier years one often quickly recalls other things sometimes only vaguely related to the initial memory. Recently my son landed his light aeroplane at Beccles airfield – the Ellough airfield of the war – and this brought back memories of another light aeroplane at Beccles, but more importantly a cluster of memories about a particular area on the outskirts of the town, to the west of the built-up area along the Ringsfield Road where the road swings left and to the south. It is known as Ringsfield Corner.

To the left the road goes to Ringsfield, another of the destinations of the family walks we took in the 1930s. Although we did not often visit it we all liked the Ringsfield church – old, rural, quiet, with at times snowdrops in the graveyard and at other times, primroses.

To the right of that point where the road swings to the left, was an old, long abandoned, virtually unnoticed, somewhat sunken road leading down to join the Bungay Road about opposite Roos Hall – said to be haunted and where a few people claimed to have seen pale, crepuscular, apparitions in the vicinity. It was an area which we as children walked past quickly! Garden fetes were held at the Hall but always ended before dusk!

It was in the fields adjacent to this old road that the Suffolk agricultural show was held in June 1937. While I expect we visited the show as a family I have no recollection of it save that the prize cows produced prize milk in such prize quantities that it had to be disposed of, and we children, Cynthia and I and maybe Dennis, with a set of as large milk jugs as the family could muster at the time, went in the early evening to the show ground where our jugs were filled to the brim with rich creamy milk, free, which we then took home. This could not have been an easy task because the journey home from the show ground would have taken us up to half an hour and the uncovered jugs were brim full. In those days, long before cholesterol and simvastatin were learned of, rich, creamy, thick milk was considered to be very good for children's health – but then so was the beef dripping which we enjoyed thickly spread on hot toast!

Straight ahead of that point where the road swings left towards Ringsfield was a narrow lane – now largely overgrown – a track between two low hedges with fields on each side. In my Leman School days this track was towards the beginning and the end of the roughly circular three and a half mile annual cross country race and it was a strategically important part of it. On the way back, at the exit from the lane and within half a mile of the finishing line, one needed to be ahead of the field if one was to win the race. On that last stretch, when the runners were really tired, few overtook the boy in the front, though there were battles for second and third place. More important, however, was the beginning of the race, for one needed to get into that lane before other runners did. This was because it was narrow and the leader determined the pace, but it was also difficult to pass one of the better runners who not only ran with his arms akimbo and his legs sticking out sideways but also seemed regularly to choose to relieve himself, on the hoof as it were, and this both slowed the pace and made it additionally dangerous to attempt to pass him. The cross country race, for boys only, took place at the end of the spring term, just before Easter, and at the morning assembly of the day of the race, the hymns always included, appropriately if fortuitously, 'There is a green hill far away'.

Although the cross country race was run only by boys, later when I was teaching at the school, Miss Collis asked me to take groups of girls out for a cross country run. She thought it would be good for them. She did not come with us, which was fortunate because there was a good deal of young feminine banter and larking about. On the whole they were an un-athletic lot. The younger ones tried to out-race each other, and the older ones – only a few years younger than me – asked for, and were given, a rest half way through, during which – trying to keep straight-faced – they wished to know, Sir, if this was the first time I had taken girls that way!

In about 1937 a light aeroplane crashed into a field on the left hand side of the lane and landed upside down with its wheels in the air. It was not badly damaged though I'm sure it needed a lot of attention before it could fly again. Fortunately, there was no fire and no one was injured. I remember going with Cynthia to look at it, along with lots of other inquisitive children and adults.

Now for what some would see as the more interesting memories of that area. The track running straight ahead was known as 'Cut Throat Lane' and I have the flimsiest of memories that after I had left school I read some of the archives in the Town Hall, and came across an old newspaper cutting which reported at the time, about the mid 1800s, or reported on an earlier event, a murder committed in Cut Throat Lane. As I recall, with no great confidence, a young man had unwisely attempted to perform what in more modern terms we would discreetly call 'a termination' on his pregnant girlfriend, using an instrument fashioned from one of the nearby hedges. The operation went calamitously wrong and the poor girl died. The distraught boyfriend fled the scene and emigrated to America but threw himself overboard on the way there. If this story was true, and I am not sure that it was, then 'Cut Throat Lane' was a severe misnomer, and it may be the reason why the track was also known as 'Lovers' Lane' – as my schoolgirl cross country tutees well knew!

Which leads me on to the last, and in some ways most lasting, of my memories of Cut Throat or Lovers' Lane. I need to pick my words carefully. Being a relatively secluded lane, with a narrow 'kissing gate' at the far end, and the little-used but conveniently located and isolated 'Black Barn' in a field to the right further on, and the disused military block-house nearer the Bungay Road, it was from time to time used by teenager and young adult, girl and boy, couples to enjoy a gentle walk in the fresh air and open countryside, communing with nature, with a low risk of being disturbed or recognized – it was, so I was given to understand, usually worth taking the risk! Alternatively, there were those who, especially in the darker and colder winter evenings, stopped off and rested a while quietly on the green-painted metal bench in Hospital Lane, or in the leafy Dell at the top of Bungay Road, rather than continue into the countryside. One learned, I understand, a good deal about life and relationships on these quiet pastoral strolls up Cut Throat Lane and at stop-offs on the way – part, one might claim, or at least pretend, of one's education.

But there were, of course, other, at least equally important, though less immediately pleasant, parts of one's education. Of what, then, did our education comprise when I was young?

EDUCATION

Home

As I expect in all families, our early education was informally at home, encouraged and guided particularly by the mother. Separate times were not set aside for this nor was there any planned structure to it. Mothers played a vital role in this respect but it went largely unnoticed and was taken for granted. It was part of what mothers did. My mother taught us, with varying degrees of success, to read, spell, write, count and draw – nothing advanced but an adequate foundation upon which teachers could build when we went to school. I remember two of my very first pieces of reading. The first was on the lid of a sweet tin: 'Jimmy Trunk has just come home, and very pleased is he, to see his Mum and Dad again, and such a lovely tea.' The second was from a little book of cardboard pages – small and quite thick – which was about a boy catching a bus in London. I think it was a 23 bus and it was running to and from Peckham. I do not recall the beginning of the little story but I do recall that the boy traveller got on the bus going the wrong way, because I clearly remember the final punch line: 'But the bus was coming back!' I was at the most four years of age, and probably a little younger, because I know that I had not yet started at Peddars Lane School and was learning to read at home. I recall, too, reading at a fairly young age, a story about Croydon Aerodrome – the leading airport long before Heathrow – and the usual stories about wonder boy football players and intrepid, jungle-defying explorers in Darkest Africa.

Not all the learning at home was of the 'three Rs' type, for inevitably there was at least a modicum of moral guidance as well. Much of this happened by chance and went beyond the 'please' and 'thank you' and general politeness level. I recall two examples which contained the lesson that one ought to act fairly and one ought not to take undue advantage of another person's weaker position. In the case of fairness, when I found a silk chiffon scarf, took it home, washed it and gave it to my mother as a present, telling her how I had come by it, my elder sister returned it to a girl who – for all I know, correctly – said it was hers. Although I was told, correctly, and accepted, that it would be unfair not to have the scarf returned, what upset me at the time was that I was not consulted or told it was to be returned, which seemed to me to be unfair. There was a conflict between our two views, Muriel's and mine, of what was fair though I was too young to see it that way. Good eventually came of it, however, because it was my trying to understand what 'fairness' really meant which started my later interest, when studying law, in the judgments of Lord Denning, Master of the Rolls – whom I later met three or four times – who always placed great emphasis on fairness and was instrumental in weaving the concept into significant parts of our law. Integral to the idea of fairness, as Denning emphasized, is the concept that one should not take undue advantage of another person's weaker position. There are, of course, many modifications and adjustments to this but let me describe the circumstances in which I became seized of the idea.

When I was at the Peddars Lane School, and probably only six or seven years old, there was a fellow schoolboy, named Salter, who lived in the country towards Ellough or Weston. It must have been coolish weather at the time because he was dressed in short thick woollen trousers and several layers of pullovers under his jacket. His trousers were held up by a pair of braces between some of the layers of his pullovers. For some reason I accompanied him on part of his way home, via Rigbourne Hill – then spelled and pronounced Rigbone Hill. Near the bottom of this hill he excused himself and went behind the hedge to vacate his bowels. To do this he had to undo the four buttons which held the braces at the front and the two buttons which held the braces at the back of his trousers. Having used a nearby dock leaf, as was the rural custom in cases of al fresco evacuation, the time came for him to reappear from behind the hedge and adjust his dress. He accomplished the securing of the four front buttons of his braces but when he tried to secure the two back buttons, especially threading the braces through the loops on his woollen underpants, such was the thickness of the layers of pullovers that he found it quite impossible to accomplish it. His plight was pitiful. With up to three miles to reach his home, he clearly did not want his pants to fall down on the way. He sought my help – I do not recall his precise words – and I willingly obliged by fumbling my way through the layers of pullovers, eventually finding the braces, and doing up the two stubborn back buttons. To express his appreciation, he took from his jacket pocket and offered to me one of those toys which are a small shallow circular glass-topped metal case in which is a series of small holes into which one tries to roll one or more small metal balls. I found this 'puzzle' fascinating and, pleased with not only my good deed but also the gift-cum-reward, I took it home and explained the circumstances of its acquisition to my mother. She said comforting words about my having helped a mate out of a difficult, weak and vulnerable situation, but after a few minutes she suggested that I ought to return the puzzle to young Salter. I did so and he seemed pleased to get it back, generously saying that if ever I found myself in a similarly embarrassing predicament and weak position he would be pleased to get me out of it, gratis. At heart he was one of the world's gentlemen. I wonder what happened to him. Given that he kept himself warm with multiple layers of pullovers, that he kept himself fit with regular exercise walking to and from school, and that his bowels seemed to be in good working order, he may well have lived to a ripe old age. I hope so.

To return to our in-home education; although there was not a really large number of books in the house, there were always sufficient – significantly more than in most of the homes of similar families I visited – and my father encouraged us to read, bringing books home, sometimes unbound discarded proof copies. He and my mother encouraged us to respect books, to cover them in paper, treat them carefully and not mark them. Strangely, I do not ever recall seeing either of them reading a book, except when on holiday, though my father regularly read the 'Daily Herald' during the week and 'Reynold's News' on Sunday, and my mother thumbed through the occasional magazine. They never suggested that we should read any particular book, and to this day I mildly resent people telling me what books I 'ought' to read: 'You simply must read such and such a book; it's on the Booker short list, you know', and giving the impression that only a dolt such as I had not already read it! At home, the books were just there – always there. They included two thickish dictionaries which we were encouraged to use; a ten-volume encyclopaedia; a Treasury of Poetry; Samuel Smiles's 'Self Help' – the importance of which I did not fully appreciate until many years later, though I enjoyed reading it at the time and making a note of some of the more apt advice contained in it; 'Fifty Great Stories of the Great War' – those were the days before it was called the First World War, because no one thought mankind would be so insane as to have a

Second World War; and 'Fifty True Stories Stranger than Fiction'. Two others I particularly recall were John Oxenbury's 'Bondman Free' – which generated the first stirrings in me of an interest in the law – and Horace Ainsley Vachel's 'The Hill' about life at Harrow School. These two are, except for academic texts, the only books I have read more than once. There are far too many books for us to spend time re-reading some of them. In which case, why do I never throw a book away?

Throughout our primary school days we had a weekly comic delivered to the house. These consisted of several sheets and we had a sheet each which, when read, rotated between us. I think that to begin with we had a comic called 'Bubbles' but later there was the 'Beano'. They were intended simply to amuse, which they did, but they also helped with our reading and spelling, and they added a visual humour which complemented that which we saw at the cinema, and the humour we heard on the radio.

One further point about our informal education at home beyond the reading, writing, drawing and counting. When she was not doing other household work, my mother – as I guess most other mothers – did a good deal of mending of worn or damaged clothes and darning of socks and the elbows of jumpers. She also did a great deal of knitting particularly while waiting for us to come home from school and father home from work, or while listening to the radio in the evenings. She even combined knitting and listening to the radio with a little magazine reading. I doubt if many, if any, of our socks, gloves, scarves, cardigans and pullovers were purchased from shops – mother, and later my sisters, knitted them. We held the hanks of wool while Mother wound it into balls ready for knitting. Very little wool was bought ready wound. I was taught to darn socks and enjoyed doing it. I was also taught to knit – 'knit one, pearl one, knit two together', endlessly repeated – and, whilst I did enjoy it, I did not have the patience to make anything really worthwhile, though, with guidance, I was able to design the pattern of a pullover with a cable patterned front which my mother knitted and which I still have.

Peddars Lane School

My early recollections of formal education are of the Peddars Lane Council School. I don't recall the use of words like 'junior' or 'infants' or 'primary' but it catered for children of about four to eleven but generally only those children who lived in the south part of the town, because those from 'the other end of the town' went to the Ravensmere School. Just as there was a senior school, the National School, fairly close to the Ravensmere junior school, so there was a senior school on the same premises as the Peddars Lane junior school, but I knew nothing of what it did or who went there, my sister Muriel having gone there for a year notwithstanding. It seemed somewhat cut off from the junior school buildings and this may have been because, with the opening of the Area School in 1939, the senior pupils from the Peddars Lane site went there, except for the very few, including Muriel, who went to the Leman School. Fortuitously, the old premises became available for the Dagenham school evacuees who came to the town at the beginning of the war, which would account for my not knowing how Peddars Lane accommodated 200 evacuees and their staff. There were certainly some evacuees in the junior school but nowhere near 200.

The accommodation of the junior school – the part I knew best – consisted of a very large L-shaped room on each of the two floors that were partitioned off with sliding doors to make three smaller rooms for classes on each floor. Each morning started with 'prayers': the reading of prayers and the singing of hymns, such as 'Fight the Good Fight' and 'Onward Christian Soldiers'. Hymn-singing at school and in church must have created a long lasting impression, because both the words and the tunes of many of them have remained entirely clear throughout my life. Incidentally, the wording of the Book of Common Prayer has always struck me as containing some of the most beautiful and striking sentences in our language: 'The peace of God which passes all understanding ...'; 'May the Lord bless you and keep you, May the Lord make his face to shine upon you and give you His peace'; 'May the words of my mouth and the meditation of our hearts be always acceptable in thy sight, O Lord.' And likewise some of Hymns Ancient and Modern: 'As pants the hart for lonely streams when heated in the chase, so longs my soul for thee, oh Lord, and thy refreshing grace.' Beautiful in its construction and in its sounds.

The Peddars Lane junior school was a two storied rather heavy looking building of, I guess, Victorian antiquity. When young, I was told that it had formerly been an ink factory but this seemed unlikely, and more recently I have gathered that it was originally a silk factory. At times it was cold and damp. The boys' lavatories were in the front playground with open, unglazed, window spaces – apertures – above eye level, which was perhaps as well because a favourite pastime of the boys was to so elevate one's trajectory that one was able to pee through the window openings from the inside. Only through great pressure, holding of breath, skill, accuracy and courage was one able to succeed and by even greater good fortune not to be caught in the attempt. Few succeeded and no one was ever caught. Indeed, I am not sure that the exclusively female and spinster staff would have known how to handle such puerile vulgarity, so they wisely steered clear both of the boys' lavatories and of noticing any such ill behaviour. All women teachers and many in other professions were required to resign on marriage. There was one exception to the totally female staff: Mr Richards was the caretaker, but, as was usual at that time, our paths rarely crossed and we had little to do with him. He functioned mainly out of school hours. It was his job to light the gas lamps in the winter afternoons, for there was no electricity, and periodically to top-up the coal-fired stoves in each of the six partitioned-off class rooms which he had lit before school hours. I understand that, probably before my time, there had been a peripatetic male teacher of handicrafts, but I did not come across him myself.

Miss Bessie Snell was the headmistress. I learned later that apart from a few years in Surrey, she had taught continuously in Beccles since January 1895, starting at the Beccles Infants Board School. She was a Deacon of the Congregational Church. She resigned from the headship in January 1941 just after I had left the school and was replaced by Miss Gertrude Fuller, headmistress of the Ravensmere Junior School where she had been in charge since it was built in 1913. This succession suggests that Peddars Lane was the 'senior' of the two junior schools in the town. Miss Fuller was said to have been an 'outstanding success teaching young children' – but I reckon Miss Snell was a hard act to follow. I recall Miss Snell as being large and ample in girth but not excessively overweight. She seemed always to wear black or dark dresses. She turned out to be a kindly lady, but I had long left Peddars Lane before I discovered this. Her form of corporal punishment was to roll back the cuff of the clothing covering one's wrist and deliver a resounding and sharp smack with the palm of her hand on the back of the malefactor's hand. I do not think she used, though she may have possessed, a cane – the wrist smack was deterrent or punishment enough.

I was always squeamish as a young person about physical pain or indeed the threat or fear or imagination of physical pain caused by the medical profession. My outlet was involuntarily to faint. Related to this, I recall an occasion at Peddars Lane, when I was about six or seven. We had to take a note home to our parents about the visit of the school dentist, and we were required to return the note to the school, bearing our parents' consent or lack of it. The note had to be returned by a certain date and I was much troubled and anxious that my parents did not give me the note to return to the school. I was convinced that I would be in trouble with the headmistress for not returning it, and in my mind's eye I could see her advancing towards me ready to roll back the cuff of my jacket sleeve. I was therefore fearful when one morning Miss Snell entered the classroom and beckoned me out. She led me to the dentist in an adjacent room. I do not recall whether any treatment was given – probably not – or whether it was just an inspection, which I think more likely. In any event I had no time to get worried or to faint. I never enquired, but I guess my parents returned the note, possibly via Muriel, so that I would not get worried about the prospect of dental treatment. I don't think they ever appreciated how worried I was about not taking the note back to school.

The school dental service, if such it may be called, was limited but good, and my earliest recollection of cleaning my teeth was that we purchased

'Gibb's Dentifrice' from the school and regularly used it for many years. The 'Dentifrice' was a hard, slightly gritty, pale pink paste in a shallow tin about two inches in diameter. One moistened the toothbrush and then applied the paste by rubbing the toothbrush over its surface. Other forms of elementary hygiene included the daily inspection of the back, front and nails of the pupils' hands, by the class teacher – although we had to pass this inspection by my mother each day before we left for school. Mother also made sure that we had washed the back of our neck rather than confine our morning ablutions to a quick wipe of the flannel across our cheeks, leaving what she called a 'tide mark' where our quick wipe ended. And she was very keen that we should look after our finger nails, keeping them trimmed and pushing the 'quicks' down into a half moon shape. Her own hands were always well manicured. At school, there was also, I believe – because I have no recollection of her or her activities – a 'nit nurse' who occasionally visited the school and closely inspected the head and hair of each pupil.

My first class-teacher at Peddars Lane school was Miss Standen, a tall, dark haired, good looking, quite young teacher, who I thought, even at my tender age, was a good teacher. I think I must have been extolling her pedagogic and other virtues at home and was provoked by some comment to say that Miss Standen was 'a very nice personage', because this remained for many years an expression in the family. I think I was a little hurt at the time that they did not seem fully to appreciate her qualities. I must have mentioned other qualities, too, because they were much amused by my saying that when Miss Standen leaned over my desk to help me, 'her lungs nearly fell out'! It may be that Miss Standen was succeeded by Miss West, because although I recall her well, I do not think she ever taught me.

Another well known teacher was Mrs. Johnson – unusually not a spinster but a widow – who had a feared reputation for being significantly nearer the vinegar end of the sugar-vinegar spectrum. She lived in Wembley Avenue in a property which partly adjoined our own. Between the two gardens was a high wooden fence in which a knot in the panelling had come out, leaving a knot-hole about three feet from the ground. I guess she did not wish to have us spying on her, but I do not think we noticed the knot-hole until she attempted to block it with a plug of putty. To ensure that the plug was adequate she pushed it well into the knot-hole, and the result was that on our side there was a 'putty sausage' sticking out of the hole. This was too much of a temptation for us, and we repeatedly pushed it back on to her side and she repeatedly pushed it back on to our side until my parents suggested that we pack it up and leave it to harden – which we did. Shortly, the putty did harden and we got fed up with trying to tamper further with it. Oddly, two other teachers lived in Wembley Avenue – Miss Jeffreys from Peddars Lane and Miss Lily Jones from the Leman School.

A little further up the school I was taught by Miss Jeffreys, middle aged – or so I thought – slender and a mixture of sugar and vinegar. My only significant memory of Miss Jeffreys is that she objected to my spelling 'they' phonetically as 'thay'. Indeed, such was the exception which she took to this error that she required me to 'write lines', spelling the word over and over again – I think perhaps fifty times. This was intended, I hope, so that I should never again spell the word incorrectly but have the correct spelling firmly imprinted on my mind, rather than as a form of punishment which was the usual motive for writing lines. With, I guess, ill grace I wrote the word the required fifty times only to be told to do it all again. This happened three times before someone – I don't think Miss Jeffreys – told me I was still writing 'thay' instead of 'they' because no one had told me the correct spelling. At least I know how to spell 'they' now! I recall this event each time I mis-key the word on the computer and it comes out as 'thay'. As an aside, I recall that the correct spelling of two words – 'February' with two 'r's and 'beginning' with two 'n's – was taught to me by Muriel, not in any formal way but in the course of conversation. I was reminded by my father that there is one 'f' rather than two 'f's, and two 's's rather than one 's' in the word 'Professor' – a lesson I learned in the nick of time because I had already spelt the word incorrectly in a letter I was writing to accept an offer of a place at university, and was able to change it. I remember, too, Dr. Gort, who replaced Mr. Glover in teaching Geography in the sixth form, telling me that a word I had used in an essay on glaciation – sérrac – did not exist. I produced a book, which he had recommended to me, containing the word, and in a slight huff, as if to get his own back, he turned the page of my essay and said brusquely, 'Well, there are certainly not two 's's and one 'c' in the word 'occasion' as you have spelled it.' It's strange the things which stick in one's mind.

Miss Watson, middle aged – or so she seemed – was senior mistress and usually taught the senior class, but I do not recall her teaching me. She was one of the Ingate Mission Watson sisters. There was also a Miss Naomi Watling, youngish, who also did not teach me, so far as I recall. The person I do remember well was Miss Hewin, quite young, short blonde hair and, it seemed to me then and seems so now, a really good teacher. We were lucky because although normally teachers taught the same age group year after year while the pupils themselves moved up to a different teacher each year, Miss Hewin stayed with my class for the last two years of my time at the school. This would account for Miss Watson not teaching me in my final year. My clearest memory is the way she encouraged us in 'silent reading'. This was a period on Friday afternoons in which we were able to choose whatever book we wished from a large box of books. Of course, if there were several children who wished to read the same book, one had to wait one's turn. The books were quite new – some of them brand new – which was not invariably the case with the set texts, not that I remember there being any set texts. I recall most vividly a few Tarzan books which I enjoyed reading. They were popular books and I recall Dennis Pegram competing to read them. My earliest recollection of reading and enjoying books other than 'baby' books was in Miss Hewin's class.

'Physical education' consisted of no more than the windows being opened, the class being required to stand and take six deep breaths, and the windows being closed! School health inspections paid particular attention to measuring the expansion of the chest when taking a deep breath. Though there may have been a few physical training sessions in the playground, there were no organized games – there was no playing field – though a good deal of exercise was obtained in walking to and from school and running around in the playground during morning break, known as 'playtime' – I do not recall an afternoon break.

Although, like other parents, my mother accompanied each of us to the primary school on our first day there, my recollection is that she and other mothers did so on no other occasion, save for one possible exception. Even on the first day at school, the parents – always mothers – stayed outside the school playground and did not enter onto the premises. Most children walked about half a mile to a mile to get to school in the morning, return home and back to school at midday and back home in the afternoon. Children from the nearby countryside walked much longer distances and could not have returned home at lunch time; I do not know what they did for food, if anything, at mid day. Children from the countryside a little further away went to village schools such as Worlingham, Shadingfield, Brampton and Gillingham. Only on rare occasions were any of the children accompanied on their way to and from school. The thought of children in the future being taken to and from school in a school bus or taxi, or car, or indeed being accompanied by an adult, would have struck everyone as being very strange. Children from the farming areas would walk three or more miles to school and only if they lived on or near a bus route at greater distances would they use a bus – at their own expense. Although my mother did not accompany us to school save for the first day, each morning, without exception, she stood outside the front gate of the house, waited until we reached the bottom of the road and then waved goodbye to us. We turned round at that point and waved back. We then turned the corner and went on to school. She returned into the house. It was much more than a ritual – it was part of the way we lived and acted as a family. Today, seven decades later, my wife, my children and I always watch from the house or the pavement when other members of the family leave, and wave as they go.

The possible exception to my mother not accompanying us to school, to which I referred, was at Michaelmas when there was an annual horse sale at the auction grounds only a hundred or so yards beyond the school in Peddars

Lane. Then lots – it seemed like hundreds – of horses would be walked by their owners to the sale ground at about the time we were going to school, and away again by their new owners later in the day. The large horses, mostly heavy farm and working horses were beautifully groomed, with shining brasses and leather work, plaited manes and ribbons woven into their tails. I guess many saw it as a beautiful and striking sight, but my mother was terrified of the horses, fearing that one or more would get out of hand and harm any of us who happened to be nearby. They were docile animals and extremely unlikely to get out of control, but Mother did not know this. On the day of the horse sale she may have accompanied us to school. I don't recall her doing so – though I think she did – but she must have been sorely torn between her fear and her need to safeguard her children. I have an enduring and colourful mental image of some of these splendid horses urinating in the road – after all they must have been awakened early in the morning and had a long walk to Beccles – with cascades of lime coloured pee hitting the road and frothing copiously as it did so and splashed back. They were also the source of a good deal of horse manure which was at all times eagerly collected from the roads with bucket and shovel to be used on the gardens. And today they think the green movement is a new idea! My mother was always careful as well to warn us about heavy lorries on the road. I think she was afraid of these, too. She referred to these as 'six wheelers' because unlike normal lorries, the big ones had double wheels at the back. Compared with modern motorway juggernauts they were mere toys in size and weight. How she would have reacted to the articulated highway monsters of today with up to twenty wheels, I can not imagine. In fact there were very few lorries on the roads in those days.

Empire Day was celebrated annually on 24 May and on these occasions we, at the Peddars Lane School – and I am sure other junior schools – were given an orange and some sweets. In the afternoon we had games and races either on the Common or on at least one occasion Green's Meadow which was part of Green's Castle Flour Mills and, through a back exit, quite close to the school.

The coronation of King George VI in 1936 was marked with great festivities in Beccles and what I recall is based solely on a photograph in the family collection of long lines of school children in neat and orderly queues being taken by teachers down Station Road in bright sunshine with lots of flags and banners being waved. I guess we were all going to the Common for sports and, hopefully, something to eat and drink – possibly Corona drinks which I recall being delivered weekly in Pleasant Place and no doubt all other residential areas of the town, and which I now learn was invented, made and distributed country-wide by two grocers in the Rhondda Valley only a mile or so from my office at the University of Glamorgan. As an aside, the conversations which I heard from adults at the time of the Abdication which led to the Coronation were overwhelmingly on Prince Edward's side, and much criticism, as I understood it, was levelled at the part the Archbishop of Canterbury played in it. While my memory of the Coronation is very thin, that of the VE Day in May 1945 and VJ Day celebrations in August 1945 is much clearer. The VE Day and VJ Day celebrations are confused in my mind but my impression is that the former was marked largely with a thanksgiving service and a victory parade, and the latter with more exuberant activities. There were sports and athletics on the Common, and National Savings certificates were given as prizes to the winners of various events. In the evening and long into the night there was crowded dancing and drinking in the streets, particularly the New Market, where people, especially young adults and servicemen let their hair down and generally abandoned themselves to jollifications, liquor, dancing, singing and the unbridled joys of the flesh. Indeed, Bubbles, with whom I was spending much of the evening, took my arm and gently led me to a short, less brightly lit, passage way just off the New Market, opposite a pub near the YMCA building, and for a few spellbound and intriguing minutes we watched a sailor and a young lady in flagrente delicto. Subsequently I passed this young lady – actually, in broad daylight she didn't look quite so young, and maybe 'lady' is too generous a word – a number of times in the town – she came from the Gillingham area – but we passed as strangers, even though I felt that, in a manner of speaking, I had briefly known her intimately.

At sometime before the war, probably about 1936-7, at a time of British Fascist activity, the town was visited by a group of Black Shirts who set up a platform in the New Market and ranted – I guess, about the evils of Bolshevism and the vastly superior merits of Fascism. They attracted a moderate crowd of curious listeners, some of whom did a little heckling, but they attracted no sympathy. The Lord was not on the Black Shirts' side, for they chose a Wednesday evening to make their speeches which was the evening on which the parish church bell ringing practice took place and their shouted exhortations were largely drowned by the church bells very close by.

One day at Peddars Lane School a Mr. 'Podgey' Palmer, a portly gentleman, came to talk to us. I had seen him a number of times before as we passed his house on our way to school. I knew he had some connection with education but did not know what. That he was important was indicated by Miss Snell introducing him to the class. I remember only one thing about what he said. He asked how many apples there would be on his apple tree if he told us that there was 'not a single apple' on the tree, 'not one'. We all, of course, put up our hands and one by one said, 'None, Sir'. He smiled benignly, and beamingly told us that we were wrong and that the correct answer was any number other than one. Being an educationalist he explained why this was so. Ah! Now we could see – the silly old buffer! What we did not know until later was that he had been a teacher at Peddars Lane School for fifty years, forty of them as Headmaster, before he retired in 1924!

My final year at the Peddars Lane school was the first year of the war but I do not recall this having much direct impact on school life. There were a few privately evacuated children from, I guess, London, but I remember only one of them. This was a pretty blonde girl, Beryl Hurren, who was responsible for the first mild fluttering of my heart, though I do not remember ever speaking with her. All I really remember, apart from her name and appearance, is that on the day she left the school to return to London, I found it difficult to sing the morning hymns because of the lump in my throat. That morning 'fight the good fight' was not against evil but against my emotions. I recall writing the young lady a note though about what, and whether it was in fact delivered, I do not know.

So far as I recall there was no surreptitious 'passing of notes' in class in the junior school. This may have been because junior school teachers realized more acutely that they had to keep a very close eye on their wards if for no other reason than their safety. The lower forms at secondary school, however, were a different matter and whilst the passing of notes was not widespread, it was not unknown. It was an interesting phenomenon, for a note might pass from one end of the classroom to the other and from one side to the other, involving its passage through perhaps a dozen pairs of hands. The note bore the name of the intended recipient and was always folded so that its contents could not easily be seen, and no one ever looked at the contents as they passed it on its way to the addressed recipient. Passing the note was a perilous operation and could only be risked when the teacher's back was turned or their attention otherwise diverted. Teachers, like mothers, often seemed to have eyes in the back of their heads! My mother certainly said that she needed at least two pairs of eyes in the back of her head when we were – or I was – small. I recall that later in the morning of a day when the headmaster called me out at the end of assembly to reprimand me – of which more shortly – Bridget Spandler (another pretty blonde!) wrote me a note, which was passed across the class, asking what had happened. Passing on these notes was relatively easy if it was passed on to the pupil sitting next to you when compared with passing it to the person either in front of or behind you, and a diagonal pass was the most difficult of all manoeuvres. Occasionally an un-addressed note, often containing a scurrilous verse or dubious drawing would be passed around. Since it had no addressee one could only pass it on, read or unread. Usually it was intended for general readership. The last person to receive it had no one else to pass it on to and, as it were, was left holding the baby. Notes usually required an answer so the difficulties and dangers were doubled. There was a remarkable bond of mutual trust and cohesion displayed by members of the class in this matter. When at school I do not recall anyone ever being caught passing a note although I guess some must have been. That there were so few messages intercepted by the staff may have been because the staff knew that they might be opening an embarrassing can of worms if they intervened.

During the two terms I spent teaching at the Leman School, after leaving the RAF and before going to university, I was foolish enough to intercept a note being passed in one of my first year biology classes. It was being passed by a small fair haired girl – yet another blonde! – aged, I guess about eleven years, who turned out to be not only the carrier of the note but also its author. She handed it over but I did not there and then look at it – fortunately. When I did open the note in private I discovered that it bore a childish drawing of the human female form with aeroplane roundels on the chest and a scribbled jungle lower down. What was I to do? I could hardly ignore the matter lest the class concluded that I was prepared to collude in the affair. Nor did I feel able to speak to the class or the girl individually – what would I say? I decided that I should hand the note to the senior mistress, Miss McCarthy. I did this as the only way out and did so with trepidation, simply handing her the folded note and briefly explaining how I had come across it. She took one look at it, folded it and calmly said, 'Thank you. I will see to this.' I don't know what I had expected her reaction to be but I now had an appalling feeling of guilt because Miss McCarthy had the reputation of being very hard on miscreant girls, reducing them to tears before she would release them. To what unspeakable fate had I sentenced this poor eleven year old budding artist? I never knew. I wonder what happened to her and if she remembers the incident.

Johnston Brown once told me that his philosophy of handling pupils was based on the 'blind eye and ton of bricks' principle: he would turn a blind eye to occasional minor misdemeanours but if this did not work or the misdemeanour was serious, he would come down like a ton of bricks on the malefactor. Not a bad philosophy. I only wish I had turned a blind eye to the note passed by my juvenile biology tutee.

The only other thing I remember clearly about those two terms of teaching biology is the girl who wrote notes in her exercise book on the frog, saying that the female laid the eggs and the male came along and sprinkled fertilizer over them. In a sense she was right, so I let it pass – it was not an area I wished to get into.

There was a fairly large number of compulsorily evacuated children, in particular from Dagenham in Essex – 'London' to us: everything south of say Colchester was London to us. I learned much later that there were getting on for 200 of them who attended the Peddars Lane School, together with their teachers, though at the time they seemed very significantly fewer. I think what happened was that, fortuitously, the secondary school buildings on the Peddars Lane site were vacated and the pupils transferred to the new Area School, so the old premises became available for the Dagenham evacuees and their teachers. The evacuees were boarded with families in the town. They came at the very beginning of the war, and did not stay long, for the local newspaper recorded that by the beginning of June 1940 a special train took 176 children and 27 teachers and helpers back to Dagenham. Not a bad pupil:teacher ratio! That these evacuees were not as healthy as they might have been is indicated by the fact that a week after they arrived in Beccles a hostel for sick evacuees was opened in Blyburgate – probably Blyburgate Hall – and an average of 16 beds there was occupied weekly. Practically all these sick children were from Dagenham. The hostel closed when they returned to their homes in early June 1940.

On the whole the relatively few Dagenham children who came to the junior school – and probably the many others who were at the secondary school premises – seemed to come from relatively deprived areas and were rather poor, not well dressed or shod, and I recall one of them asking a fellow pupil if he could have the core of an apple that was being eaten, rather than throw it away, and received the reply, 'There ain't gonna be no core, mate.' I think it must have been some of these evacuees who introduced to the school a strange but enjoyable game called, I think, 'hijimmynacker' or something like that, in which a boy or a pair of boys would bend down, leaning their head and shoulders against a wall. Other boys would form a line several yards behind them and one at a time race up and throw themselves on the backs of the first boy or boys. As each additional boy leapt on top of those who had gone before him, the pile of boys became bigger and bigger, heavier and heavier, until the whole pile of them collapsed – and then they started again! It was not a competitive affair although I guess the longer they could avoid collapsing, the more successful they were. It was good, if strange, fun.

All sorts of tales, most of them untrue or exaggerated, were told about the Dagenham evacuees. They were reckoned to sleep under the bed rather than in or on it because this was what they did in their own crowded homes. They were said, too, to be amazed to find local people using the bath to bathe in because in their own homes the bath was used to store coal. And they wanted to know what cows, which they had never before seen, were, and they argued that it was from bottles rather than from cows that milk was obtained.

There were also school boys – grammar school boys and, it seemed, rather more affluent – from Gravesend evacuated en masse to the Beccles area. Although all I remember – and maybe all I actually knew at the time – about the Gravesend pupils being evacuated to the area was that a class of them, maybe up to twenty, all boys and aged about 16 or 17, with their master, used the Leman School for one or two practical science classes a week. There was, however, a great deal more to their story, as I learned much later.

On 3 September 1939, 400 boys, their headmaster, Mr. Samuel Lister, and their teachers from Gravesend County Grammar School for Boys were evacuated on the recently-launched MV Royal Daffodil (with a passenger capacity of over 2000) from Gravesend in Kent to Lowestoft and were then taken by rail to Beccles. I recall seeing from the promenade a few of these pleasure steamers coming into Lowestoft, and one of them was the Daffodil. We must have been taken by our parents to Lowestoft specially to see this. A search was made for suitable premises for the school, and 'Shipmeadow House' was selected as a distinct possibility. This was a disused workhouse – closed in January 1938 – currently being used to store ARP equipment for the Beccles and Bungay area. During the first term the building was improved, altered and generally 'spruced up' but still remained rambling and cold, for it was a severe winter. At the same time furniture and equipment was taken from the Gravesend premises and installed at Shipmeadow. The boys were billeted with many different families in the town, up to at least three to a home, and were, so some of them remembered, fed almost exclusively on baked beans on toast – which they claimed to love. The term ended with two parties – one for the senior boys and one for the juniors – being given in the Public Hall in Beccles for the Gravesend scholars. Similar parties were given for the Dagenham children.

Meanwhile, during that first term, the Gravesend school occupied various halls in the town, such as the 'Red Triangle Club Hall' – the YMCA – which was blacked out, cleaned and heated for the purpose. The Club also provided lunch for the mothers of those evacuees who were accompanied, but this scheme failed because the mothers preferred to spend time with their children in their billets at lunch time. Early in January 1940, at the start of the new term, the school moved lock stock and barrel to Shipmeadow House. The boys travelled daily from Beccles to Shipmeadow, a distance of 3-4 miles each way, by bus or cycle or, more frequently, on foot, which was a particular burden during that winter when there were heavy falls of snow through which the boys had to trudge.

In May 1941, Beccles was included in a new 'defence area' to protect against the possibility of a German invasion, and all compulsory evacuees within that area were ordered to move out of it. Moving to the Midlands or to South Wales was recommended but the Gravesend grammar school headmaster pressed for and received permission to move to Bungay, which was outside the defence area. A line had to be drawn somewhere. It was drawn at ten miles from the coast and fell between Beccles and Bungay, though the evacuees would have been no safer in the latter than in the former unless the steadfast citizens of the ancient borough of Beccles had been able to repel the invaders! The school continued to use Shipmeadow House, the boys and staff travelling the slightly shorter distance from Bungay each day. They continued to do this until the summer of 1942. By this time quite a number of the boys had left the school, especially after the summer examinations, and several members of the staff had been conscripted into the forces. Even as early as February 1940 almost a quarter of the 400 unaccompanied evacuees – that is without their parents – and half of the 94 teachers (again, not a bad pupil:teacher ratio!), together with almost all the 158 mothers who had accompanied their children from Gravesend had returned home. As a consequence of these factors, the whole school went back to Gravesend. They were happy to return to their homes and families and acknowledged that they had received great kindness and care from the families with whom they had stayed. One of them recalled that he had found the streets of Beccles 'very clean but very narrow' – he missed the wider streets of Gravesend. Shipmeadow House then became a pig farm and later still a chicken farm, and is now converted into apartments.

Two of the many things which surprise me about the evacuees are, first, the high proportion of teachers to pupils, both from Dagenham and from Gravesend – maybe the teachers were as keen to leave the threatened areas as were the children; and, second, the high proportion of evacuees who were accompanied by their mothers, certainly in the case of those from Gravesend. I am not clear where these mothers stayed or under what arrangements, but it was natural for them to want to be with their children and away from the dangers in Dagenham and Gravesend.

When Beccles was included in the 'defence area' from which compulsory evacuees had to be moved, the question naturally arose as to whether the children of Beccles families ought also to be moved – be evacuated. The authorities very quickly announced that there was 'no intention whatsoever to evacuate Beccles schoolchildren', though they did intend to evacuate children from Lowestoft and Great Yarmouth. Although some of the original Dagenham evacuees returned to their homes within the first year of the war, a new influx of hundreds of evacuees and their mothers arrived in the parishes near Beccles – presumably outside the 'defence area' – towards the end of 1941 to join the large numbers who had not left. These were children whose homes in London had been destroyed in the blitz. They came by train from London, were taken to the Area School in Beccles where they were medically examined and given a hot meal before being taken by bus to their new homes in the surrounding parishes.

Within eighteen months of the war starting Suffolk and Norfolk took in a third of a million evacuees in official parties and many more privately. It was a massive operation. Inevitably there were problems; some children refused to board the train at the last moment; large families, of which there were many, refused to be split up; several mothers were expecting babies, in some cases imminently, and premises and facilities for their confinement had to be found.

In July 1944 there was another and unexpected influx of evacuees from London – 436 children and 94 adults fleeing from the new threat of the flying bombs.

Although there was no official evacuation from Beccles, a number of parents considered sending their children to Canada for the duration of the war. I recall my parents discussing this and deciding not to do so. The only children I know who were evacuated to Canada or the USA were Micah Clarke's three children, Patrick, Shirley and Prudence.

The Area School

In September 1940 I moved up to senior school and went to the Area School. I had not been allowed to sit the scholarship examination to go to the grammar school because 'the authorities', whoever they were, said I was not up to it and would not pass the examination. Not being given the opportunity to try the examinations was a source of concern to my parents, though I do not recall being much troubled by it myself. My elder sister, Muriel, had also not been allowed to sit the examination three years earlier. They had to intervene a year later for me to be allowed to sit the deferred scholarship examination. This they successfully did against the strong opposition of Miss G M Woolner, the senior mistress, known – with rare vulgarity for Beccles at that time – as 'Titty' Woolner, a disrespectful but striking tribute to her outstandingly top-heavy anatomy. Today fourth form wags, noticing that her initials were G M, might well claim that she had been genetically modified and would ponder on the endless possibilities G M might have for anatomical modification. She had joined the staff when the secondary school part of Peddars Lane School – where she had been Muriel's senior mistress – closed and staff and pupils were transferred to the Area School. Shortly after I left the Area School a year later she was appointed head of the Ravensmere School. Muriel had also taken and passed the deferred scholarship examination but I am not aware that my parents intervened to enable her to sit it, though they may have done.

The Area School was a new one, opened in 1939. The teachers I remember at the school included the headmaster Mr. George Odam who seemed to me to be very strict and who took an enormous pride in his school – he was, after all, the head of a large, innovative, type of educational institution, occupying a brand new, up-to-date, set of buildings with science laboratories and other dedicated classrooms, for example for woodwork, metal work – including a blacksmith's forge – and domestic science, new and modern furniture, excellent equipment and large playing fields, although I do not remember playing any football or other games there. There were also an excellently equipped assembly hall and gymnasium, changing rooms with showers, which were great innovations at the time. All pupils were required to take to school each Friday a small piece of fine sand paper and a square of cloth with 'Brasso' on it in order to remove ink stains from the woodwork and to polish the brass covers to the inkwells of the new desks. Mr. Odam demanded high standards of behaviour and shouted at, and threatened to clip the ear of, anyone running in the corridors especially the 'crush corridor', a term we had never heard of before – it was a wider corridor than the rest and located where the volume of pupils passing was at its greatest.

Among the teachers, I also particularly remember Miss Horne, from Lowestoft, a retired, kind, mathematics teacher who had returned to teaching because of the war. She was a good teacher and I learned later that she had taught one of the mathematics teachers who later taught me at the grammar school: Johnston Brown. Miss Horne was our form mistress and did not simply teach mathematics, for she also taught us English and some simple acting. I recall of the English, that she dealt with pronunciation by getting us to repeat carefully and well mouthed, 'Let me see, said Mr. Jimmy at the butcher's shop. Give me some suet, please, and then I think I'll take a chop. You see how well he ends his words, this careful Mr. Jimmy? He never thinks of 'Lemme see' or dreams of saying 'Gimme'.' And of play acting I recall my own lines, 'Here come I, Mr. Jack, with my wife and family on my back.' Heaven knows what the play was about, and now it seems rather juvenile for the first year of secondary school. It must have been difficult for the staff to judge how much each of us had already learned and the level at which to pitch their teaching when we came from different schools from a somewhat wider area than the primary schools covered. Our reading was certainly at different levels, but we were all given the chance and encouragement to read as much as we liked, or could. I and others read books which were significantly more advanced than the 'Here come I, Mr. Jack…' level would suggest. Miss Horne was able to take over and further encourage my own growing interest in reading which had been started at home and had been further stimulated by Miss Hewin.

I faintly remember a Mr. Squirrel who taught science and joined the Area School staff from the old National School. He subsequently caused a bit of a stir in the town by committing suicide – then looked upon as much as a criminal and frighteningly evil affair as a personal tragedy, about which one talked, if at all, in hushed tones.

The only other name among the teachers that I remember was Mr. Leslie Easter. I do not even remember what he did or what he looked like. He was, I believe, one of the few surviving teachers who had taught at the old Beccles College and had then gone on to the Ravensmere National School until the Area School opened.

I do not recall much about the deferred scholarship examination which I must have taken in the spring of 1941, except that it was considered an important occasion and one was told that fish for breakfast would enhance one's brain power! My father encouraged me to use my imagination in writing essays – then called 'compositions' – and this was advice which I did not appreciate until very much later in life. It seemed to me in my earlier years that one ought to deal in facts and not to imagine too much. I was seriously mistaken in this view for many years. I now see imagination not as fantasy but as creativity. Being creative has become an important value to me and I much admire creative people – people who make things and leave something worthwhile, whether tangible or intangible, behind them.

Just over a year after the war began and just after I had started at the Area School we were abruptly awakened early one Sunday morning by a loud bang. Dennis, who was sleeping next to the bedroom wall, felt the house shake badly – I felt nothing. We soon learned that the town had had its first air raid and that bombs had fallen on houses in Kilbrack Road – very close to where my Uncle Harry (Grandfather Ward's brother) and Aunt Annie, lived – and had killed Mr. and Mrs. Tricker who lived in one of the houses. It was a semi-detached house which suffered a direct hit from a high explosive bomb and was destroyed. Mrs. Tricker was thrown out of bed onto the pavement outside her house and died immediately. Mr. Tricker, who was a veteran of the Boer War and the First World War, was badly injured and died a little later in hospital. The family in the adjoining house were relatively unscathed. Another house in Kilbrack Road was also destroyed and another two were badly damaged but mercifully the occupants of both these houses were not badly injured. Several additional bombs exploded nearby. Before dropping its bombs the enemy plane had flown low over the town dropping flares and incendiary bombs – which were soon put out. It was presumably hoping to hit either the Elliot and Garood works nearby where munitions were being made or the railway station. The Trickers had six sons, all of them had played for the Beccles Football team and one of them, a school teacher, had joined the Arsenal Football Club. The town, naturally, was much shaken by this bombing and these fatalities.

Memory is strange and forgetfulness is stranger. For example I recently learned from a Beccles newspaper that during the evening of 3 March 1945, a lone German bomber flew over the town and dropped fifty anti-personnel bombs in Kemps Lane. Now, I lived with my family not more than a hundred yards from Kemps Lane across an open field but, wrack my brains as I have, I have absolutely no memory of the event, or of anyone mentioning it – there is not even the distant muted tinkling of a tiny bell in my mind. Had it not been recorded in print in the local newspaper at the time, I would have dismissed it as utterly untrue.

The Sir John Leman Grammar School

I must have passed the scholarship examination – which probably meant simply that fees were not charged. In any event, in the autumn of 1941 I went to the Sir John Leman grammar school – founded in 1631. Sir John, a bachelor, lived to the age of 98. Going there was a strange experience and I still, many years later, cannot work out what was different about it. One could not say that the pupils were invariably cleverer than others I knew at the Area School because many of them manifestly were not. Indeed, a number of my contemporaries at the Area School went on to college and became school teachers, and one became the works manager of a large engineering works. These were accomplishments greater than a significant section of the Leman School population. A number of the children were sent to the Leman School for social rather than for educational reasons. The tradesmen of the town and nearby farmers tended to send their offspring there rather than to a non-grammar school, and the entrance examination was considerably less demanding than the scholarship examination. Additionally, those who went at the age of about eight years into the preparatory class – Form One – and presumably without having to pass an entrance examination, were guaranteed entrance to Form Two, the first year of secondary school. Form Two therefore had a mixture of pupil entrants – those fee payers entering from Form One, those fee payers who passed the entrance examination, those who passed the scholarship and those who passed the deferred scholarship. None of this was the subject of comment but there probably was an underlying difference in the general ability and aspirations of the four groups. So far as the aspirations are concerned, most of the children of the tradesmen and farmers were expected and destined to enter their parents' business, so how well or badly they did at school was unlikely to affect their careers. This applied whether the child was a scholarship pupil or a fee-paying pupil. I guess non-tradesman and non-farmer parents of the fee payers and scholarship children had other aspirations and expectations, but I repeat, none of this seemed to be of any importance or consequence at the time. The school was beginning to pass into a new era, from the small, select institution which it had been to a larger, more varied school. I think Muriel, who preceded me at the school by three years, was at the end of the former and I was at the beginning of the latter.

A marked superficial difference from the Area School was that the Leman School had a uniform. For the boys this consisted of a grey shirt and flannel trousers; a light blue, dark blue and white striped tie; a navy blue blazer; and cap. For short periods in really hot summers boys were permitted to remove their blazers and ties while in school. The blazer and cap bore the school badge: three dolphins, marking the membership of the Fishmongers' Guild of the founder of the school – Sir John Leman, who had also been Lord Mayor of London. The girls wore a white square-necked blouse, navy square-necked gym tunic and in winter a strange close-fitting navy cap or, in summer, a straw panama hat. Those boys and girls who won school athletics championships wore a distinctive badge: a pale blue, single dolphin, in the case of boys on their blazer and in the case of girls on their gym tunic. If one won more than one such annual championship one wore more than one such badge. Curiously, I recall at least one girl wearing three such badges but no boy wearing more than two. In the case of the boys, the award of first eleven cricket or football colours was marked with the right to wear a pale blue ribbon round one's cap, or two such ribbons if one possessed both cricket and football colours. Rex Butcher and I were fortunate to win two annual championships each and to have first eleven colours for both cricket and football. Those few boys who sported two single-dolphin blazer badges and two pale blue rings round their caps formed the school's sporting elite, though that distinction was not always accompanied by similar academic distinction. One was expected to wear full school uniform during the week when on the way to or from school. Any default on this was met with Saturday morning detention, no matter how high up the school one was. By the time a school photograph was taken in March 1948, while the girls all wore a uniform – which varied in design depending on whether they were sixth formers – few of the boys wore a blazer.

There was another difference in dress at the Leman School in that the staff wore black academic gowns – not all the staff, and in decreasing numbers as the years passed. They were not always the older teachers who wore gowns but I recall Dr. Wood, Mr. Glover, Miss McCarthy, Miss Budd, Mr, Johnston Brown, Mr. Clarke, but I am sure there were others. 'Twas said that in the case of the men the gown was used to cover up the frayed cuffs and elbows of their jackets. They certainly kept the chalk dust off their clothes.

In retrospect, there was an interesting change in the friends we had as primary school children – when our friends were our brothers and sisters and those children in our road – to our friends when we went to secondary school when they were our class mates and fellow sports players. Many years after I left school and went to a reunion I found that the old students I knew best and with whom I talked most were not my class mates but contemporary football and cricket players whether they were in the same class and age group or not.

What do I recall of my early days at the Sir John Leman School? In Form Two, on my first day there, the woodwork master, Mr. Pierson, 'Percy', Cross, was teaching us how to saw a plank in the school woodwork room which was much smaller and considerably less well equipped than that at the Area School. In the course of this demonstration a large wooden-framed picture of various types of indigenous tree fell from the wall to the floor. Percy scarcely looked up as it crashed, and certainly did not stop sawing, but merely – presumably by way of explanation – muttered 'Vibration'. Percy was a strange, if kindly, man. He had joined the school staff in 1914 and taught part of the week at the Bungay Grammar School and part at the Leman School. He was, I believe, the only member of staff then to possess a car, and a very ancient one at that. The younger of his two daughters died at an early age of meningitis, and this, affecting him badly, may have accounted for some of his strangeness. The first skill we were required to master, if indeed we ever did, was to plane a block of wood and mark it with a pencilled 'loop', then plane the edge at right angles to the first surface, marking it with a 'v', the former being called 'face side' and the latter 'face edge'. I have never known these technical terms to be used outside Percy's classes but I am sure that no boy passing through his hands ever forgot the instruction to 'plane face side' and 'plane face edge'. The first artefact we made was a spade cleaner for use in our horticulture lessons – as gardening was known at the Leman School. It was fashioned from a single piece of soft wood, crudely shaped and requiring neither joints nor skill. Next we made a pot stand whether for a tea pot or a flower pot I never learned. Probably it made no difference. What surprises me today is that none of the wits, of whom there were plenty, asked Percy if the thing could be used for chamber pots. The spade cleaner soon disappeared but the pot stand remained in my parents' possession, albeit in the garage or garden shed, for many years. I inherited a partially completed small table or stool made of oak from a boy who had left the class the previous year, and I completed it, largely, I recall, by screwing the parts together and finishing it with a coat of linseed oil and polish. This piece of furniture still graces our house, and members of the family, believing that I was totally and solely responsible for its construction, much admire it. I also made a small corner shelf of dark walnut wood which lasted several years but is now no longer. Although a good deal of soft wood was used, there seemed to be plenty of oak and walnut wood available too. Woodwork classes – for boys only – were confined to the first two years and had to be given up for more academic pursuits thereafter – a pity, I have always thought. Two enduring images of the woodwork room remain in my mind's eye. The first is the ancient and much used black cast-iron glue pot in which lumps of resin-like glue were heated and softened ready to be used. There seemed as much old glue stuck to the outside of the pot as there was new glue inside the pot. Those were the days before propriety brands of impact and other glues in tubes were manufactured. The other memory is of Percy expertly honing chisels on an oiled stone block, moving the blades rapidly back and forwards and occasionally turning the block as he did so. None of us ever mastered the technique and we made a frightful mess of trying to do so. Unlike the Area School, the Leman School did not teach, or have equipment for learning, metal work.

Writing of woodwork reminds me that there was a boy in our class named Woodcock who was gifted at fretwork of which he did a great deal at home. One of his specialities was to make a well crafted wooden handgun which used elastic bands for firing the 'bullets'. These were not in any way dangerous and they were much sought after and their maker made a tidy income from selling them. Fellow pupils – the boys – will recall that he was known as 'Timber Diddle'!

We were taught gardening during our first year, a subject taken far more seriously by our teachers than by most of the pupils. These lessons took place in the school garden. There was a succession of teachers. Miss Lily Jones, a rather stern, prim and proper person, taught us to start with and she was followed – I forget in which order – by Mr. 'Posy' White, Mrs. Palmer and Mr. Pottenger. We were shown the only 'proper' way, we were told, to cultivate the garden which was 'double digging', the excavation of a spit's depth of soil and then the digging and turning of another spit's depth on top of which was then returned the soil from the first trench. It seemed a waste of time and energy to me, or at least not, as one might say today, 'cost effective'. I recall of Mr. Pottenger that he taught us composting, in which horticultural art he cautioned us to be careful lest the decaying material 'heat up like buggery'. Save for one occasion much later, when a master hurt his hand at cricket, I do not recall any other member of staff even mildly cussing.

In my first year at the Sir John Leman School, the headmaster, Mr. Gordon S Humphreys, took a grave dislike to me. He took us for what might be called elocution lessons and seemed to enjoy humiliating me and poking fun at my accent – which may well have been markedly Suffolk-oriented though I should not have thought more so than most others. In particular he ridiculed my pronunciation of the word 'Daisy' in the song 'Daisy, Daisy, Give me your answer, do.' He corrected me and corrected me, and in the end I gave in and pronounced it 'Deezey, Deezey,' which seemed to satisfy him, or at least he laid off for a while. If it was Deezy he wanted, who was I not to give him Deezy? How he would have handled, or expected me to handle the pronunciation difference between Daisy and Breezy, I do not know. He would have done much better to have dwelt on some of the unusual aspects of local language, for example the locally widespread use of the word 'funny' to mean 'very' which led to such curious expressions as 'funny serious'. The man was not half the teacher Miss Horne had been! Ah. I feel a little better now!

Then at a later date, still in my first year, he suddenly walked into the classroom, dismissed the girls and said – correctly – that there had been a practice for some time in the school of boys smoking, that Baker was one of them, which was also true, and he told all those to whom Baker had given cigarettes to stand up. All but a few stood up, and I was very nearly expelled. What he must have known, or should have found out, was that most of the boys in the class took it in turn to buy cigarettes and share them with the rest. He could have asked them if any other named boy had given them cigarettes, and the same number would have stood up. None of us smoked during school hours or on school premises. Incidentally, I acquired my first cigarettes by chance. In the window of a small confectionary-tobacconist-stationery shop in Newgate I saw a notice selling 'Five Darts for Two Pence'. This struck me as a very reasonable price for darts so I went in and bought two penny worth. They turned out to be five cigarettes which went under the trade name of 'Darts'. Had I had my wits about me I should have remembered that darts, as used on dart boards, usually came in threes and not fives. The shop keeper ought not to have sold them to me because I was only twelve at the time but I guess he had his living to make and he took the risk of prosecution. For my part I guess I took the view, 'Why waste the cigarettes?' and so shared them with some of my friends. Humphreys, who I am sure would not have been impressed with this explanation had I been sufficiently unwise to proffer it, accused me, too, of gambling, which was not true.

On another occasion, a Monday morning, he called me out after assembly and reprimanded me for talking in church the previous day. I was then a member of the St. John's Ambulance Brigade and he was in charge of the Air Training Corps, and both had been at a church parade. Whether this had anything to do with his reprimand I do not know. It certainly had little or nothing to do with him. I do not think I had been talking in church, at least not solely or excessively. This was the occasion on which Bridget sent me a solicitous note in class enquiring as to what had happened.

I have thought a lot about this over the years and have concluded – though with no great confidence – that Humphreys, in the particular case of talking in church was aiming his ill temper not only at me but at the Area School, because it was from the Area School that the St. John's Ambulance Brigade and the Army Cadet Force mainly drew its members, while the Air Training Corps drew its members mainly from the Leman School. I guess he saw the Area School as inferior to the Leman School and therefore the Army Cadet Force and St. John's Ambulance inferior to the Air Training Corps. I have found it difficult to see things this way or to understand his reasoning. I am not sure, but what might have been better at the Leman School was its provision to pupils of opportunities and a wide range of educational and social experiences, which was very good. There seemed at the Area School too ready a willingness to dismiss the perceived weaker pupils, those who did not learn as quickly as others. To have one's children dismissed by the headmaster as capable of becoming 'only a domestic servant' in the case of girls, and 'suitable only for manual work' in the case of boys, I know riled all hell out of some parents. Even so, a number of the boys from the Area School, by determination and personal ability did extremely well in their careers after they left school. I cannot think of any other difference which might have justified the view that the Leman School was superior to the Area School.

Early in 1941 the Air Ministry announced a pre-entry scheme for boys over the age of 16 who were interested in becoming aircrew or ground staff members of the RAF. Humphreys was quick off the mark, formed an ATC Flight at the Leman School, got himself made officer – though only a Flying Officer – in charge, and within the first two months had recruited 70-80 sixteen to eighteen year old members. I wonder how many of them he bullied into joining – Meiau! A year or so later, and many of his earlier recruits having been called up to the RAF, the recruiting age for the ATC was dropped from 16 to 14 and maybe even 13, and it was from this age group that he determined to increase his numbers even if, as I suspect, he poached them from the St. John's Ambulance Brigade.

Whatever the roots of his dislike of me, I did later join the Air Training Corps but only after Humphreys had left in 1943. I am not aware of being disliked in quite this way by anyone else. No other person at any stage of my life has been deliberately and gratuitously nasty to me. Humphreys was the exception to the general rule that none of our teachers was a bully, vindictive or given to victimization. Strangely, though I did not look at it this way at the time nor for many years later, becoming a member of the ATC did me a great deal of good. I learned a lot – but not of such useful stuff as I did with St. John's Ambulance; it gave me the opportunity to learn something about leadership; and I rose quite quickly to become the Flight Sergeant, the senior rank open to non-adults. Furthermore, it was the ATC which provided me with a good deal of athletics, meeting other teenager athletes, and travel within England – Kettering, Purley and London. There was also a number of annual camps for the ATC – at Mildenhall, Aylesbury and Margate. These were great fun; we met cadets from other parts of the country and felt quite grown up, sleeping in barracks and eating in the messes, as well as having 0.22 rifle shooting competitions and flying in various types of aircraft.

The senior mistress when I first went to the Leman School was Miss 'Granny' Barton, a spinster lady close to retirement, somewhat frumpish in appearance and old fashioned in manner. She taught us English but I have no recollection at all of her teaching, though I do have a clear recollection of the final stages of one of her classes. There was a small member of the class, a boy – let us call him Brown – who I believe even in his early teens was an accomplished organist. He was also quite a humorist in his way – skilfully, for example, distorting the words of 'The Ancient Mariner' to describe Percy Cross's car: 'And now 'twas like old cocoa tins, now like a burning tyre ...' – though on this particular occasion he was, intently serious – seriously, if indecorously, picking his nose! Granny Barton espied him doing this and had an attack of the vapours, disbelieving her aging eyes. Recovering her composure, if only partially, she ordered the errant Brown out of the class, and as he stretched out his hand to open the door to leave she realized to her additional horror that the very hand with which he imminently proposed to open the door was that to which was attached the finger which so recently and horrifyingly had been half way up his right nostril. Warding off a swoon, she rallied and called on her inner strength to instruct young Brown to take a piece of paper from the waste paper basket and with it carefully open the door and depart before the wrath of the Almighty descended upon us all. Brown did as he was bid, and the class of hooting boys and tittering girls would have settled down had not the distraught Miss Barton, steadying herself on the edge of her desk, summoned up sufficient strength to beg to excuse herself and end the class early in order that she might revive herself with the smelling salts which she habitually carried in her ancient and commodious handbag should the need arise as it did on this lamentable occasion. She left the school soon after this, though whether because of reaching retirement age or because of the woeful Brown incident, I do not know.

It was this self same Brown who invented, designed or discovered the once – for a brief period – well known but now virtually unheard of 'Blunderance'. What on earth, you may well ask, was a 'Blunderance? Let me explain its essence. At the end of a morning or afternoon's classes, when the pupils were ready to leave the room, a boy, selected or volunteering in advance, would 'accidentally' stumble or blunder as he went through the doorway. The boy following quickly behind him would blunder over him and fall next to or on top of him. Others would follow, 'unable' to avoid the growing and growling mass of writhing boys beneath them, shouting well practiced and insincere expressions of regret and protestations of helplessness. Both the act of blundering and the pile of blunderers were known as a 'Blunderance'. The fascinating thing is that the Blunderance was perfect in its original form. There was no proto-type. There was no gradual evolution. It was immaculate from the very beginning. The only variation in executing the Blunderance was the decision – which was made by a kind of silent vote, a kind of unspoken tribal unanimity, often made at the very last moment – whether to blunder before the girls left the room so as to trap them in the room and enhance the mayhem, or to let the girls leave first so as to gain time to prolong the Blunderance. A few of the girls asked to join the Blunderance, but despite the keenness of some of us to agree, this was reckoned to be going too far, was indecorous and unseemly, and heaven knows where their participation might have led. I wonder what happened to young Brown? He must surely have gone on to greater things in life, unless of course Miss Barton left a note on his file.

In some respects George Lacroix, a French boy whose family escaped to England early in the war, provided the antithesis of the Blunderance. He was a member of our class and, apart from his being a friendly lad who fitted in well, all I remember of him is his ability, which he demonstrated only a few times – to escape from the classroom without the teacher noticing that he had gone until it was too late. I am sure he did this only with certain teachers, for most of them were too vigilant not to see that something as startling as a boy creeping out of the room was going on. Without explanation or warning and seemingly on the spur of the moment, he would duck down between the desks and crawl towards the door. Then when an appropriate moment arrived he would quietly open the door – and he was gone! The pupils who he had to crawl past on his way to the door pretended not to notice, and without their loyal silence he could never have succeeded. Having escaped from France, escaping from a classroom in Beccles must have been kid's play to him! As with so many others, I wonder what happened to him.

There are significant, unfortunate and lasting gaps in my understanding of English grammar and this may possibly, though not of course wholly, be attributable to the lack of continuity in the teaching staff. Miss Barton started us off but there then followed several others. Miss C Proudlock, a Manchester graduate, came at the end of my first term at the Leman School, was young, timid and did not last long. She was followed by Miss Mearns who came in 1943, departed the following year and left no footprint on the sand between my ears. Then there was Mr. Sowerby – splendid Dickensian name – who spoke with a marked northern accent, drawing out some of his vowels – 'Loook here, Wooodward, where's your boook?' for example. In class he lost me in a miasma of iambic pentameters, which I understood neither then nor now, though he easily convinced me of what I was fully to appreciate only later, that even in the absence of rhyming endings, the beauty of poetry lies in its sounds. I fear that I much embarrassed him on the train to Bungay one Saturday morning when he was accompanying the football team playing against Bungay Grammar School, by asking him to expand on some of the 'Seven Deadly Sins' which somehow had cropped up in one of his lessons. He obliged but his normally mild stammer increased when he got to lechery, and he eventually leaned towards me and whispered, presumably so that the other boys present could not hear, 'excessive sexual intercourse'. Indeed, so quietly did he whisper that I could not hear him and I asked him – 'Excessive what, Sir?' He repeated his reply, slightly more loudly, thereby attracting the attention of our fellow passengers. I had not intended to embarrass him, and I regret that I put the poor man at considerable ill ease.

When Mr. Sowerby left the school, his place was taken by Miss Mary Mercer, who I mentioned earlier in passing. She, also, came from the north of England – the third one in a short period of time – but different and, so it seemed to us, virtually without an accent. She was young and pretty, refreshingly modern in her dress and in her approach to young people and their education. She was like a breath of fresh air and her arrival coincided with the ending of the war, with the start of our School Certificate course and with what Johnston Brown saw as my timely 'seeing the light' and for the first time taking school work seriously. Who else would have taken us out of our classroom in summer to sit on the grass outside and talk about Masefield's 'Lost Endeavour' and Shakespeare's 'Henry the Fifth', the set books in English Literature; who else would take my homework example of a Spoonerism, 'Ruddy Blush = ****** Rush' and write on it in red ink 'We pronounce it Bluddy up north'; and who else so easily could conjure up for us – brought up in the pancakean landscape of north Suffolk – the variety and beauty of the Cumbrian Lake District's landscape while introducing us to Wordsworth's 'Michael', 'an old man, stout of heart and strong of limb' – it was almost as if she was taking us by the hand to meet this old shepherd and wander with him in his countryside.

> If from the public path you turn your step
> Up the tumultuous brook of Greenhead Ghyl,
> You will suppose that with an upright path
> Your feet must struggle; in such bold ascent
> the pastoral mountains front you face to face.
> But courage! for around that boisterous brook
> The mountains have all opened up themselves
> And made a hidden valley of their own

It was Mary Mercer and her personality rather than the subject matter itself – which in her hands came to life – that, in many ways for the first time, made English lessons attractive and interesting. The wags no longer fooled around. Yet she never had occasion to comment on or to correct our behaviour. Most of us listened spellbound. Many of her pupils – I'm sure she would have called us 'students' – owe a great deal to her. She did not stay at the school for more than a few years, but her impact was extraordinary.

Probably the greatest and most memorable of all the 'characters' on the staff and one who taught at all levels, from the second form to the upper sixth form, was Mr. 'Micah' Clarke. Any group of boys who passed through – or rather under – his hands could write a long and very amusing book about Micah. The anecdotes, handed down from generation to generation of schoolboys, are legion. He taught by rote, writing what appeared to be all that we needed to know about French grammar on the board every day throughout our school career. It was, it seemed, all scribbled on the board during our first term and then repeated daily for the next four or five years. He was a great man for 'endings', 'exceptions' and 'sounds'. The 'endings' were attached to verb roots: -s, -s, -t, -ons, -ez, -ent; or, for example, -ais, -ais, -ait, -ions, -iez, -ient. He scribbled them and we recited them. The 'exceptions' to his rules always seem to have numbered a dozen. He would give us the rule and then add the dozen exceptions: things like -age ending words which happened, I think, to be feminine. We would recite, for example, 'nage, plage, rage, … une image'; and there was another which I think had the plural ending in 'x' and which sounded like, 'bijoux, cayoux choux genoux, hiboux, something, cocoux, poux.' I had little idea at the time what it was all about and I have less now. Micah taught us – by disturbingly over-mouthed recitation – the 'sounds', the pronunciation of vowels, by getting us to recite, daily, 'Un bon vin blanc' and 'con-son-ant'.

These recited sounds immediately followed his entry to the classroom and his 'Bonjour mes elèves.' Outside observers would have been puzzled as to what on earth was going on – but then so did some internal observers!

He translated the French word 'assez' as 'somewhat, rather, fairly, enough' – so that when a boy asked a friend, 'How are you?' the reply was often 'I am somewhat, rather, fairly, enough well, thank you.' And he invented the verb 'to must', meaning 'to have to' or 'to be obliged to' because it fitted into his way of teaching verbs – and it worked!

I recall that Micah brought copies of a Free French newspaper called 'La France' which we read in class or maybe during the Friday afternoon 'clubs' sessions. There was a poem which included the words 'J'écris ton nom: La libertée', the beat of which was dot, dot, dot dash, the morse for V, i.e. V for Victory – 'repeated. Clever stuff! 'La France' also had a serial story in play form about a French super-detective and we acted the play. This detective used his own officers to pretend that they were bandits in order to catch the real bandits – I think robbing a bank – and I had to recite 'Bon! Les veritables bandits n'auraient pas fait mieux!' – 'Good! Real bandits could not have done better!' The trouble was that those who robbed the bank were not the detective's men but real bandits! Whether or not I could, or can, remember their correct tense and spelling, the words certainly have stayed in my mind!

At the end of all this – endings, exceptions and sounds – with a bit of luck we could read and write the language tolerably well but certainly not speak it well. I recall that as part of our preparation for the School Certificate examination in oral French, a Swiss priest gave us dictation and he invariably used what sounded to me like 'leur' when I would have expected 'le'. The dictation was a catastrophe. Up till then we had been using the sound 'luh' for the word 'le' and had reserved the sound 'ler' for the word 'leur'. He was a kind and most interesting man. He confessed that in his sermons in church he often got the French word for 'horns' muddled with the English and consequently described the devil as having 'cornes'. He later made a sculpture of Sir John Leman, the school's founder, which graced the headmaster's study for many a year. But from our point of view, he was brought in too late to save us, because at the actual oral examination, where we were examined in pairs, the diminutive and grizzled examiner ended by saying 'Allez-vous en' and the two of us, utterly lacking in comprehension, sat tight. He then shouted at us, 'Allez-vous en' so ferociously that we leapt up and rapidly left the room, trembling. We discovered only later that he was telling us in French to leave, and we learned this only because the other boy's mother was French and asked us how we had got on. On reflection, his having to shout at us may have saved us because we did leap up and leave as he had, unknown to us, intended us to do! In any event we both passed with credits.

Incidentally, another cleric who was called in to help teach us during the run up to School Certificate was a long-retired Anglican parson who taught us Scripture, or Religious Education or Religious Studies as the subject was variously known. Two things about him stay in my mind. First, the old boy had 'bottom trouble' of some undisclosed description because he brought a soft circular cushion with him and set it carefully on his chair before he sat down, with an audible sighing groan of relief, and started to teach. This was the source of much ribaldry among the boys. Second, he did not distinguish between preaching and teaching, and his delivery was that more suited to the pulpit than the classroom. The Acts of the Apostles was the set New Testament text and his first words to us in the very first lesson was to shout, 'Good News! Good News!' Startled, we paid closer attention to the words that followed than we might otherwise have done. He did not stay long.

Micah Clarke often pretended to be furious and was mock-brutal. He would bring errant boys out to the front of the class, crouch down, fix them with his penetrating gaze and enquire, 'What's your little game, Boy?' Irrespective of the answer – and there usually wasn't any – he would draw in a sharp, hissing, somewhat moist, intake of breath through his bristly grey moustache and appear to wallop the miscreant a resounding clout across the cheek, shouting, 'Go to your place, Laddie'. In fact, as we soon learned, it was a stage blow taken, without our seeing it, on the palm of his own hand which he placed close to the boy's face. The accents were drummed into our skulls in the same way: a stage blow with the right hand for an acute accent, one with the left hand for a grave accent, both hands for a circumflex, and a mock kick up the backside for a cedilla. If we were making no progress he would say that we were 'no furrudder', no further forward. And he would caution us, usually when it was already too late to do much about it, 'What you don't know now, you won't know next Monday', but equally one of his favourite and more encouraging sayings was, 'You'll fail in your exams if you don't revise.' He always said 'silence' instead of 'quiet', 'cease' instead of 'stop, 'proceed' instead of 'go on' and 'How do you blow?' instead of 'How are you?' Few of us escaped being addressed as a 'blithering idiot'. He of all the members of staff gave regular homework and was renowned for giving homework even during the short half-term holidays and the evening before the last day of term. He may appear to have been brutal but we knew that he was certainly not, though it is true that the girls thought less of him than did the boys. He was assisted in the lower forms by, first Miss G Lisle, a recent graduate who joined the staff in September 1941. I liked her – sufficiently to ask her to sign my autograph book, which she did with a charming and warm entry in French. She was the only teacher I saw who broke down and cried in class. This was not typical of her and I think she must have been under some strain or other. Some said that she had become pregnant which is possible but in any case she left after what seemed only a short time at the school. Her place was taken some time later by a young French mistress called, I think, Miss de la Montaigne. Micah remained clearly in charge of teaching us French and at this distance I have no idea what precise part his assistants played.

Micah taught at the school for nearly forty years and, it is said, never missed a day. When the Waveney River was flooded one winter he cycled from his home at Kirby Kane, via Lowestoft to Beccles, and arrived on time for his first class. He habitually kept his cycle pump in the inside pocket of his ancient and much worn jacket. But then he also kept school records covering many years in those pockets. On small strips of paper he would record the results of everyone's School Certificate examinations since the day he arrived at the school in, I believe, 1919, and was able to produce them from his jacket pocket at any time.

My own School Certificate examinations were held in the YMCA hall in Beccles, close to the parish church, because there was not a sufficiently large room to hold them at the school. A number of different papers, of different lengths, were being sat at the same time in this hall and the church clock outside struck every quarter of an hour – or most of them because it missed a few. During the written French examination, I wrote my answers out in rough and, thinking I had plenty of time, I started to write them out neatly on the formal examination paper. I was about half way through when the invigilator, Solly Firth said the French examinees had only five minutes left. With the variety of times being called out and with the church clock striking only some of the quarter hours, I had misjudged the time for writing out the answers neatly and, indeed, I did not complete the task. Angry with myself and despondent, I went home and threw the papers containing my rough answers in the fire place. Shortly, Micah, who save for two other occasions, never called at our house, cycled up, knocked on the front door and asked what had gone wrong. I told him and he asked where the rough papers were. I pointed to the fire place – where, by great good fortune, there was no fire burning, it being the 'front room' and summer time – and he took the papers, climbed on his bicycle and pedalled off down the road. I've no idea what he did with the papers, but he must have done something pretty dramatic because I passed with a credit. Without his intervention I should have failed. He was a man who, just below his mock-ferocious exterior, and what by today's standards was his appalling teaching technique, took infinite pains over his pupils and their welfare – far more than any other teacher. During the summer vacations he would make it his business to find out which universities and which of their departments still had vacancies. In this way, if any of his pupils – including those who had not done French in the sixth form – had done rather better in their higher school certificate examinations than they had expected and as a result were looking for places rather late in the day, he could advise them where and how to apply.

Several years after I had left school I was on holiday in Beccles with my wife and two small children, none of whom Micah had previously met. We happened to meet Mr. and Mrs. Clarke in the town and after a few minutes he said, 'Come for tea. We shall expect you at four.' We were startled by this invitation-cum-injunction, but before we could reply, whether to accept or to beg to decline the invitation, they had moved off along the street. We went for tea and arrived precisely at four o'clock. They were charming, we chatted easily, they made us completely at ease and had a present for the children. I had never been to one of the teachers' homes before, except for one brief visit to the headmaster's house after I had left school. They were beginning to get old and their furniture was worn, but they were excellent hosts. It was said that he took every newspaper every day, had done so for very many years and kept them all neatly stacked and catalogued in his garage. Although we took a walk with them round the garden we were not, to my regret, invited to see the inside of his garage. He was later knocked down and killed by a passing lorry outside his house: a sad ending.

Although Micah Clarke was the greatest of the 'characters' on the staff, the one most widely looked up to and admired, and was considered the most influential male teacher – at least by the boys though less clearly by the girls – was Frank, 'Pop', Glover, the senior master. He joined the staff of the school in 1914 when it moved to its current site and was called up and commissioned later in the First World War. He had played county cricket for Suffolk, had captained Lowestoft cricket team for many years, and taught geography, athletics and games at school. He had been called up with other male teachers early in the Second World War, but for some reason did not join the forces, instead becoming a Captain in the Local Defence Volunteers (unkindly named 'Look, Duck and Vanish') later renamed the Home Guard. He was a very large man and much respected both in the school and generally in the town. His teaching was largely by rote – of the 'capes and bays' variety – but effective. For example, he taught the geography of Ireland by describing the island as saucer-shaped with the mountains round the edge, penetrated by rivers flowing to the sea. The mountains, clockwise from the north-west included Antrim, Mourne, Wicklow, Kerry, and Connamarragh; and the rivers, which I remember much better, were Erne, Foyle, Bann, Lagen, Boyle, Liffy, Slaney, Blackwater, Lee and Shannon. These were drummed into us and remained drummed in ever thereafter. My grandsons tell me that today Wikipedia on Google also gives the mountain names in geographical order but does so anticlockwise from the south-west.

I recall an occasion when, after the morning assembly, the girls were dismissed and the boys were told to remain behind to be addressed by Mr. Glover. The headmaster was disturbed by the appearance of 'writing' on the walls of the boys' lavatory. He very briefly spoke of this 'writing', simply said 'We don't do that sort of thing' and told us to leave. Naturally, many of my fellows took an early opportunity to be excused and go to the lavatory to observe this 'writing' which by then had been expunged by the caretaker. Glover's simple 'We don't do that sort of thing' ensured that there was no more writing on the walls. He had an extraordinary influence on people. His only son had Down's syndrome and was never seen in public. This may have affected his approach to schoolboys, and we admired him greatly. Many of us who took to cricket did so because of his reputation on the field and because he taught the game to us, rather than for any other reason. He was able to get us automatically to go to the school each Saturday morning during the summer to roll the cricket pitch ready for the afternoon's match. He never had to ask and none of us resented it or tried to dodge it. He would pull the heavy roller from between the shafts and we would push from behind the roller. On the occasion of one annual athletics match against Bungay Grammar School, the Leman School had won every single event right up to the final event, the tug-of-war. Just before this, Glover asked me – I was athletics captain – to call the team quietly to one side, and he said, as an instruction rather than a prediction,, 'We will lose the tug-of-war', which we did, but it was very difficult pretending to be toppled and to fall all over the place and make it look real. It was the sort of pantomime that the comics in the school, had there been any in the team, would have exploited and made the most of. The Speech Day programme of 17 December 1946 shows that the athletics match was on 13 June 1946, and simply says, 'Bungay Grammar School defeated in Annual Athletics Contest.'

At football and cricket matches when we played at home half a dozen or so of the girls from our school made and served the two teams tea and cakes at half time. They were often the more sociably inclined of the girls, including Bubbles. This might be seen today, mistakenly, as a sexist approach but the girls seemed to enjoy doing it – as we would have, had we ever been invited to make and serve tea for the girls' hockey teams! They were all keen volunteers – and they met new boys. When we won a match on the basis of our second half performance, we often said that the opponents were still thinking of the girls who had served them tea at half time, although this possibility was not mentioned at assembly the following Monday morning when the team captains reported on the Saturday matches.

There were a few cricket matches against visiting forces teams and I recall particularly the match against the Royal Australian Air Force 'Test' team. For this occasion, as on a few others, the school team was strongly augmented with a number of masters, including Pop Glover who captained our team, and I think we had twelve men against their eleven. All I remember clearly of this match is that I was caught at first slip with the first ball which zipped off the edge of my bat before I knew it was coming. The bowler's name was V E Jackson and I saw him a few years later at a match at Lords when he was bowling for

Leicestershire. If you look him up in Wisden, as I have recently, you will find that Victor Edward Jackson was a right arm break and medium paced bowler who in his first class cricket career played 354 matches, scored 15,699 runs with an average of 28.43, including 21 centuries and 73 half-centuries. He bowled 64,389 balls and took 965 wickets, including seven innings taking ten wickets and 43 innings taking five wickets, his best being eight wickets for 43 runs. In the 1940-1941 season he played for Donald Bradman's XI, and after the war he played for Leicestershire. It was a great experience to play against him and his colleagues even though I was not long enough at the crease to get to know him better! Incidentally, at one stage Bungay Grammar School's cricket team had the psychological advantage over us when their bowlers included the nephew of the well known Bedser twins.

Relating the story about losing the tug-of-war competition against Bungay Grammar School brings back another lesson learned on the sports field. Surprisingly, again Micah Clarke was involved and equally surprisingly Solly Firth. The occasion was a cricket match in which the Air Training Corps played against the Army Cadet Force. The bowling against the ATC, for whom I was playing, was not of the highest quality and I enjoyed my innings. After a number of the strokes I replayed the stroke I should have played which today is quite common but at that time unusual, and I guess was the result of my enthusiasm and enjoyment. Micah watched the match and Solly was one of the umpires. On the Monday morning Solly went out of his way to say that although I had scored well I had made only one good stroke during the whole innings. Did I know which one it was? That was his main concern. I did not say so but I thought there had been a few more than one but I picked out a cover drive and he simply said 'Good. Don't boast about the other strokes!' Micah also spoke to me on the Monday morning. He was concerned about those 'rehearsal' strokes after playing a shot. 'Were you showing off?' I assured him that I was not, and after a momentary pause during which he looked penetratingly into my eyes, he said, 'Alright. But be careful.' That they should go out of their way to speak with me about that match indicates that they were as much concerned with their pupils' personal development as they were with their academic development, and concerned with their education beyond classroom learning.

Equally but in a different way, the school broadened our education by organizing social evenings in which we were taught to dance and to discuss current affairs occasionally in the form of debates, including political debates. Sometimes there was a sausage and mash supper cooked for us at the end of the evening, which was great. I was not keen on the debates and recall, as many of us do, clever responses only after the event, being too slow or tongue-tied to reply at the appropriate time. There was just one exception, when to a rather right wing claim that in society the cream always rises to the top I too loudly expressed the view which I had intended to be a whisper to the person next to me, that scum too always rises to the top. The dancing was fun and I recall our excitement and surprise when Miss Collis, the girls' physical education teacher, taught us the tango. Daring thigh-pressing and knee-interlocking in public – what more could teenagers ask for? And for once boys had a legitimate excuse for walking a girl home, albeit with diversions, at night. One lad, younger than me – let's call him 'Billy', though that was not his real name – told me that he and his girl friend went home via the London Road cemetery – to which access was easier during the war when the iron railings were taken away as scrap metal – and they agreed that they would kiss only when they saw a shooting star in the skies. Billy reckoned that on school dancing lesson evenings the Milky Way did a roaring trade in shooting stars!

Education in sex matters was virtually non-existent and even the sixth form biology classes did not mention them save obliquely in connection with the earth worm and the frog. But the December 1946 School Speech Day programme says that from 26 to 28 November 1945 Miss E Taylor ran a course in sex education for girls at the school, and from 4 to 7 December Mr. Cyril Bibby ran a similar course for boys. I have no recollection of this and would be very surprised if I attended the course. If I did attend, it could have had little impact on me and none on my memory. I do recall the name Cyril Bibby but only vaguely as a socialist health educationalist. Maybe the courses were confined to the sixth form. It would not be surprising if they were run at the instigation of Dr. Wood, the headmaster, for he came to the school from Bedales School, an independent co-educational boarding and day school set up in the late nineteenth century as a reaction to the Victorian limitations of the English public schools. It became famous for its liberal ethos and relaxed attitudes. Dr. Wood was a good headmaster and most of us got on well with him, but I do not remember his being noticeably liberal or relaxed in his attitudes, though the 1946 Speech Day programme suggests that he was quite modern in his running of the school. Had he arrived at the school a few years earlier I might have been spared the trauma of being vilified and bullied by his predecessor!

Though I am oblivious of Cyril Bibby's tuition, I remember clearly that two of us – Dennis Pegram and I – at about the age of fourteen or fifteen, two of the few openly known to have a girl friend, were taken aside on a couple of afternoons after school and Johnston Brown spoke with us about sex though that word was not mentioned. His tuition consisted solely of going through some of the pages, especially the drawings, in a largish book he had on sex matters. It was confined to the relevant parts of the human body and there was no mention of morality or relationships. He would not let us borrow or even handle the book. I do not know if our tutor felt better at the end of it but, even on reflection now, it told us little that we did not know or could not guess and it afforded us some mild amusement. Much more enlightening and enjoyable was the book, 'Life Long Love' which one of the girls possessed and which she kindly passed round to others in the class, girls and boys. This is in no way to say that sex education was not necessary, and I can illustrate this quite easily. At about the age of thirteen a group of four of us, two boys and two girls, went to the cinema to see a film in which a woman excitedly told her husband that she was pregnant. He was delighted and very surprised: 'Darling, I didn't know. How wonderful' – sort of thing. We, both boys and girls, discussed this after the film and puzzled over how the husband could have been unaware that his wife was pregnant. To us intercourse inevitably resulted in pregnancy – not a bad deterrent – so if she was pregnant how could he possibly not know? The explanation we eventually came to was – and this came from one of the girls – that the wife must have made love to her husband whilst he was asleep. Satisfied that this was the explanation, we did not go into the anatomical mechanics of how it was actually accomplished.

I have mentioned Pop Glover's cricket coaching. This started on the second day of the third term of my first year, early in May 1942 and I was looking forward eagerly to being taught and playing the game. During the afternoon, a Friday, I was on the playing field with other boys, though maybe not all of those in my class, when the school caught fire, and smoke billowed and flames burst from the upper storey. I and most others watched from the playing field as the staff and senior boys threw as many of the movable contents as possible out of the classroom windows, and the building was hurriedly evacuated. One of the senior boys had a nasty cut on his forehead but there were no other significant injuries. The fire brigade was called, arrived, and soon slurped up the muddy contents of the school pond. Fortunately the Beccles Water Company had a large tank at its premises on the far side of the boys' playing field and this source was used, but not in time to avoid the upper storey of the building being seriously damaged. I recall, at what seemed a long time after the fire, being at David's home when he opened a cupboard and out tumbled heaven knows how many copies of 'The Merchant of Venice'! I remember little else directly about the fire. I went home, disappointed that our first cricket coaching had been so rudely interrupted. Over the weekend Micah Clarke cycled round the town – or at least our part of the town – to tell us that arrangements had been made for the Leman School to share the premises of the Peddars Lane School and the Area School, part time, and that we should initially foregather at the Parish Church on Monday – just three days after our school was burnt down. I learned more details later from local newspapers. The fire started in the false roof of the building. It was the timber merchants across the road on the other side of the boys' playing field who, noticing smoke coming from the roof of the school, first raised the alarm and did so before anyone in the school or any of us on the playing field noticed that anything was amiss I guess that although they were not in danger of the fire spreading to their premises, they were accustomed to look out for signs of fire on nearby premises. Although there were 300 pupils enrolled at the school only 220 of them were in the building at the time of the fire. Fire damage was confined to the roof and upper floor. The main hall, the caretaker's house, the headmaster's office and the staff room were undamaged except by smoke. The property taken or thrown out of the building was put first on the tennis court and later taken for safe keeping to neighbouring houses and garages and some was taken into safe custody by staff and pupils. The school records, including an old school bag from 1549, were saved as was all the ATC equipment. Unfortunately, the text books and notes of the sixth formers, due soon to take their Higher School Certificate examinations, were lost or damaged. Nonetheless, four out of the five candidates, including the injured senior boy, passed the Higher School Certificate as did all 25 pupils taking the School Certificate, 16 of them matriculating, including my sister Muriel. Arrangements were quickly made for the 150 pupils who had lunch at school to use the British Restaurant. In its borrowed and shared multi-site premises, the school soon adjusted to the new circumstances and settled down to routine school work.

Our cricket tuition during the whole of that summer term in our first year was devoted to Pop Glover teaching us the standard batting strokes – forward and backward defence, forward and backward attack, the hook, the pull, the drive, the cut and, a little later, the leg glide which was the only fancy diversion from the path of correct cricket which he, I think reluctantly, allowed. He taught us how to field and to back up, and how to catch the ball. In throwing in from the field we were told to throw it in 'hard over the top of the stumps' where the keeper could gather it easily, ready to knock the bails off. He paid less attention to teaching us to bowl, save, at least in my case, to wallop the ball high over the boundary and say, 'If you will bowl the ball like that you must expect me to hit it hard.' There were only three permitted calls – 'yes', 'no' and 'wait' – called by the striker if the ball was in front of or level with him and by his partner if not. A slow ball to cover was 'yes' (some times accompanied by 'Come one') a fast one 'no'. The non-striker was told to 'follow up', as the bowler bowled so as to be ready for a quick single. The striker ran up the leg side of the wicket, the non striker up the off. They never crossed on the wicket. One never took a step to leg when batting, and to ensure this, Pop put a stump immediately behind the batsman's legs. When, more than sixty years later my teenage twin grandsons went to a summer coaching course at Lords they were taught exactly the same basic strokes. Pop Glover would be appalled today to see the atrocious running between wickets – up the middle, crossing over and generally getting in each other's way on tight runs – the frequency with which batsmen 'wander away to leg', and fail to follow up sensibly. He would also smile in puzzlement to see the helmets, face guards, leg pads, arm shields, thigh pads, cuff bands, dark spectacles and strapless, slip-in 'boxes' – which I tease my grandsons by pointing out that the boxes are smaller than they were in our day! They each, and all their fellow players, carry huge leather bags full of gear when they practice or play a game, bags which are larger than the single bag we took for the whole team! But Pop would have delighted in the skill displayed by batsmen in the modern game and I know that my grandsons, one a batsman, the other a bowler, play better cricket than I did.

In seeming to pay much less attention to bowling, maybe Pop thought that either we could or we could not bowl and that he could do little about it, but he could do something about everyone's batting: batsmen won or lost games, not bowlers. The concentration was overwhelmingly on teaching us how to bat – usually in small groups – and I don't recall us playing a single game that first season. He graded us on our ability and progress, placing Rex Butcher first in bowling and me first in batting. We both played first eleven cricket – and soccer – for the last four or five years of our time at the school.

The only other thing I remember about that first summer at the Leman School was that Bridget Spandler invited June Gibbs and me to a party at a riverside house near St. Olaves. It was a Sunday and we travelled by train. The party had been arranged by the owner of the house who was, I believe, an opera singer. It was a lovely sunny day and some of the afternoon, apart from eating the sandwiches and cakes and drinking the lemonade, was taken up in the opera singer throwing gramophone discs like frisbees across the lawn, breaking some of them and losing others in the river. It was not the riotous afternoon which these capers might suggest but it was a memorable and very enjoyable one.

Possibly because of the interest I took, and was encouraged by the school to take, in games and athletics, I do not think I paid much attention to school work until I went into the lower fifth form and began work for the School Certificate examinations. For example, I have no detailed recollection of doing any homework other than French before then although I am quite sure we had regular homework in all subjects from the very beginning of the first year, and I am equally sure that there was no way of my dodging it – the school and my parents were too vigilant. I don't know the reason why there was a sudden change. One of the masters – Johnny Brown – several years later said that I saw the light in the nick of time. I don't recall any such metanoia but I do recall finding several of the subjects much more interesting than I had previously. I suppose having a pattern to the work and a goal to aim at – School Certificate – helped. I liked the structure of studying and laying out of our work: this particularly applied to geography, history and science. I think we were encouraged from that point onwards to be more systematic, methodical and organized in the way we learned – or at least in the way we remembered things ready to reproduce in examinations! (I can hear Micah at this point saying, 'But what's the use of learning, Laddie, if you don't remember it?') Hence the satisfaction of committing information to maps in geography, the arrangement of material in history under headings and subheadings, and the drawing of diagrams of laboratory apparatus in science. And there was fun and value in designing, remembering and using mnemonics. I have already written of Micah Clarke's 'ending' and 'exceptions' and 'sounds' in French, and of Pop Glover's 'Capes and Bays' approach to geography, which were of long standing. But these other matters were new. In history, for example, I still remember that there were 13 causes of distress after 1815 – the date from which our course started – but I have long since forgotten just what those causes were. At the time the number helped me to work out what they were. In the case of the Chartist movement there were six main aims which I believe I could recall with a few moments to think about them. In science, it was the physics which most interested me. I liked biology less, though I recall most of a mnemonic which helped me to remember eight somethings or other in the brain – 'On Old Olympia's Towering Tops, Old something Stands'. And I could never make head or tail of chemistry.

Miss Teverson joined the staff to teach science in my second year at the school and stayed for some years. Mentioning her reminds me of three things. At one stage we were issued with new hard-backed exercise books for biology, and one of our class mates partly used it to hide a number of 'Art Studies', that is pin-up girl photographs. It was a good collection, I understand, but it fell into the hands of Miss Teverson who not unnaturally was, or appeared to be, appalled. I don't recall how she handled it but it caused the young art collector great consternation and acted as a warning to the rest of us. The other two memories relate to chance sayings of Miss Teverson. One day when she discovered a boy near the front of the class turning round to have a chat with the boy behind him while she was writing on the blackboard, she ordered him to 'Turn round square' much to our guffawing amusement. Better still, on the occasion when her class was being interrupted by some boys at the back of the room talking and at the same time some boys talking at the front of the class, she lamented, 'Now I've got boys talking at both ends!' The class collapsed, hooting with hilarity. These accounts should not be taken to suggest that classes were ill-disciplined, for they were not, but pupils, especially the boys, rarely missed an opportunity to distort a perfectly innocent remark from a teacher. Nor was talking in class widespread. Again it was not, though taking the opportunity to have a brief word sotto voce with one's closest neighbours when the teacher's back was turned or their attention otherwise diverted was – like the passing of notes – sometimes thought worth risking. Boys seized the opportunity to use and emphasize publically words and expression which would normally be frowned at. For example, from Shakespeare, 'Tennis balls, my liege' and 'Then be thou damned inexorable dog', and in hymns, 'And Mary bore sweet Jesus Christ our Saviour for to be'. And they brought into common language words which for some reason or other amused them such as the French verb, 'oublier', to forget: 'I've oublied my book'. I'm beginning to wonder as I recall some of this, whether we ought not to have been at a specialized institution rather than a grammar school!

The first School Certificate examination which we sat, in the summer of 1946, was Geography in the morning. In the afternoon I played cricket and, fielding at first slip, I reached high for a ball coming fast off the edge of the bat and, whilst I did not catch it, it caught me and I dislocated the third finger of my right hand. I was taken to the Beccles hospital by Miss Collis, the unattractive gym mistress who was reckoned to have an unusual relationship with her equally unattractive black dog, Sam. The finger was straightened out under ether and I clearly recall the click as it was pulled straight. All was well except that the examination the next morning was Art, and I found this very difficult since the finger was heavily bandaged. Apart from the French examinations of which I have already written, I do not remember anything else about those examinations. When the results came out I had distinctions in Geography, History, Science and Extra Science, credits in English Language, English Literature, French, Mathematics and Religious Knowledge. In Art, where I had been expected to do well, I got a pass only. These results, miraculously, were a good deal better than anyone, so far as I know, had expected, including me. Although I usually revised fairly thoroughly for examinations, neither then nor later do I recall being anxious about the outcome. It certainly was not confidence or bravado but rather a strange form of indifference. We sat examinations and that was that. Having sat them, there was nothing more we could do about them. If I had thought about the future – and I don't think I did – I guess I would have thought it would take care of itself.

When I was in the fifth form I was taken with a party from the school to see a ballet performance at Norwich. It was the Ballet Rambert and they danced 'Les Sylphides'. The School Speech Day programme for 1945-1946 tells us that the visit to the ballet was on 25 October1945. It was unusual that a party should be taken to the ballet and almost inconceivable that boys like me would have any time for it. Yet the staff who arranged the visit were clearly much more far seeing than I gave them credit for, because I was captivated by the performance. The integration of music, movement, costume, decor and story struck me then, as it does now, as extraordinarily beautiful. I recall that we must have sat very close to the stage because I remember the way in which the dancers' tights and the toes of their shoes were darned. In the case of the former, it was just after the war and they obviously had to economize, but in the case of the latter, it was very many years before I realized that ballerinas habitually and deliberately cut the fabric off the points of their shoes and darn them to get a better grip. I have often wondered why they are not made with darned points. During the course of 'Les Sylphides' at Norwich, a wing of the scenery toppled over and a male dancer simply reached up with his hands as the wing descended and held it up in an elegant pose while others gracefully helped to move it out of the way. I was so transfixed by the dancing that it was not until I saw the ballet again a little later that I realized the falling wing and the pose and recovery were not part of the ballet itself. It must have been this visit to Norwich which stimulated my interest in ballet, because for several years thereafter I read all I could about ballet and the great dancers of the past, and it is an enjoyment and a fascination which has stayed with me. As I listen now to ballet music – that is music specifically written to be danced to, rather than music to which dance has later been added – I 'see' and 'feel' the ballet movements and shapes.

When I was in my early teens, for a brief period and at David's instigation, I joined the League of Labour Youth. I recall no discussion of politics or of any other matter or function, save for a social evening-cum-dance in a room over the Co-op grocery department, and of that I remember no details. Joining the League was for me a lark rather like going to Spiritualist Church meetings but I think it was more serious for David. Party politics interested me neither then nor subsequently, although as an adult I enjoyed studying political philosophy. Save for Miss Pulsford who took no steps to conceal her socialist beliefs, I do not know what the political leanings of any of our other teachers were. Micah Clarke was anecdotally reckoned to be a Liberal but he was a canny enough person quite honestly to give us one impression, or even more than one impression – and believe another. During a discussion in an English class the question of communism and joint ownership somehow arose, and Miss McCarthy, who was taking the class, said that she had no wish to share her toothbrush with everyone else. Some of those present felt that either she had missed the point or was trivializing what might have been an important issue and one worth discussing. I could no more rely then on a guess of a teacher's – or most other people's – political orientation than I can nowadays. It still gravely offends me to see politicians – of all major parties – on television giving political speeches on school premises to school children. I come very close to despising professional politicians as a class, though in fairness I guess some are not as bad as others! Nonetheless, on a number of occasions in my Royal Air Force and later career, when I was positively vetted for various reasons, the question of the Labour League of Youth cropped up as did a single copy of 'Soviet Weekly' which I bought when I was in the sixth form because of an article on Russian industrialization which was part of the Higher School Certificate scholarship paper in Geography. There, now, how do you reckon I vote, assuming that I do vote? Incidentally, being in Africa for twenty years, I was not entitled to vote in Britain or elsewhere until I was nearly fifty.

In my early to mid teens I also became a member of the 'Tute', the Men's Social Institute in Fair Close near to David's home – again, it was he who introduced me to it. I spent in total many half hours playing billiards there –

and less so snooker. Both games taught us a good deal about solid geometry and the physics of motion, though we were not always aware of it. I recall a number of the other players including a one-armed man who I think was on the staff, who used a block of wood with a groove cut into it on which to rest his cue. He was a good deal better with his one arm and his cue rest than most other players. I did not play much snooker as an adult though I did win a match when in the RAF but only because – undiscovered until after the final – my opponent could not distinguish between red and brown.

Up to the time when the School Certificate results became known my future had been seen in the family to lie, if I was good enough, in one of the more 'elite' or 'refined' Beccles employments which at that time were seen to be a clerk in a bank, a clerk in the post office, or a reader in the printing works. I should have liked none of them, but fortunately the question did not arise because it was decided, presumably by my parents and the school, that I should stay on and go into the sixth form. I don't know how or why this decision was reached. From my point of view it was easier just to stay at school, though clearly it had significant financial implications for my parents. There seemed to be little discussion, and none to which I was privy, either about it or about what might happen thereafter.

I, with Rex Butcher, was made a prefect as soon as we went into the sixth form. This was the first time prefects had been selected from the lower sixth. The school was getting bigger and I suppose more prefects were needed. I never discovered what a prefect was supposed to do and I do not recall that we did anything special. In the sixth form, too, I was made house captain and captain of the athletics team, and continued my first eleven soccer and cricket and cross country running.

I enjoyed the sixth form academic work, leading up to the Higher School Certificate which I took in the summer of 1948. It seemed much more a case of learning rather than preparing for the examinations, though examinations and a set curriculum must have been driving forces. We were left more to our own devices. There was some question of which subjects I should study. In those days we 'did' either science or arts. They were not mixed. The head master, Dr. Leslie Wood, who had mercifully replaced Mr. Gordon Humphreys in 1943, obliged everyone in the sixth form to study Economics, which he taught. The course was based on Honor Croom's 'The Approach to Economics', a manageable, easy to read and well written text. I decided to take Geography and Art as main subjects and Biology, French Literature and Economics as subsidiary subjects. The Geography was because I liked it and much admired the master who taught it – Pop Glover. Unfortunately, he left at the end of the second term of my first year in the sixth form to become senior lecturer at Wymondham Training College. He was replaced by Dr. Gort who I think must have been aware of how difficult it would be to fill Pop's shoes – in my view he never did. Incidentally, he also took over as senior master, but when, only two years or so later, he left the school he was replaced as senior master – surprisingly at the time but wiser on reflection – by Johnston Brown. I learned later that Micah Clarke and Solly Firth, both of whom were Johnston Brown's senior, were distinctly put out when neither of them was asked to fill the senior master vacancy. I took Art because I was reckoned to be quite good at it, despite the School Certificate results. I took Biology because, with my athletics and games, it was thought I might become a physical training teacher. The Economics was taken because the headmaster said so. And I took French Literature because Micah Clarke had not got enough students to fill even a small class so when he asked me and one or two others to take the subject I guess we were too afraid, and certainly too compliant, to refuse. He taught us at the end of the upstairs corridor rather than in a classroom. The whole combination, lacking as it did in cohesion, was really designed to enable me to play a lot of football and cricket and to continue my athletics. I was not, then or subsequently, unhappy with the selection of subjects

For some reason, probably because of staff shortages at that level, we took some of our Biology at the Lowestoft Grammar School – which by that time had reopened after the war, and we travelled to Lowestoft by train. I do not remember any details of the Higher School Certificate examinations save the practical in Biology which was taken at Lowestoft. Over the preceding two years we had learned how to dissect the earth worm, the frog, the dog fish and the cockroach. When we entered the examination room for the Biology practical we were relieved to learn that the animal to be dissected was a cockroach. We were pleased because the cockroach was fairly simple to dissect, did not take long and could be approached in a gentle, leisurely, methodical fashion. Although I have forgotten all subsequent steps I remember that one began by fixing the insect in a bed of wax, waited for the wax to harden and then start the dissection, the first step of which was to remove the wing scales so as to expose the 'innards'. I accomplished these steps quite easily but when I got to the 'innards' part I discovered to my horror that the body cavity was completely empty save for a little dust! Fortunately, the Biology invigilator had a spare cockroach – she was more amused than surprised and said she had a spare one up her sleeve! – which had the correct contents, and I guess I got on with the dissection as I had been taught.

There was a group of us who travelled by rail to Lowestoft for Biology classes: Ralph Keeler, Frank Wilkin, Rex Butcher and me. I recall an occasion when Frank took with him a stick of white chalk and when we boarded the train to Lowestoft, he lowered the roll-up blind in the carriage and on it he drew a reasonably accurate, though somewhat ambitiously dimensioned, representation of a skyward-pointing penis. He then let the blind roll up to its normal position and we pictured in our mind's eye the next poor old dear who had the misfortune to pull down the blind and be faced with the fruits of Frank's Rabelaisian artistry. Even as sixth formers we could be deplorably fourth form-minded!

During my first year in the sixth form, the school put on a concert in which most of the pupils did some sort of act. I sang as part of a trio, 'The Two Gendarmes' and Longfellow's 'Excelsior' – 'The shades of night were falling fast as through an alpine village passed a youth who bore mid snow and ice a banner with a strange device – Excelsior!' Also during my time in the Sixth the form performed Shaw's play, 'Arms and the Man' – 'The Chocolate Soldier' as it was called when it was later adapted as a musical – on the stage of the Regal cinema. I was not one of the cast – and would have been terrified to be one – but I was a stage hand or prompter or something like that. The leading lady was Betty Martin and she, with the rest of the performers, was a great success. I remember her worrying lest instead of the famous words, 'I am a Petkoff' she might say 'I am a Ketpoff'. She didn't. The copy of the School Speech Day programme tells us that the performance was on speech day and was later repeated at the Public Hall. These are yet other examples of the wide range of extra-curricular activities in which the school encouraged and supported us.

At the end of the sixth form, in the Summer of 1948, I had sufficiently good grades in all papers – still to the astonishment of most, including me – that being awarded a major scholarship and going to university became a possibility to be considered. The headmaster advised me to dismiss from my mind a career in the law on the grounds that it involved a great deal of memory work – which was true – and that I did not have a good enough memory for it – which turned out not to be true. He also dismissed the suggestion of the Art master that I consider a career in Art – the idea of doing so would not have crossed my mind. Rather, he believed my future to be in physical education – as at that time so did I. It was, however, a decision which could be put off for a while because I was required to do national service as soon as I left school.

THE SECOND WORLD WAR

Of the fourteen years I spent at school, from 1934 to 1948, six of them, 1939 to 1945, were during the war. For a year or so before the war there was much talk in the town and there were many articles in the newspapers about its inevitability and for a year or so after the war it took time for the effects of war to wear off. The war, therefore, dominated a good part of our growing-up years.

When the war started, Muriel, aged thirteen, had been at the Leman School for a year; Cynthia, eleven, was about to leave Peddars Lane and go to the new

Area School; Dennis, eight, had two more years to go at Peddars Lane before going to secondary school; I, just ten, was in my final year at Peddars Lane. My father was 41 and was outside the call-up period, though as the war progressed – does war ever 'progress'? – the service registration age was lowered perilously close to his age. My mother was just 37. We were a relatively young and I guess fairly typical family.

Some time before the war a system of national registration was set up and every person in the country was registered and given a National Registration number, which consisted of three parts – four letters indicating the town and the part of the town, followed by a number for each household and then a number for each member of that household. For example my number was TWBG.227/5. David has recently shown me his autograph book and inside the front cover is his NR number, TWBD.65/5. TWB was for Beccles, G for my part of the town and D for David's; his family was 65 and mine was 227; he was the fifth member of his household and so was I of mine. It was a well worked out system and was accepted by everyone as being necessary and of benefit to us all. Today some folk are worried about a similar system, albeit containing many more 'biometric' personal details, but in wartime 'Big Brother' was looking after us, not prying into our personal affairs – or was he?

It seems that we knew war was really imminent because Dennis and I began to dig an air raid shelter in the garden at home a few days before the war was declared. We used a small coal shovel to do this and, although we could not have dug it very deeply, the location we chose became the site of the more permanent shelter which my father shortly made. During our digging we uncovered a number of pieces of old white clay smoking pipes – no whole pipes but parts of the stems and of the bowls. These were not really uncommon because we had found pieces in the garden and elsewhere locally earlier on. I am not sure where they came from nor what the land was used for before our house was built there. I recall carrying to school our gas mask in a rather flimsy and increasingly tattered cardboard box, and a tin box of 'iron rations' containing a bar of chocolate – which had to be replenished from time to time! – and some tough biscuits and barley sugar sweets. On a number of Saturday mornings I went to the Area School with Cynthia to help with the war effort by cleaning out rabbit hutches and helping to dig cabbages in the school grounds.

I recall listening with the rest of the family and just about everyone else to the radio broadcast by Neville Chamberlain, the Prime Minister, telling us that Britain's ultimatum to Germany had had no effect and that we were at war with that country. The only immediate thing I remember thereafter was, just a few minutes after the broadcast ended, Mr. Simper, two houses away from ours, cutting masses of chrysanthemums from his garden, tying them into bundles – bouquets – and giving them to many of the neighbours, saying, we might as well enjoy them as have them destroyed by gas.

Within days, my father, with our 'help', converted Dennis's and my juvenile attempts to dig an air raid shelter, into something more likely to protect us – a deep trench, perhaps eight feet long, four feet wide and four or five feet deep, plus another two or three feet above ground level, covered with soil, with steps to get down into the shelter. Piece by piece over a period of several months the shelter was lined with wooden boards, a paraffin lamp was installed, with candles and matches, and some iron rations left there. I guess we took blankets and pillows from the house each time we used the shelter at night. There must have been something for us to sleep on but I do not remember a bed or bunks – maybe a chair or two. A few other people also built their own shelters in their gardens – Mr. Keable, next door, had a well appointed shelter, but most did not. Indeed the less healthy and widows would have found it impossible to make a shelter below the ground level. It was a matter of criticism in the family that when the time came for the Government to provide free Anderson shelters – corrugated iron structures only partly sunken into the ground, but covered with soil and grass – and usually free Morrison shelters – indoor iron reinforced tables under which one could take shelter – we were not allowed to have one on the grounds that we were adequately catered for, albeit at our own cost.

The people to whom Anderson shelters were provided were fined if they did not erect and cover them within a specified period. To start with, each time the air raid siren sounded – an up and down wailing – usually at night, we would all get up, and go down into the shelter and wait until the all clear siren was sounded – a prolonged, single note. Somewhat later, there were times when the siren sounded so frequently and we were less worried about air raids, that we were not sure whether it was 'on' or 'off', and we made a little sliding contraption of cardboard which we altered each time so as to remember whether there was a warning or whether it was 'all clear'. Eventually the warnings became infrequent and in due course stopped altogether. But there was always the possibility of an air raid, as the Kilbrack Road and Kemps Lane bombings show, and towards the very end of the war there were the V1, doodle-bug unmanned flying bombs, and V2 rocket bombs, to worry us. I recall seeing the flames from the exhaust of doodle-bugs flying northwards towards Lowestoft, and the vertical vapour trail of the V2s reaching high into the sky further south. The doodle-bug became dangerous only when the 'put-put' of its engine stopped, for then it would fall to ground and explode. Early in the war, during the year I was at the Area School, I saw a clearly marked German bomber flying quite low from east to west over the school playing fields, but this was the only one I ever saw.

I have no recollection of our having used an air raid shelter at the Peddars Lane School and indeed I am not sure that there was one, except that I have a vague recollection that there was a small brick building at the far end of the back playground – the girls' playground – which might have been, or been used as, a shelter. On the other hand, air raid warnings were frequent during my year, September 1940 to July 1941, at the Area School. Then we all trooped, unhurriedly but with expedition, class by class, into the underground, brick lined, shelters which had been recently built – the previous year Cynthia and her class mates had to run across the playing fields to take shelter in Sandy Lane, a sunken lane at the far edge of the school premises. A teacher accompanied us and remained with us in the shelters until the all clear sounded. To pass the time, our teacher, the Miss Woolner to whom I have referred, read to us a number of Biggles stories which we enjoyed and she played with us a spelling game in which each successive pupil would add a letter to the letter given by the preceding pupil in such a way as not to end a word but to extend it as far as possible. If one's proffered letter did end a word one was 'out'. If one wished, one could challenge the preceding pupil on the grounds that the letter suggested was not part of a real word. A successful challenge would also result in one being 'out'. I recall an occasion when the two preceding letters were 'ac' and I suggested 'n' as contributing to the word 'acne' but I was challenged on this and was told by Miss Woolner that there was no such word. I didn't like the woman before that and liked her less after it! I recall this event very clearly and even remember that the girl who challenged me was June Gibbs who thought I was trying to make the word 'acknowledge'. I liked June, who also had not been allowed to take the scholarship examination the previous year but was then successful in the deferred scholarship examination. From those early days in our first year at secondary school, she was the girl friend of my friend Dennis Pegram. They stayed together, were married, and had a family. Dennis unfortunately died when he was, I think, in his fifties. June died some years later. They had been good friends.

At the Leman School, things were different again. I have no recollection of air raid warnings and having to evacuate the premises and take shelter outside. Though there must have been air raid warnings there were no shelters except for one small brick shelter – maybe two – at the far end of the girls' playing field which had flooded a year earlier and was no longer used.

The differing provision for, and need of, air raid shelters in the three years covered by my last year at Peddars Lane, the year at the Area School and the first year at the Leman School may well have reflected the changing circumstances of the war and its changing impact directly on Britain over those years, 1939-1942, rather than different attitudes to the need for shelters displayed by the school authorities.

The war naturally had its effects on school life. Some of the masters were called up but relatively few because most of them were beyond call-up age or were in some way unfit. On the other hand, there was not the inflow, no matter how slight, of new masters which one might have expected over a period of 4-5 years. The gaps in the staff were filled by women teachers and for the first time some of them were married. Robert White, who taught art at the Leman School and Bungay Grammar School, was called up in August 1940, was married on a Saturday and joined the forces on the following Wednesday. He had disappeared before I got to the school but returned later at the end of the war. His place teaching art was taken by Miss Varley from the Lowestoft Technical School who was an expert in handwriting. Her own Lowestoft students had been evacuated and the school closed. Although she taught my sister Muriel I do not think she taught my class. Muriel's handwriting was a great deal better than mine is. In any case, Miss Varley did not stay long at Beccles and she was replaced by Miss Roper and later by Mrs. White, Robert's wife. A Mr. Thomas, whom I scarcely knew, left the staff of the Leman School to join the forces very shortly after I got there. I recall the elderly but charming Mr. Woosnam returning from retirement to teach us, and when he left, he asked the whole school, which was assembled to bid him farewell, to sing 'Shenandoah', which we did lustily and with some emotion since he was a much liked man.

Within the classroom at the Leman School, in the case of French, economies were made at the instigation of Micah Clarke. He required us to rule extra lines at the head and the foot of the writing paper we used. Few of us will forget his stentorian injunction as he handed out the single sheets of ruled paper, taking the utmost care, Scrooge-like, not to give more than one to each pupil, to 'Rule extra lines top and bottom.' We competed with each other to see who could get the most extra lines drawn on the paper and how much writing we could crowd into them and the margins. The economy was potentially surprisingly large. On a page about nine inches wide, the one inch margin took up eleven percent of it, and, additionally, if one could add – as one did – up to four extra lines at the top and another four at the bottom of the normally twenty line page one increased one's writing area, and saved up to forty percent of the paper needed. Together the extra lines and the margins reduced the paper used by about a half. This is another example of what a remarkable man Micah Clarke was.

Out in the playground and on the playing field there were changes to our 'break' or playtime, for the general larking about by the boys in the lower forms now included 'playing commandos' when we would, at least in the drier weather, crawl through the grass at the far side of the field and attack those coming at us from the opposite direction. Much of our youthful playing became war-oriented. And some of it was gladiatorial – I and a thickset boy from the year above me, John Seago, had wrestling matches during the lunch break. These became quite serious and were watched by a ring of others. Neither of us harmed, or harboured any ill will towards, the other but we were serious about wrestling our opponent to the ground. We must have somehow been selected by the crowd to do the fighting. He seemed immensely strong and I expect won most of the contests. It was during these that I acquired, through Dennis

Pegram, the nick name 'Bruzzo', a name which stuck for a while, though I disliked it and did not think it was 'me' at all.

The war had its affect not only on school life but also on the town's social life. Ironically, there was a great deal more public entertainment during the war than there was either before or after it. This was partly to keep up morale and partly to raise funds for the war effort. I have already mentioned the 'holidays at home'. Miss Maureen Smith – Mrs. Youell – managed and taught a very successful dance school for well over fifty junior and teenage girls – I don't think there were any boys – and she gave public dancing performances with ballet dancing, tap dancing and all sorts of other dancing, including dances from other countries. In my family photograph album there is a photograph of Muriel taken by the leading local photographer, Mr. Leyneck, in her Spanish dancing costume. Bubbles was also an accomplished member of the dance school. Mr. Youell, Maureen's husband, played the musical saw. This was an ordinary, but good quality, carpenter's saw which he played in cello-like fashion, holding the handle between his knees, bending the blade with his left hand and drawing a violin or cello bow across the back of the blade. The result was a moaning monotone which varied in pitch with the degree of bending of the blade. It sounded much better than this description might suggest and the tunes he played, some of them classical, were easily recognizable. The signature tune which introduces the television series 'Midsomer Murders' is partly played on a musical saw. There was also a number of concert parties given and I recall a group organized by the Leggett Brothers, known as the Leggetonians. At their concerts there were comedians, solo singers, monologues, small orchestras made up of piano, violin, accordion and drums. Some unusual musical instruments were also played. For example there were the 'bones' performances. The bones were a pair of cow rib bones about six inches long and an inch wide which were held between the fingers of each hand and vigorously 'clacked' together, a little as castanets are played. There was a common variation on the bones, when dessert spoons were used instead of the bones. Several boys at school could play both the bones and the spoons but to my great disappointment I could never master the art. Neither have I ever been able to 'click' my fingers as most other people seem able to do.

The war undoubtedly forced families, even more than schools, to economize, especially the mothers in respect of their house-keeping: 'Make do and Mend' was a frequently used expression and if one complained one was often asked 'Don't you know there is a war on?' Not all the economies were the result of war time restrictions but were part of the way of life at a more frugal and thrifty period of our history. Worn bed sheets were repaired by turning sides to middles, and tears in the cloth were patched. The heels of worn socks and the elbows of worn woollen garments were darned. I remember with great admiration the skill with which Mrs. Pegram, Dennis's mother, took threads from the material on the inside of a jacket and used it to darn the elbows – the result was extraordinary and the darned area was very difficult, virtually impossible, to distinguish from the rest of the cloth. The collars and cuffs of shirts were 'turned' so that the frayed part from the outside was concealed on the inside of the collar or cuff. 'Rag mats' were made by collecting fragments of old cloth, cutting them into strips about five inches long by an inch wide, and 'sewing' them on to a backing of hessian – disused sacks – by threading them through the hessian with a tough pointed wooden peg-like tool about six inches long. With a carefully selected range of rag strips some of the women made attractive patterns on their rugs. The ashes from the domestic fires were more thoroughly sieved each morning and any useable fragments of coal were re-used, We chopped the kindling – the fire wood – into thinner slices partly to economize and partly because it was easier to get a fire 'going' in this way. Families, like my own, who did not normally keep chickens in their garden, did so during the war, and men, like my father, who previously had not cultivated an allotment, did so during the war.

The production, conservation and careful use of food was of great importance to an island nation subject constantly to the threat of blockade by sea during the war, and a number of steps were taken by the Government, voluntary bodies and individuals to secure foodstuffs. Crops, and their storage, especially of grain, were preserved by the Young Farmers' Clubs paying a half penny for each sparrow killed, and the local council paid a penny for each rat tail handed in to them; thousands and thousands of sparrows and rats were killed in this way and tons and tons of foodstuffs conserved. People were exhorted to 'dig for victory' and those near the river were encouraged to 'fish for victory'. To increase the number of people working on the land, the wages of farm workers was increased from 38 shillings and 6 pence a week to 48 shillings and 6 pence and then 54 shillings a week. Allotment holders were encouraged to grow more food, those previously without an allotment were badgered into becoming allotment holders, and unused land was taken over to provide more allotments. Wasting food or buying too much food was forbidden by law. Individuals and groups were urged to make as much jam as possible, and I have already mentioned the huge amounts made by volunteers at the Area School. Shop owners could be fined for selling foodstuffs over the regulated prices and for selling sausages containing more than 45% meat.

It was obviously important that enemy aircraft should not be helped at night to learn where they were by seeing lights from the ground, and the blackout rules were rigorously enforced. Those who broke the rules were fined and they included prominent members of society: Dr. Wood-Hill, a leading GP in the town and a senior magistrate; Mr. Odam, the headmaster of the Area School; Percy Cross from the Leman School and many others were fined and 'named and shamed' in the local press. Repeat offenders were sent to prison. There were frequent and urgent cries, sometimes colourfully expressed, from individuals and ARP Wardens of 'Put out that light!' The lights did not have to come from lamps but included light from fires and burning rubbish in the garden. In the case of my home, great care was taken each evening to put blankets over the windows – which had strips of paper glued over them to reduce shattering if bombs fell – because the ordinary curtains and blinds tended to leave chinks of light at the tops and sides. There were no street lamps, and personal torches used in the streets at night had a metal cover over them with a small and narrow opening to let a restricted amount of light show through. The headlights of the few vehicles being driven at night had similar masks over them. Humorists used to say that since the windows of buildings had strips of paper stuck over them to reduce the glass shattering and to prevent it flying about and injuring folk, in the event of nearby explosions, some people –'no names mentioned!' – cleaned their windows much less frequently and this lessened the risk of lights shining through them and breaking the blackout rules. Those unnamed window non-cleaners argued that there was little point in cleaning windows which might be blown to smithereens the next day.

So far as evacuation and evacuees are concerned I have already written about the Dagenham and Gravesend school children. The authorities recommended that those billeted with families should be moved on to another family for three months and then return to the first family for three months, and so on, but I doubt whether this was either a good idea or whether many people accepted the recommendation. The children and their mothers had endured enough disturbance to their lives without having to put up with three-monthly up-rootings. About nine months after the war began, Lowestoft and Great Yarmouth school children, accompanied by teachers and helpers but not parents, and not 3 or 4 year old infants unless they were accompanying their older siblings, were evacuated to Hereford and Wales under an official scheme. The Lowestoft and Great Yarmouth children were required to take with them, according to local newspapers, the bare essentials, 'their gas mask, identity card, ration card, food for the day, a change of underclothing, handkerchiefs, stockings, plimsolls or house shoes, comb, tooth brush etc.' It was an emotional and highly worrying time, putting stress on parents and children alike. The Mayor of Lowestoft appealed to the parents to keep calm when they saw their children off. A few children from Lowestoft and Great Yarmouth were privately evacuated to Beccles, often to stay with relatives or family friends. Several of them – including Ralph Keeler and Frank Wilkins both of whom went to Birmingham University with me – became close personal school friends. It was made clear from the beginning that there would be no officially organized evacuation from Beccles.

Britain in the days of our youth was not the multi-ethnic society which it is now. The only thing I learned about non-white people was the Africans

I learned about from Sunday School books on David Livingstone, and the Chinese people I learned about from missionaries returning from the Far East and giving lantern shows in the church hall. Indeed, I did not see any black people until the war when a fairly large number of African-American soldiers were stationed at Ditchingham, I think in a disused maltings. I clearly recall cycling to Ditchingham, probably looking for 'souvenirs' – pieces of metal from shot-down aeroplanes – and visiting the African-American soldiers there. We enjoyed the visit and returned later for other visits. They were completely isolated from their white fellow soldiers and most of them seemed to be employed on cleaning and maintaining army vehicles. They smoked, 'Camel', 'Silver Star' and 'Lucky Strike', cigarettes in packets quite different from the British cigarette packets, and they gave us chewing gum. We told them about ourselves but I have the feeling that they did not tell us much about themselves. I don't think we were intrusively curious about them – just interested in talking with new, friendly, different people. On reflection I think they were more curious about us than we were about them. As for the more numerous white American soldiers we met in Beccles, usually at matins on a Sunday morning, I remember being surprised to see that their uniform trousers and tunics were often of different shades of khaki and how glamorous their women soldiers looked in their smart uniforms and silk stockings! I guess I ought not to have been surprised – although I was – that whilst there were many local 'G I Brides' – girls who married American soldiers – I never heard of a 'G I Husband'!

I recall a number of sad fatalities in the town during the war. A young primary school boy was knocked down by an armoured car when he was walking in the Ellough Road area and was killed. And a soldier standing on the back of an army lorry was seriously injured and died when the lorry was driven under the low railway bridge in Ravensmere and the soldier failed to duck in time. Mr. Sidney Day, the father of a friend, Derek, in Pleasant Place, was killed early in the war when a lorry tyre which he was fitting burst and threw him onto an adjacent lorry. A young man working at one of the maltings in town fell into a hopper of barley, was sucked down and killed. A very similar fatal accident occurred at Green's flour mill close to home when a man was sucked down into a container of wheat. A parson in one of the nearby villages was challenged by an armed sentry as he left the village in his car after taking a service there. Whether or not he answered the challenge, the sentry shot at the tyres of his car, the minister was badly shaken and shortly died of a heart attack.

There were two other sad fatalities of which I know, though in these cases they were not accidental and only one of them occurred during the war, the other after. The first was towards the end of 1944 when Arthur Heys of the RAF was convicted of the murder of Winifred Evans of the WAAF, at Ellough air station. I heard some details of this at the time but I soon forgot them. Some five years later, however, when I was in the Provost Marshal's Branch of the RAF Police, I was put in charge of the criminal records of No. 4 Wing which covered the Beccles area. From these records I learned that there was a dispute over jurisdiction, the murder having taken place on RAF premises and both the perpetrator and the victim being RAF personnel. The dispute was soon settled and Inspector Green of Scotland Yard took over the investigation, but the case had been initially investigated by the RAF Police. Their records, which included some of the very earliest statements taken, told a slightly different story as to the facts from that reported in the local newspapers, though they did not in any way cast doubt on Heys's guilt. In those days, when a sentence of death was passed, the judge wore a 'black cap', a nine inch square of black cloth placed over his wig, as he did so. Heys was hanged in Norwich prison.

The other murder was a very sad affair. It took place towards the end of 1949. I knew both the culprit (who had been in the same class as Cynthia at the Area School) and the victim (who had been in a class or two below me at the Leman School) though not well. Jimmy Rivett, a builder's labourer, son of a local market gardener and fruit and vegetable merchant, and a 17 year old Leman School girl had been on 'close terms of friendship for four years and on terms of intimacy for several months'. One evening they went to the cycle shed at the Leman School and had intercourse, after which he killed her by strangling her with her school scarf. The murder site was only a few hundred yards from Cut Throat Lane. The trial took place in 1950, when I was a temporary teaching at the Leman School after leaving the RAF, and I recall Miss Pulsford, who had taught me Physics, organizing a petition to have Jimmy's sentence of death commuted. I do not recall whether I signed the petition – I probably did – but I do know that I hesitated over it. I recall more clearly, too, that when some years later I was reading law I studied the case of Rex v Rivett, which had become a leading case in England, Canada and Australia. The only motive suggested for the crime was that the accused knew the girl's parents did not approve of their relationship, whether on account of youth or of differences in social status or career aspirations and expectations, I know not. He was certifiably insane and the defence relied on this for their main arguments. Two juries found him fit to plead and the third convicted him, all of them rejecting the expert opinion of qualified psychiatrist witnesses, as they were entitled to, since it was for them, the jury, not the judge, to make this decision. In the Court of Criminal Appeal the Chief Justice, Lord Goddard, held that in order for a defence of insanity to succeed, the accused must show that he had a disease of the mind such that he was not responsible for his actions – that he did not know that what he was doing was wrong, that is legally, not morally, wrong. I am not sure, but I think Jimmy went from the school cycle shed to the police station and told them what he had done. If this was so, then it would have been strong evidence that he knew he had broken the law. Among the stories that circulated in the town at the time I recall two. First, that at least some members of the jury were deeply distressed that the legal guidance and instructions from the judge prevented them from acquitting the accused of murder. Second, that Jimmy's jailors were much saddened by the way their prisoner seemed utterly indifferent to his fate, calmly playing cards with them in his cell and acting as if nothing untoward had occurred. These reactions of the jury members, jailors and petition-collectors indicate that there was a great deal of sympathy for Jimmy, not for what he had done but because he was insane. It was a tragic case. He too was hanged in Norwich prison.

To return to the economies of wartime, I learned later a number of details about rationing during the early part of the war. Food rationing started very early in the war and at the time it was introduced the rationed items consisted of four ounces of butter; twelve ounces of sugar; four ounces of bacon or uncooked ham, or three and a half ounces of cooked ham a week. The meat ration was initially on a purchase price basis, every person over the age of six years being entitled to buy up to a shilling and ten pence worth of butcher's meat a week. Those under six years got half the adult ration. A family of three could buy 'four pounds of best English sirloin; or eight pounds of boiling cuts of best home killed beef, such as brisket or flank; or five pounds of imported sirloin.' But there was no limitation on buying liver, kidneys, tripe, heart, ox-tail and sausages. And if one ate in a restaurant one did not have to use ration coupons.

Clothing was rationed from June 1941 and a system of clothing coupons, issued at the Post Office, was introduced with 66 coupons being issued to everyone with which to buy clothing and cloth. The first coupons to be used were the margarine coupons in the existing ration books –margarine was not yet rationed. With these coupons a woman could buy two dresses (18 coupons), a skirt and a jumper (12 coupons) and a pair of pyjamas and still have 28 coupons left for underclothes, stockings and shoes. A man could buy a sports jacket, two shirts, a pair of flannels, a pair of pyjamas, underclothes, two pairs of socks, a cardigan and two ties and still have six coupons to spare for other items. Raincoats or overcoats cost 16 coupons. There were no extra coupons for wedding dresses, mourning clothes, or clothes for other special occasions.

There were very many other changes that took place during the war of which I also learned later, several of them from the very beginning. Whit Monday was no longer a Bank Holiday and folk were urged to travel as little as possible on other holidays – goods traffic was more important, they were told, than passenger traffic. Holiday makers, day trippers and others were forbidden to enter within five miles of the coast unless they could prove that they had a good reason for doing so. The Beccles regatta was cancelled. Popular concerts with songs, instrumental music and monologues were held in the town. Cinemas were opened on Sunday evenings. Local fascists were arrested but there were only three of them in the whole of East Anglia and none from Beccles. Farmers were asked to grow more flax, and to build their haystacks in the middle of their fields to prevent enemy aircraft landing. 'Buy a Bomber' and 'Buy a Spitfire' weeks were held to increase National Savings. National Savings drives were held, and there were National Savings poster competitions for school children and, as the local paper reported, the winning posters were exhibited in London (Gordon Eady, David Soames, John White and Colin Baker) and locally at the YMCA Hall (Mary Odam, Michael Judge, Peter Keeley, Reggie Youngman, Anne Clarke, Peter Lawson, Alastair Robertson, Rodney Hutchings, Austin Bates, Derek Briggs, Jean Harvey, William Feavyour and Olive Thompson.) Petrol was rationed. Householders were given bags of dry sand and asked to keep it in buckets, handy to deal with incendiary bombs. Fire-watching duties became compulsory and stirrup pumps, sandbags and rakes were issued. Waste paper was collected by the hundreds of tons. Private building and construction works required a licence. Public air raid shelters and static water tanks were constructed in various parts of the town. Doctors gave first aid lectures at schools. People driving vehicles within five miles of the coast without a licence to do so were fined. Life boats from all Suffolk coastal towns went to Dunkirk to evacuate the troops. Iron railings were cut down and used for scrap metal, including those from around tombs in graveyards, the railings in the Peddars Lane School and the gates of the Leman and Area schools, church gates and cemetery gates, all the railings down the Avenue except those where livestock were grazing, and round the war memorial. Details were issued instructing the population what to do in the event of an invasion – which would be announced by the ringing of church bells which otherwise were silenced during the war. Those refusing to accommodate evacuees were bound over or fined. Locally, the Women's Voluntary Service collected thousands of garments and boots and distributed them to the evacuees. A Scottish military pipe band gave a number of performances including sword dances. A 'War Weapons Week', with exhibitions of war material and weapons, was organized and yielded £136,000 in Beccles. Minutes of council meetings were written or typed on both sides of the paper, minutes were read out rather than copies sent to every member and when documents were sent out, the envelopes were handed in at the end of the meetings and used again. The Beccles Town Football Club closed down as so many playing members joined the forces. Instead, Beccles United was formed out of several of the local clubs. National days of prayer were held in churches throughout the country and congregations were large – up to 1500 in St. Michael's church in Beccles, where the national anthem was sung and the rector ducked out of preparing a suitable sermon by saying that it was a time for praying, not preaching.

From the end of the war onwards there was a marked change in the urban landscape of Beccles as new housing areas were created, away from the older and more crowded parts of the town and in the more open areas to the south. This was not an entirely new development because between the wars large estates had been built in the Ellough Road and Castle Hill areas. The post-war development started informally, surreptitiously, in a small way. Young married couples, where the husband was returning from the war, found themselves without a home of their own and in many cases simply with nowhere to live. They saw the now empty buildings on the now disused airfields close to Beccles, and they moved in. They were far from comfortable dwellings but they would do. All sorts of innovative individual ways were found to get access to electricity and water and to move odd pieces of abandoned furniture and curtains from other buildings into their new quarters. There was a good deal of official tut-tutting and arguing the toss but the squatters stayed put. You don't fight and survive a ghastly war away from your loved ones and return to them with nowhere to live and just sit on your hands and look longingly at empty buildings! British and Beccles people are made of sterner stuff! The first official step to ease the housing shortage was that the Council erected about a score of 'Pre-fabs' – prefabricated, single storied houses, near Swine's Green – where Rip our dog had provided us with an out-of-Christmas-season chicken dinner a decade earlier. These lasted many years longer than originally intended and provided very welcome homes for a number of people. Then in the following years larger housing estates were built in the Sandy Lane-Castle Hill-Rigbourne Hill triangle, with many well-built, brick, double storied houses. As a smaller part of this housing expansion, Crickmore's meadow at the top of Pleasant Place was turned into a small estate and a road driven across it to join up with Kemp's Lane. Pleasant Place was no longer a cul-de-sac. 'Our Road', which in our childhood had been our haven, our playground and indeed our 'world' was no more.

PART THREE

WHERE ARE THEY NOW?

DAVID

In May 1948 David left for National Service in the Fleet Air Arm branch of the Royal Navy . He did his initial training at HMS Royal Arthur, Corsham in Wiltshire. He served ten months on HMS Illustrious, the Home Fleet training and trials Carrier which went regularly to the Moray Firth where young trainee pilots flew from Lossiemouth to make their first carrier landings. The ship also went to the Azores on exercises with other British and American warships. Other trials took place north of Bergen in the Arctic under extreme cold conditions at night. With fellow mess-mate David Lee (Worlingham), he was fortunate to get a joint posting with the Naval Air Fighter Development Unit at RAF West Raynham , Norfolk. They manned the refuelling bowser and maintained the camp bicycles! On release to the Reserve he studied at the Essex Institute of Agriculture at Writtle where he had a thorough grounding in crop and animal husbandry and farm management. Finally, he made his initial foray into theatrical production, writing and directing at the college end-of-term review. In the early 1950's he worked for a time for Mr. Frank Chipperfield at Ellough Hall near Beccles. Leaving to join the CWS canning factory, Lowestoft, he became an agricultural fieldsman. Fourteen years later he joined Ralph Tuck Promotions, working in advertising where, amongst other things, he met and worked with Alan Smethurst, The Singing Postman. In 1968 he became an unlikely civil servant in the DHSS, remaining there for twenty years. Over the years he has been involved with many theatrical productions - Beccles Border Players, Lowestoft Players, Broadland Players, Gilbert and Sullivan Society, historical pageants and youth clubs. He was a member of the Beccles and District Arts Society for over thirty years until it discontinued. Poetry and prose readings have been a particular love of his. Since retirement he studied with the OU and gained a BA and Diploma in European Humanities, fostering his lifelong interest in local literature and the arts. His great love of the East Anglian sound and culture has led him to broadcast on local and national radio for many years. He continues to write and record CDs, to foster the dialect that he loves. He has been a local representative for the National Centre for English Cultural Traditions. For 25 years he was a member of Keith Skipper's Press Gang, a group of local entertainers who toured Norfolk and the Waveney Valley. He is a member of the Robert Bloomfield, Adrian Bell, John Clare and the Parson Woodforde Societies, giving many public readings from the latter's diary. He met his future wife Shirley in 1955 although he had noticed her growing up before this! They became sweethearts during a Beccles production of The Mikado (Gilbert and Sullivan) and were married in 1957, living in Beccles until 1964 when they moved to Lowestoft. In 1980 they moved to their present home, Owles Hall, Frostenden. Their son Michael is a social care worker in Norfolk. He is married to Treeza who works for WEA. They have three children – Jonathon, aged 25, Aaron, 24 and Martha, 18.

COLIN

When Colin left school in the summer of 1948 he was called up to do National Service. His conscription had been delayed for a year after his eighteenth birthday to enable him to complete his Higher School Certificate studies. After his initial training at RAF West Kirby in Cheshire he went to the RAF Police College at Pershore in Worcestershire and was assigned to the Provost Marshal's Branch. Much of his subsequent service was at RAF Horsham St. Faith near Norwich. He was demobilized very early in 1950 and at the Headmaster's invitation spent two terms at his old school, teaching biology and coaching cricket. In September 1950 he went to Birmingham University to read honours geography and graduated three years later. He spent the following year at the London School of Economics and Political Science reading African Studies and at the School of Oriental and African Studies learning Chichewa, the main language of Nyasaland. In August 1954 he sailed for Cape Town in South Africa and then drove the 3000 miles to Nyasaland. There he spent the following seventeen years in the Colonial Administrative Service in a number of different districts in the south and the centre of the country, becoming District Commissioner of the Fort Manning District, then Under Secretary in the Cabinet Office, and finally he was appointed founder Principal of the new University of Malawi's Institute of Public Administration. In 1971 he was appointed Director of the large post-graduate Institute of Administration in the University of Ife, Nigeria, and three years later returned to Britain where he joined the staff of the University of Glamorgan. Here he was appointed Professor, founder Director of the University Business School, Dean of Professional Studies and Assistant Director of the University. He retired from these concurrent posts in 1995 and was made Professor Emeritus, Honorary Fellow and Research Professor, posts which he still holds. He has devoted the latter part of his career to research and writing, focusing on Nyasaland-Malawi and using biography as the medium for exploring political and social history.

He has published nineteen books and over a hundred articles. He holds the degrees of Bachelor of Arts of Birmingham University; Bachelor of Laws, Master of Philosophy and Doctor of Philosophy of the University of London; and Doctor of Letters of the University of Glamorgan. He was awarded the MBE in 1967 for services to Public Administration Education and Training in Malawi. He met his future wife, Shirley, on their first day at University and they were married in Nyasaland in 1956. They have two children: Daryll who is Consultant General and Vascular Surgeon at the Royal Free Hospital in London, and Lynette who is an Optometrist practicing in Norfolk and who with her husband also owns, manages and performs in, the Circus Ferrel. Shirley and Colin live in Rhiwbina in Cardiff where, inter alia, they enjoy many orchestral concerts, opera and ballet performances. They have three grandchildren: Charlotte, aged 21, and twin boys, William and Edward, aged 15.

THANKS

We are conscious that there is a great deal more to producing and publishing a book than simply writing it, and we are deeply grateful to a number of colleagues and friends who have helped us to transform our handwritten and word processed accounts of our Beccles Schooldays into a book. In particular we are grateful to:

Menna Price, Post-Graduate Student in of the University of Glamorgan for word processing David's manuscript

Catherine Wright-Jones, Visual Communications Officer of the University of Glamorgan, for designing and processing the cover

Michael Davies, Senior Photographer in the University of Glamorgan, for processing the photographs

Sheila Butcher, Sharon Carter, Christopher Elliott, Joyce Keely, George Odam, Brian Patrick, Monty Pitkin and Robert Tilney for access to their photographs and permission to use them.

A REQUEST

We would be very pleased to hear from any readers who knew Beccles during the 1930s and 1940s, or who knew us, and we hope they will get in touch with us and tell us their recollections of those days and what has happened to them since then. We would like that very much indeed. Our e-mail addresses are, in David's case, woodward.owleshall@btinternet.com, and, in Colin's case, cabaker@glam.ac.uk